Racism and political action in Britain

This volume does not represent the views of the Social Science Research Council, nor does it necessarily reflect those of all members of the Research Unit on Ethnic Relations.

Racism and political action in Britain

Edited by

Robert Miles and Annie Phizacklea

Routledge & Kegan Paul
London, Henley and Boston

First published in 1979
by Routledge & Kegan Paul Ltd
39 Store Street,
London WC1E 7DD,
Broadway House,
Newtown Road,
Henley-on-Thames,
Oxon RG9 1EN and
9 Park Street,
Boston, Mass. 02108, USA
Set in 10 on 12pt Press Roman by
Hope Services, Wantage
and printed in Great Britain by
Lowe & Brydone Ltd
Thetford, Norfolk

British Library Cataloguing in Publication Data

Racism and Political Action in Britain, Conference,
1977

Racism and political action in Britain.
1. Great Britain – Race relations – Congresses
2. Racism – Great Britain – Political aspects –
Congresses
I. Miles, Robert   II. Phizacklea, Annie
III. Social Science Research Council Great Britain.
Research Unit on Ethnic Relations
323.1'41   DA125.A1   78-40778

ISBN 0-7100-0035-9
ISBN 0-1700-0036-7 Pbk

For mum and dad (RM)

For mum (AP)

Contents

Contributors

Michael Banton: Professor of Sociology, University of Bristol since 1965; Director of SSRC Research Unit on Ethnic Relations, 1970–8.

Christopher T. Husbands: Lecturer in Sociology at the London School of Economics. He received his doctorate from the University of Chicago where he carried out research into George Wallace's support in Wisconsin and Indiana. He is currently engaged on a four-nation comparative study of recent and contemporary right-wing electoral movements.

Roger King: Principal Lecturer in Sociology at Huddersfield Polytechnic. He is co-author (with Neill Nugent) of *The British Right* (Saxon House, 1977).

Caroline Knowles: Research student at City University in a research unit investigating race as a political and administrative issue in the British labour movement. She also teaches sociology and social anthropology at City University.

Michel Le Lohé: Senior Lecturer in Politics and Chairman of the Postgraduate School of Studies on Social Sciences at the University of Bradford. He is author of a number of articles on the electoral behaviour of immigrant groups in Bradford and has contributed to L.J. Sharpe (ed.) *Voting in Cities* (Macmillan, 1967) and I. Crewe (ed.) *British Political Sociology Yearbook: The Politics of Race* (Croom Helm, 1975).

Robert Miles: Lecturer in Sociology at the University of Glasgow and previously Research Associate in Sociology at the SSRC Research Unit on Ethnic Relations. He is working with Annie Phizacklea on a research project on political conceptualization and political action among the English and West Indian working class in London; together they have also published work on the British trade unions' attitudes and action with regard to black workers.

Neill Nugent: Senior Lecturer in Politics, Manchester Polytechnic. Author of several articles on British right-wing politics and co-author (with R. King) of *The British Right* (Saxon House, 1977). He is also co-author of a forthcoming book, *The Middle Classes in Revolt* (Hodder & Stoughton, 1979).

Annie Phizacklea: Research Associate in Political Science at the SSRC Research Unit on Ethnic Relations. She has received a doctorate for her thesis on the political socialization of black and white adolescents in Britain and is currently working with Robert Miles on a research project on political conceptualization and political action among the English and West Indian working class in London.

John Rex: Professor of Sociology at the University of Warwick, President of the International Sociological Association Research Committee on Ethnic Minorities, and a former Chairman of the British Sociological Association. He is author of *Race Relations in Sociological Theory* (Weidenfeld & Nicolson, 1970), *Race, Colonialism and the City* (Routledge & Kegan Paul, 1973) and, with Robert Moore, *Race, Community and Conflict* (Oxford University Press, 1967). He also writes on sociological theory. He is currently engaged on a research project on race relations in Birmingham with Sally Tomlinson and David Hearnden.

Stan Taylor: Lecturer in Politics at the University of Warwick. He is currently engaged in a study of British political party responses to New Commonwealth immigration and its economic and political effects.

Robin Ward: Deputy Director of SSRC Research Unit on Ethnic Relations since 1972 where he is leader of a research programme on race relations and housing. He was previously a lecturer in sociology at Manchester University. He is a joint author of the Penguin books on introductory sociology and is currently revising his doctoral thesis on race relations and housing for publication.

Acknowledgments

A number of the essays collected here were originally given as papers to a conference on 'Racism and Political Action in Britain' in September 1977, held by the Social Science Research Council Research Unit on Ethnic Relations. We would like to thank those members of the unit's administrative and secretarial staff who helped to organize the conference and ensured that it ran smoothly and according to time-table. Thanks must also go to Sue Whitmore and Sarah Pegg who have kept us amused for so long and who have typed and retyped the manuscript so many times. Finally, we thank Michael Banton for his enthusiastic support and assistance in so many ways, Ivor Crewe for his encouragement and comments, our colleagues at the research unit who are always ready to provide constructive criticism, the conference participants who thought it worth while to attend, and Philippa Brewster of Routledge & Kegan Paul who made the book a reality. Responsibility for what you are about to read, however, remains with us.

RM
AP
January 1978

CHAPTER 1

Some introductory observations on race and politics in Britain

Robert Miles and Annie Phizacklea

In the wake of the events of the 'hot summer' of 1976[1] we began to organize a conference on 'Racism and Political Action in Britain'. The conference was held a year later, soon after the political violence in Lewisham in London and Ladywood in Birmingham. These events had indicated, once again, that racism in British society could still provide a motive force for political action amongst a minority of the white population and, by implication, for the counter-action of other groups, including black people in Britain. The conference brought together a number of academics who had ideas and data relevant to these issues and some of their material is presented collectively in this volume.

This material makes a threefold contribution to ongoing discussion of this area: first, it shows that events in Britain in the 1970s are not, historically speaking, novel but have precedents in the past hundred years of British political and social history; second, it outlines some of the features of white racism and its modes of political expression; and third, it assesses some of the impact of white racism on the British political system and upon black people in Britain. In this introductory chapter[2] we intend to comment upon the context of and the relationship between race and politics in Britain today, beginning (for those readers who may be unfamiliar with the evidence) with some remarks about the reaction within the national political system to New Commonwealth immigration. In what follows, we shall aim to identify what we see to be some of the main issues in this field of study and to show how the various contributions extend our knowledge in these areas.

We feel that it is important to alert the reader at the outset to the fact that the concept of racism has been given many definitions and has been used in many ways. Indeed, the contributors to this volume are not agreed on a single definition, and one, Michael Banton, is disinclined to use it at all within social science. In our own contribution to this volume we define racism in relation to the social process which creates a racial category (Lyon, 1972). Thus, we use racism to refer to those arguments and beliefs which serve to identify and set apart a minority group or groups on the basis of some physical and/or hereditary characteristic(s) and then attribute to that group(s) some other negatively evaluated feature.

In addition, the reader should be warned that the concept of race is also problematic. It was popularized in the mid-nineteenth century as designating a permanent human type but Darwin demonstrated that there were no permanent types in nature. Scientists sometimes use 'race' in the sense of 'sub-species' but their whole conceptual vocabulary is now much more sophisticated so that a great gulf has been created between the scientific and popular understanding of what constitutes race. When the word 'race' is used in this book, therefore, it relates to a category shaped by social beliefs and perceptions. Finally, in this chapter, we shall refer collectively to New Commonwealth immigrants and their children as black, although where necessary, we will separately identify the specific ethnic or national group. In using the word 'black', we are aware of the difficulties of this terminology (Banton, 1976).

Race, immigration and British politics

So much attention is paid to New Commonwealth immigration that the history of immigration to Britain prior to the 1950s and the type of opposition which these previous immigrations provoked is often overlooked. In the past 130 years the Irish, Jews, Poles, Ukrainians and Cypriots have constituted the largest immigrant groups, with smaller numbers of Italians, Spaniards, Greeks, Maltese and Chinese (Watson, 1977). Of these groups it has been the Irish (who currently constitute the largest immigrant minority in Britain) and the Jews who appear to have provoked the most widespread opposition from the 'native' British. Karl Marx wrote of the impact of Irish immigration in 1870 that:

> Every industrial and commercial centre in England now possesses
> a working class *divided* into two *hostile* camps, English proletarians

and Irish proletarians. The ordinary English worker hates the Irish worker as a competitor who lowers his standard of life (1965, p.236).

And Engels was less than complimentary about the Irish and their effect on the condition of the English working class when he wrote in the middle of the nineteenth century: 'it is easy to understand how the degrading position of the English workers, engendered by our modern history, and its immediate consequences, has been still more degraded by the presence of Irish competition' (1972, p.125).

In chapter 2 Neill Nugent and Roger King refer to the hostility towards Jewish immigrants in the late nineteenth century. To illustrate, one contemporary commentator, W. H. Wilkins, wrote of the 'destitute and degraded immigrants from East of Europe, or the vagrant and vicious aliens from the South' who 'add in a manner altogether out of proportion to their numbers to the miseries of our poor in the congested districts of our great towns, to which they invariably drift' (1892, pp.10–11). Another, the Reverend Reaney, wrote that 'wherever the foreigner comes in any number, the neighbourhood in which he settles speedily drops in tone, in character and in moral' (1892, p.91).

This historical evidence therefore suggests that immigration *per se* is likely to provoke a hostile response. Moreover, both the Irish and the Jews entered the economic system as semi- and unskilled workers, and it is therefore not surprising that most hostility was shown by those with whom they were in competition, the English manual working class, a point to which we shall return. That New Commonwealth immigration provoked English hostility therefore fits the historical pattern but it is still necessary to explain why the political repercussions of this immigration have been so much more resounding than those of previous groups.

New Commonwealth immigration is said to have produced a 'race relations' situation in Britain, and it would therefore be of great relevance to chart in detail the way in which this definition came to prevail. There is some evidence to suggest that up until the mid-1950s, at least in the eyes of civil servants and academics, matters of race and race relations were seen to affect only certain other member countries of the Commonwealth. When in 1952 the Race Relations Board (which became the Institute of Race Relations in 1958 and which was in no way related to the Race Relations Board set up by legislation in 1965) was established at Chatham House, it was not thought that Britain would be an area of study. The board's Director, Phillip Mason, looking back on its formation, wrote:

> it was assumed that Britain was a tolerant society in which this kind of thing did not happen. Concentration was on South Africa, Rhodesia, Kenya, the West Indies; it was problems of the end of the Empire that we considered, although no part of the world was specifically excluded (1969, pp.193–4).

But by the mid-1950s, the director and staff had taken the view that there would be 'an increase of tension between the races in Britain' although, even after the disturbances in Nottingham and London in 1958, their concern about race relations in Britain was not reflected in the new Institute's work, focused as it still was on Africa.

However, by the mid-1960s race certainly was a domestic issue and was intimately related to immigration. This is clearly reflected in the writings of two politicians, published in 1965. For example Norman Pannell suggested:

> Few things are more damaging to the reputation of immigrants generally than the prevalence of certain serious crimes amongst a relatively small number of them, and inter-racial relations would greatly benefit if the offenders were sent out of the country (Pannell and Brockway, 1965, p.32).

And Fenner Brockway wrote: 'One of the principal activities of the present National Committee for Commonwealth Immigrants is the encouragement of local inter-racial councils to deal with problems in terms of large immigrant communities' (Pannell and Brockway, 1965, p.111).

Although in disagreement about immigration control, these two MPs were nevertheless agreed in believing that New Commonwealth immigration had brought about, in Britain, circumstances where different 'races' were having to 'relate' and that this was a problem.

Ideas about race were threaded into the language in which New Commonwealth immigration was debated for at least two reasons. The word race has historically come to be a means of classifying people in terms of physical characteristics, from which developed the idea that the world's population was divided into permanent and distinct racial types (Banton, 1977, p.27). That this notion of racial types is now without justification (Banton and Harwood, 1975) does not prevent it from lingering in some form or another in the minds of both public and politicians. Immigration in the 1950s brought West Indians, Indians and Pakistanis to Britain who were, like the Jews and the Irish, both semi- and unskilled (in British terms at least) and culturally distinct, but the New Commonwealth immigrants were also physically distinctive and this made the indigenous, white British population more conscious of their presence.

Moreover, one of the effects of the development of mass communications on an international scale has been to focus public attention upon conflict between different races elsewhere in the world, notably in the USA and South Africa (Hartmann and Husbands, 1974, pp. 133–6). In addition, within a single country the mass media has made it possible for local events to become national news, with the result that a large section of the British population can now develop opinions on the issues selected by the media for attention, even if they are not directly affected. Hartmann and Husbands' study shows how the media coverage of race in Britain has defined the situation, and thereby shaped the public consciousness, in such a way as to make black people appear to be a threat and a problem.

It is within this context that we believe New Commonwealth immigration has, unlike Jewish and Irish immigration in the past, both become so inextricably entwined with the idea of race and has developed into what is commonly referred to as an 'issue of high potential' (Butler and Stokes, 1974, pp.303–8). But there are other factors too: New Commonwealth immigrants come from former British colonies, they are the 'natives' who were conquered, and their arrival in Britain serves to symbolize the decline of the British Empire and current economic ills. Thus, the very presence of the black man in English cities testifies to the conclusion that the world order, and Britain's preeminent role, is not what it was. Finally, as Michael Banton observes in chapter 10, there is in Britain, much more than in countries more accustomed to immigration, an expectation of social conformity and a rejection of claims of distinct ethnic identity. We would suggest that this is partly due to the fact that until very recently Britain, because of its size, has not been a nation of great heterogeneity, and because of its history and insular position in the North Sea, has not experienced movements of different peoples across its boundaries.

The attitude of successive Conservative and Labour governments to the question of New Commonwealth immigration is best understood against this background. It is possible to argue that, up until the violent clashes between black and white residents in Nottingham and Notting Hill, London, in 1958, the issue of immigration and therefore of race was viewed as of minor importance by both Conservative and Labour politicians and was characterized by paternalistic attitudes. One commentator illustrates this by quoting from the Minister of State for Colonial Affairs in 1954 when he pronounced that, 'we still take pride in the fact that a man can say *Civis Britannicus sum* whatever his colour may be, and we take pride in the fact that he wants and can come to the Mother Country' (Katznelson, 1973, p.127). The 'hooligans' responsible for the violent clashes in 1958 were subjected to exemplary punishment, but the activities of such persons as Sir Oswald Mosley and Colin Jordan in the Notting Hill area were not widely publicized, let alone restrained.

Later that year, the Conservative Party Conference passed a resolution calling for immigration controls, and over the next three years increasing pressure for controls was applied on the Conservative Government by a small but highly vocal Conservative parliamentary party lobby with the tacit support of some sections in Whitehall. It is difficult to gauge how effective this agitation for controls was in winning public support for such measures, or in stimulating the rate of New Commonwealth immigration as the threat of controls was raised. What is certain is that however reluctant the Conservative Government had been to introduce a bill proposing immigration controls, it did just this in October 1961. The volte-face was complete, a position the Labour Party was to arrive at within three years and which resulted in a classic political consensus between the two parties in the handling of what became to politicians the same issue: immigration and race relations or the control of black immigration and the introduction of measures to aid 'integration'.

Even though the Labour Party shifted its position in 1963 to one which tacitly accepted controls on black immigration, it was the shock result at Smethwick in the General Election of 1964 which undoubtedly brought home to the Labour Party that it could not afford to let the electorate think that it was anything but strongly in favour of strict controls on black immigration. In Smethwick, Peter Griffiths had stood as the Conservative candidate against Patrick Gordon Walker who had previously represented the constituency. Griffiths campaigned on a platform which exploited the concerns and uncertainties which had already given rise to a local anti-immigration organization and to a local Conservative party prepared to exploit the issue. Griffiths argued that the Conservative Party in Smethwick was 'acting as a safety-valve – a function which otherwise might be undertaken by right-wing groups' (Deakin, 1965, p.6). This argument is all the more interesting in the light of the support given by John Bean and Colin Jordan (of the extreme right-wing British National Party) to Griffiths' campaign. In doing so, it appeared that they were helping the Conservatives to exploit the only issue on which they themselves might have gained popular support. In response, Jordan is quoted as saying, 'I was certainly aware of this danger, but equally aware that once people started to think racially, their own logic would take them well beyond any position the Conservatives could ever adopt' (Walker, 1977, p.55).

Thus, while the Conservative Party's reaction to Griffiths' victory was somewhat embarrassed, and the Labour response condemnatory, Griffiths' campaign could be seen as simply encouraging a type of anti-black sentiment which both parties were already tacitly supporting in their acceptance of the need for controls on black immigration.

The new Labour Government and the Conservative opposition were by early 1965 in complete agreement on the need for even tighter controls, thus giving further ground to the anti-immigrant, and hence anti-black sentiment and agitation in the country. It is argued that agreement between the parties on a dual policy of strict immigration control and integration measures was the chosen strategy for 'de-politicizing' the race issue (Katznelson, 1973, pp.148–51). While it may have appeared to do this in the short term, it cannot be denied that the dual policy effectively played into the hands of anti-black sentiment. First, as we have already noted, by tightening controls on black immigration both parties were by implication accepting that black immigrants were a problem and second, the introduction of ineffective race relations legislation allowed the racist lobby to claim that freedom of speech and action, so dearly defended over the centuries, was being drastically curtailed, the latter argument becoming a cornerstone of the rhetoric of the right.

The apparent consensus between the Labour and Conservative parties did leave the immigration and race issues open to further exploitation by the right. But it was not until 1968, and the intervention of Enoch Powell, that a further and important twist was given to the legitimation of white hostility. Condemned though he was by the majority of both Labour and Conservative MPs, the popularity of his appeals were readily recognized by the Conservative Party leadership who lost no time in calling for stiffer controls. What had appeared to be a period of levelling of the slippery slope was over and the rest is a matter of legislative history (i.e. Commonwealth Immigration Act 1968; Race Relations Act 1968; Immigration Act 1971; Race Relations Act 1976).

But that is not the end of the matter, not least because issues and conflicts are not automatically resolved by Acts of Parliament. The 'race/immigration' issue, along with issues such as hanging, 'law and order' and sexuality, has the capacity to suddenly return to the centre of the political stage, as the Ugandan Asian 'crisis' (Humphry and Ward, 1974; Bristow, 1976) and the events during the summer of 1976 showed. During the 1970s, the National Front and other racist parties have played a part in ensuring that race remains a political issue although, as Peter Evans (1976) shows, the press have much to answer for as well, and it is therefore possible to view the 'rise' of the National Front in Britain as yet one more lurch down 'the slippery slope'. Certainly we would argue the intervention of Powell in 1968 made racism more respectable and, in the process, prepared the ground for a party within the fascist tradition. But slippery slopes do level out and although we would not argue that the 'race/immigration' issue has lost its potency to bring about further political and social developments, we would draw attention to the following points which suggest that it may not be as steep as in the past.

First, legislation has created an administrative structure which can represent black interests (although this is not to say that such representation is either adequate or successful) in the process of decision-making, both at national and local level. This means that government and administrators do have somebody with whom to consult and may therefore be more sensitive to black interests and demands; it may also mean, as we suggest below, that there is a more adequate means of containing and limiting black protest. Second, that 'race/immigration' is an issue means not only that it can be exploited for specific ends but also that politicians and decision-makers in Britain are now aware that they have to proceed with caution (witness the pronouncements of Peter Walker within the Conservative Party), even if their knowledge and understanding is limited. This does not in itself guarantee that they will act and decide 'wisely', indeed it implies that a low profile will be adopted in relation to white racism, but it may also mean that concessions will be made to black demands (as the content of parts of the 1976 Race Relations Act suggests). Third, New Commonwealth immigrants have now lived in Britain for twenty-five years or more, and have produced black British children. What is now an established black population may produce an active political response: the passage of time has meant that what was in the 1950s an uncertain immigrant population, bewildered by new surroundings and unexpected discrimination, is now a population with a sense of history in Britain, albeit short in length but most certainly rich in content. Events such as the response in Southall to the Chaggar murder in 1976 demonstrate that there is an interaction between white racism and what might be called black politics. Fourth, there is a new bi-partisan consensus, a condemnation of the activities of the National Front which are seen to be beyond the pale.

Historical continuities

The political arguments and issues surrounding racism and the emergence of the National Front (NF) in Britain as a racist political party and the strategy it has chosen to pursue are far from novel as chapter 2 by Neill Nugent and Roger King, and chapter 3 by Caroline Knowles demonstrate. Nugent and King show that both the British Brothers League (BBL) established in 1902, and the British Union of Fascists (BUF), active in the 1930s, conducted political campaigns which alleged a decline in the economic and social position of the British people as a consequence of, respectively, Jewish immigration (in the late nineteenth century) and the Jewish presence (in the 1930s), both nationally and internationally. Both organizations were especially active in the East End of London, and it is therefore of interest that the NF seems to be obtaining electoral support from the same area; in the Greater London Council (GLC) elections in May 1977, the NF obtained about 30 per cent of its total London vote from the East End and in certain seats, obtained more than 20 per cent of the poll. Christopher Husbands comments on this continuity in chapter 7.

There are both similarities and differences between the British Brothers League, the British Union of Fascists and the NF, as Nugent and King point out. We would add that the BUF and NF contrast with the BBL in the following respect. The existence of the BUF, most obviously, and the NF, less clearly, can be understood in relation to a central development in twentieth-century European politics, the emergence of fascist political parties. Martin Walker (1977) indicates that the NF, in terms of its leadership, organization and parts of its ideology, borrows from the fascist tradition and in chapter 6 Stan Taylor comments on this question in more detail. For example, both the BUF and the NF advance a world political view which stresses the supposed international conspiracy of world Jewry, a world view that was central to the programme and strategy of the National Socialist Party of Germany (NSDAP).

Thus, while the BBL was an organization which both reflected and encouraged local grass-roots anti-Semitism in East London, the BUF in the past, and the NF currently, have had wider political horizons related to a facist world view and have utilized anti-Semitism and white racism with the aim of realizing broader aims. The BBL could be more usefully compared with the British Campaign to Stop Immigration (cf. Nugent, 1976), discussed by Michel Le Lohé in his chapter on the effects of the presence of immigrants on the local political system in Bradford, in that both organizations have their origin and *raison d'être* in anti-immigrant feeling in a particular area and have gone on to channel and organize similar feeling elsewhere in the country (cf. Gainer, 1972, pp.67–73). An ultra-right political party, with an interest in utilizing this grass-roots opposition, will obviously be interested in such organizations because, potentially, they can deliver an immediate membership; for instance, most of the members of the British Campaign to Stop Immigration joined the NF. However, the ideological transition from being anti-immigrant to 'fascist' is not a necessary or automatic process, as statements made by disillusioned NF members testify (see *Guardian*, 11 August 1977; Walker, 1977, p.59).

It is also interesting to reflect on the fact that the claims of the extreme right-wing organizations centre on similar themes. Part of an explanation for this historical continuity stems from the argument that these claims are not simply ideological constructs imposed from above but are, as we argue in our contribution, generated, in part, in the realities of working-class life. The Jews, who were forced to leave Eastern Europe in the late nineteenth century and who settled in England were, in the main, poor and had few skills, those they did have being largely irrelevant to English production methods (see Gartner, 1973, p.57). They had little alternative other than to swell the ranks of those trying to find what accommodation there was in poor working-class areas and to find any economic role that was open to them. There are similarities here with New Commonwealth immigrants although the latter were not political refugees, but economic migrants. Thus, in the same way that the white English worker of today can interpret the presence of black workers as taking 'our' houses and 'our' jobs and thereby creating the housing problem and unemployment, so did the white English worker some eighty odd years ago in relation to the arrival of Jewish workers. The causal connection may not be correct but it is based on a concrete reality which is directly experienced. Thus, it can be argued that the ideology of the British Brothers League was, in part, a political manifestation of the views of sections of the manual working class in East London.

Parallels with recent events are also evident in chapter 3 by Caroline Knowles. She is concerned with the way in which the various elements in the Labour Party responded to anti-Semitism in London in the mid-1930s and one can see from her essay that the different strategies to oppose fascism voiced within the Labour Party and the labour movement more generally in the 1930s are now being repeated with regard to the National Front. These different strategies are ultimately premised on competing world views which have conflicting ideas about the nature and role of the state in capitalist society. Strong though these parallels are, there are a number of important differences between the two periods.

First, as we have shown, the appearance of the NF as a political force has followed a period of between ten and fourteen years during which race has been, in varying senses, a political issue in British politics. Thus, in contrast to the BUF (see Benewick, 1972), the NF is able to play the 'racist card' in an already prepared arena in which blacks are already nationally defined as '*a* problem', if not '*the* problem'. But, second, there is today government legislation which makes it possible, under the Public Order Act 1936, to ban marches if they are likely to lead to a breach of the peace (used in 1977 to ban an NF march in Manchester) and which, under the Race Relations Act 1976, makes it an offence to publish or distribute written material or use, in public, words which are 'threatening, abusive or insulting in a case where, having regard to all the circumstances, hatred is likely to be stirred up against any racial group in Great Britain by the matter of words in question' (Section 70).

However, the existence of a law does not guarantee its enforcement. The Public Order Act, itself a response to political violence in 1936, has been used rarely and warily, and whether Section 70 of the 1976 Race Relations Act will suffer a similar fate is difficult to say. The history of Section 6 of the Race Relations Act 1965, which instituted the offence of incitement to racial hatred is not an encouraging one (Lester and Bindman, 1972, pp.343–74), although it may be relevant that the 1976 Race Relations Act specifically removes certain of its limitations. In the eyes of at least sections of the black communities, the existence of a strengthened provision in the form of Section 70 will be interpreted as an intention to act against incitement to racial hatred, but if the provision remains unused, and if black people continue to feel threatened by white racism, they may well conclude that this has been yet another example of government hypocrisy. In particular, this will further confirm the beliefs of a proportion of the British-born blacks that it is white authority in general that is their real enemy.

Racism and black politics

Most chapters in this book deal in one way or another with white racism, and the political action to which it is related, and there is correspondingly less attention paid to the black response. Elsewhere we have argued that it is possible to distinguish three main processes by which blacks may organize themselves politically: the class unity process, the ethnic organization process and the black unity process (Miles and Phizacklea, 1977a). We concluded on the basis of the evidence then available to us that black unity was an unlikely development and that although there was some evidence to support the view that class unity was perhaps becoming a reality, it was nevertheless the case that racial discrimination in the industrial sphere had forced black workers to pursue their interests through ethnic organization. In chapter 4 John Rex provides evidence relevant to these arguments and conclusions.

His argument is that the disadvantaged position of blacks in *all* spheres of social life is causing them to adopt a position of defensive confrontation. Thus, in our terms, it is not only because of events in the industrial sphere that ethnic organization is a necessity. Moreover, Rex's chapter raises issues (the reality of racial violence and the political activity of young British-born blacks) which we did not discuss in any detail in our earlier contribution, mainly because the available evidence was patchy and far from clear-cut. As a result of considering these issues, it becomes clear that a substantial part of the political activity of blacks in Britain is a reaction to white racism and its expression through political action.

Attempts to measure the level and scale of any form of violence are difficult, particularly when it is sporadic, local and fails to produce an organized response on the part of those attacked. The task is doubly difficult when one is attempting to measure racial violence. The fact that a West Indian is physically attacked outside a public house in Birmingham by a white Englishman may mean nothing more than it was unfortunate that he was walking past the entrance when the latter was being ejected for being drunk and disorderly. But of the very same incident, it could be argued that a West Indian stood more chance of being attacked than a white Englishman because of the racism that is an important feature of English culture. The recognition of racism is somewhat easier when, for example, bookshops selling ethnic literature are vandalized and daubed with racist slogans (see *Guardian*, 28 April 1977).

The media have given particular attention to violence by blacks, particularly at the Notting Hill Carnival in London in 1976 and 1977 and in the form of 'mugging', a media-constructed concept which suggests the appearance of a new 'black' crime although it refers to nothing more than robbery with violence from a person in a public place, an activity not uncommon in certain white working-class areas. This emphasis is consistent with the general pattern of media reporting of race (see Hartmann and Husbands, 1974) while the minimal attention paid to white violence against blacks can scarcely counter the resulting image which associates blackness with violence. Yet white violence against blacks is a reality, and in certain areas it has forced minority members to organize in self-defence. For example, Bengalis in the East End of London have experienced considerable violence and their community leaders estimated that there was an average of ten attacks a week during 1976. In the early summer of 1977 self-defence groups were set up and the situation was considered so serious by the High Commissioner for Bangladesh that he demanded an urgent report on racial violence in the East End of London (*Guardian*, 31 May and 6 June 1977). Once a feeling of being under physical attack by whites has developed within cohesive black communities (although it is often the case that it is such violence that makes them cohesive), it need not necessarily matter whether any further incidents are actually racially motivated because that is how they will be interpreted. This feeling of being under attack clearly developed in Southall in London in 1976 following the murder of an Asian youth by a white gang which contained one youth of part West Indian decent. In the context of other developments referred to earlier, this murder came to be defined by a large proportion of the Asian population as racial, and brought forth demands for protection from all forms of racism. There was not, however, agreement on the best means of ensuring protection: on the one hand the established community leadership sought protection and support from the government and the police, while on the other, many of the younger members of the population were distrustful of (white) authority and urged the Asian communities to defend themselves.

The demands for self-defence in both the East End of London and in Southall furnishes further evidence for John Rex's notion (chapter 4) of defensive confrontation, but it would be unwise to infer that this is now the general posture of black communities, for support for such actions is by no means unanimous, as was evident in Southall in 1976. Additionally, there are reasons for believing that the black population as a whole will find it difficult to generate a coherent, single strategy to oppose white racism and that, when it comes to action, those who are immigrants, are as likely to withdraw from the political process as to participate.

Elsewhere we have argued that it is unlikely in present circumstances that West Indian and Asian workers will organize collectively to pursue common interests because, first, the cultural characteristics of the Asian ethnic groups are as different from the West Indians as they are from the English; second, there is evidence of substantial hostility between Asians and West Indians, and third, West Indians and Asians do not themselves constitute homogeneous communities (Miles and Phizacklea, 1977a). It is particularly relevant here to also bear in mind that the black population constitutes no more than 2 per cent of the total British population and that over half of the former are immigrants. That 2 per cent of the British population, although residentially concentrated, is nevertheless a small minority, and when the cultural heterogeneity is taken into account, we are, in fact, talking about even smaller ethnic minorities.

The fact that the black population is divided into immigrants and black British is also significant in that the former do not necessarily regard Britain as 'home'. Moreover, the black immigrants have come from ex-British colonies where an ideology about the 'Mother Country' was deeply rooted: this ideology included the beliefs that Britain was a fair and just society and that all were equal before the law, beliefs which are still echoed in the black communities, although less often than in the past. In the event of more generalized conflict, those who are immigrants, although they may vociferously demand equal treatment in Britain, may not be willing to pursue an active strategy against racism when they are very aware of being not only a small *minority*, but also an *immigrant* minority. In the final analysis they may be unwilling to take part in any action which they think might lead to 'trouble', and which could worsen their situation. They may even prefer to return to their country of origin. There are, of course, exceptions, particularly the Kenyan and Ugandan Asians who were forced to leave East Africa and whose options are therefore more limited.

It is here that we turn to the second issue which could not be broached while we were reviewing the political strategies available to the immigrants, the political strategy of black youth. The position of the British-born blacks is somewhat different from their immigrant parents in that India, Pakistan or the West Indies cannot be 'home', at least not in the same sense. On the basis of our own experience, we argue that a proportion of British-born blacks are well aware and, indeed, contemptuous of their parents' desires to avoid taking any action which would provoke 'trouble'. For West Indian youth, as well as for young people from some of the Asian communities, their parents' country of origin is very distant, both physically, culturally, and indeed emotionally, so there can be no notion of 'return' to a 'homeland'. One consequence of this is that they may be more prepared to defend their position in British society. There are two aspects to this, the reality of white violence, and the existence of institutional racism and a structure of disadvantage. With regard to the former, it is now clear from events in Southall and from our knowledge of other parts of London and elsewhere that both West Indian and Asian youth are prepared to meet violence with violence.

The existence of institutional racism and a structure of racial disadvantage is equally important to an understanding of the strategies pursued by black youth in Britain, particularly West Indian youth. We argue that both street crimes and the emergence of Rastafarianism amongst West Indian youth are understandable responses to unemployment, homelessness, police harassment and a socio-economic system which confines the black worker to certain low-status and low-pay sections of the economy (see Smith, 1976). Moreover, a substantial proportion of West Indian youth has been culturally alienated, having neither the support of the idea of 'home' (which has been an important emotional support for their parents) nor any avenue into white working-class culture since the mid-1960s (see Hebdige, 1975). What might be called the 'Rasta' culture of sections of West Indian youth in Britain is itself a modification of the Rastafarianism that originated in Jamaica (see Smith, Augier and Nettleford, 1960) and need not contain the religious aspect that is central to its parent. The wearing of locks and a green, red and yellow woolly hat in the British context is more likely to be a 'political' expression of a rejection of white society and an identification with an alternative way of life than an indication of religious belief in the strict sense.

However, the evidence for arguing that both Asian and West Indian youth is more likely to adopt an active strategy of defensive confrontation needs to be placed in perspective. Not all, indeed not even a majority of British-born blacks with West Indian parents adhere to a Rasta culture and we currently have little evidence to suggest which political strategy the majority may pursue. A study (albeit dated) of political beliefs of school-age West Indian adolescents indicated that only a small, although significant, minority of those questioned indicated an ethnically-specific conceptualization of politics in Britain, the remainder either showing little interest in politics or exhibiting remarkably similar beliefs to their white working-class counterparts (Phizacklea, 1975). Additionally, and this applies to both West Indian and Asian youth, the activity of young blacks in Britain will be mediated by at least a section of their elders. Sivanandan has argued that the Race Relations Board and the Community Relations Commission (now merged to form the Commission for Racial Equality) have created 'a black bourgeoisie, especially West Indian (the Asian bourgeoisie was already in the wings), to which the state can now hand over control of black dissidents in general and black youth in particular' (1976, p.364). Whether it is correct to label those black 'race professionals' (Heineman, 1972, pp.126—9) who have entered the state's employ as a bourgeoisie is irrelevant here. The point is that there is now a sufficiently large group of blacks who, like representatives of other interest groups, are able as a consequence of their personal structural positions, to request that both government and civil service take account of their own views (and, therefore, to an extent, black interests) on relevant matters. Some of these black 'race professionals' are employed in the Commission for Racial Equality (CRE), an organization that might usefully be compared with the Trades Union Congress (TUC). Like the TUC, the CRE will claim that it should be consulted on all matters affecting its constituents and will want to discourage any rank-and-file activity which is unconstitutional. We must wait to see whether they can discourage black youth from pursuing direct action as a response to their disadvantaged circumstances.

In sum, we are arguing that what we have previously called the process of ethnic organization, and what John Rex (chapter 4) calls defensive confrontation, is *inter alia* a reaction by blacks in Britain to racial discrimination and violence, and to the structure of racial disadvantage. We are also arguing that, in the current circumstances, it is some of the young British-born blacks who are most likely to be active participants in this process. Thus, in the case of Southall, we are suggesting that the conflict over strategies to oppose racist violence can be seen as both a generational conflict and a conflict between immigrant and British-born. However, we also want to draw attention to the evidence which shows that, in certain circumstances, class unity is also a reality. Robin Ward shows in chapter 9 that there are circumstances in which white and black workers are able to organize collectively to pursue their interests as residents. This serves to support our argument elsewhere that class unity can develop locally and 'spontaneously' in response to a specific issue or problem and, as with much working-class political action in the informal sphere of politics, people with little or no experience of political activity are drawn together to pursue a joint interest (Miles and Phizacklea, 1977a). It is therefore inaccurate to view the development of black politics in Britain as being solely in one direction and with only one impetus.

Racist ideas and racist political action

So far in this introduction we have not discussed the relationship between racist ideas and racist political action. It is a truism to state that there is no simple relationship between attitudes and action: an attitude must be viewed merely as a behavioural predisposition and the balance of evidence is that situational factors are as, if not more, important in explaining action than personal beliefs (cf. Wicker, 1969). Thus, it may be that racism is widespread in British society, but it does not follow that a large majority of the British population, or indeed, the British working class, is willing to engage actively in racist violence or to support or join a racist political party. If Stan Taylor's analysis (chapter 6) is correct, support for the National Front, expressed in terms of voting and membership at least, would appear to be limited and not subject to steady growth. Furthermore, as Christopher Husbands points out in chapter 7, it does not necessarily follow that a vote for the National Front is an expression of racism, although this may be more true in the late 1970s than in the earlier part of the decade.

One reason for the lack of 'fit' between racist ideas and racist action is that racist ideas are held in association with a wide range of ideas about other issues. As we take care to point out in our paper, only a relatively small proportion of our working-class sample consistently relate their self-defined disadvantaged position to the presence of black people in Britain. For the majority who hold racist beliefs, their racism rubs shoulders with other, often contradictory, explanations and beliefs. One might therefore argue that, for this majority, their political ideas make possible a range of political actions, but which is actually pursued at any one point in time depends upon both the context and the relative importance to the individual of the various contradictory ideas. The holding of racist beliefs therefore carries the potential for racist political action although the potential is only rarely realized. It is against this background that one can view the march of some London dockers in 1968 to the House of Commons to express support for Enoch Powell and his views. The march was, by all accounts, spontaneously organized, a quick response to the speech of a national politician which 'activated' racist ideas to the extent that they assumed such an importance that they could only be expressed in some form of action. The account given by Pearson of 'Paki-bashing' in a Lancashire mill town also supports this view. 'Paki-bashing' has not been a permanent feature of life in this town but occurred during the summer in 1964 as a response to a particular incident: the incident, in the context of the socio-economic circumstances of the area and the racist beliefs of the local working population, stimulated the action (Pearson, 1976; see also Horobin, 1972).

If this sort of explanation is correct, it gives support to those who argue that the media can have a profound effect on the relationship between the white British and New Commonwealth ethnic minorities. In drawing attention to, for example, the allocation of homeless Asian families to a luxury hotel, without paying equal attention to the fact that white British homeless families were also allocated such accommodation (Evans, 1976), the national newspapers both brought to the fore and confirmed racist beliefs. In such circumstances, individuals and political organizations can more easily stimulate active support for racist politics. Stan Taylor's chapter contains evidence for this argument with regard to the wide press coverage given to the entry of Malawi Asians in 1976 and the National Front vote in the Metropolitan District Elections.

In this context, it is therefore significant that racist ideas in the white British population find an echo in the ideology of particular political parties. By comparing both Stan Taylor's (chapter 6) and, more particularly Neill Nugent and Roger King's (chapter 2) analysis of NF ideology with our analysis of the content of contemporary working class racism in the inner city, one can see that the manual working class could well transfer support to the NF. It does not follow, however, that non-manual workers are less likely to support the NF, if only because, as Stan Taylor suggests, the appeal of the NF to this group may be based on the more abstract ideas of race and nation. However, as both Stan Taylor's and Christopher Husbands' (chapter 7) papers confirm, large-scale support for the NF is, at best, potential rather than actual, at least as measured by membership and votes. Future research would therefore do well to concentrate upon identifying the circumstances in which racist ideas are translated into racist political action.

Working-class racism

In our contribution to this volume, we imply that it is possible to identify a distinct working-class racism, a view which receives some support from Stan Taylor's paper. However, as Michael Banton correctly points out in chapter 10, the question of whether one can identify a working-class racism remains unproven in the absence of comparative studies. But behind this apparently straightforward empirical question there also lies the more general issue of the relationship between class consciousness and nationalism.

The formation of the British working class has occurred within the boundary of the nation state which in turn structures class conflict. Because of this, it is possible for the working class, in common with other classes, to identify with the national structure that both surrounds and supports British capital and, hence, one finds within sections of the working class strong support for both the Royal Family (for example, as demonstrated by the Jubilee celebrations in 1977) and British political institutions. Similarly, the arrival of black immigrants from the New Commonwealth has brought forth a negative response from all classes in British society. However, the structural position of the working class (cf. Westergaard and Resler, 1975) gives rise to specific conflicts and particular images of the socio-economic structure (Parkin, 1972, pp.88–96; Bulmer, 1975) with the implication that working-class views about New Commonwealth immigrants are likely to be situated in a quite distinct belief system. It is therefore possible for a working-class consciousness, shaped and constrained within the nation state, to accommodate negative beliefs about 'outsiders' who, in the case of New Commonwealth immigrants, are physically distinct.

This is well illustrated by the case of the decline of the cotton industry in Lancashire. Economic competition between British and Asian manufacturers is long standing and consciousness of this is widespread in the local working-class communities in the mill towns. The boundary of the nation provides the context for the demand from both mill owners and mill workers for import controls: capital and labour come to stand united against 'foreign' competition. The recent decline of the cotton industry has coincided with the arrival of Pakistanis in these towns and this, according to Pearson

> provided a concrete and visible manifestation of the economic issue of import control. Thus, the importation of low-cost cotton goods and low-cost labour merge, and the Pakistani worker takes his place in the drama of the 'poor cotton weaver' – in a crude, common-sense form of economic rationality – as a symbol of the problems of a troubled working community (1976, p.70).

For the local, white working class, the Pakistani worker becomes a visible symbol of economic and social processes of decline which are not easily intelligible in local and concrete terms, with the consequence that 'Paki-bashing' can be seen as 'a primitive form of political and economic struggle' (Pearson, 1976, p.69). Physical attacks on blacks by whites in such areas therefore exhibit a form of rationality when considered within the context of the working-class condition and experience which is, in turn, constrained by a national boundary.

Nationalism and ethnicity

Several chapters in this book refer to nationalism in connection with the problem of how to conceptualize the response of a large section of the British, or perhaps more correctly, the English to New Commonwealth immigrants. It is relevant to recall here that we are considering a social process in which the English have been brought into contact, through immigration, with a number of quite distinct groups, but that large sections of the English population have found, and still do find, it difficult to distinguish between them. Perhaps the most common distinction drawn is between West Indians and Asians, although the precise words used and, indeed, the specific groups referred to, vary from place to place.

But it is not simply a matter of distinguishing the Asians from the West Indians, or even the Pakistanis from the Bangladeshis: Verity Saifullah Khan (1976) has argued that although Pakistanis in Britain share a common nationality and religion, they are differentiated in terms of ethnic/regional origin and class. One can therefore neither talk of Pakistanis as an ethnic group, nor assume common identification and solidarity amongst them. Khan sees ethnicity as 'something to do with people of one culture realizing its distinctiveness and utilizing its distinctive resources . . . in interactions with outsiders. Both presuppose an awareness of difference and a degree of contact and interaction with outsiders' (1976, p.223).

But if ethnicity is a reaction to contact with 'outsiders', with people from another culture, can we define English racism as an expression or aspect of an emerging English ethnicity? Is it the case that the arrival of black immigrants in Britain forces not only the various migrant groups but also the English to develop an ethnicity? We would not agree, and for the following reasons. First, in Khan's terms, ethnicity would seem to be *inter alia*, the response of a group to its new minority status *vis-à-vis* the majority: 'The new minority situation demands resources inaccessible to, or distinct from, those available to the majority' (1976, p.223). In the case in question, it is the English who are the majority and the Pathans, the Mirpuris, etc. who are the minorities. Second, to anticipate a point made by Michael Banton in chapter 10, the negative response of the English to New Commonwealth immigration often implies some kind of territorial right which has been transgressed. Evidence for this is found in the responses of some of our white respondents in terms of 'our country'. It is because the majority can claim territorial rights and allegiance to an historical nation state, that we would argue that the 'we' in this instance is an expression of nationalism. One can therefore argue that, in the case of New Commonwealth migration to Britain, the immigrants have, partly as a consequence of their contact with the English, developed their *ethnicity*, while sections of the English population, in reacting unfavourably both to the immigrant's presence and their maintenance of difference (that is their ethnicity), have come to assert a *nationalism* which, as we suggest elsewhere in this book, is at least implicitly, if not explicitly, racist.

Reflections on the future

> As I look ahead, I am filled with foreboding. Like the Roman,
> I seem to see 'the River Tiber foaming with much blood'. That
> tragic and intractable phenomenon which we watch with horror on
> the other side of the Atlantic but which there is interwoven with
> the history and existence of the States itself, is coming upon us here
> by our own volition and our own neglect. Indeed it has all but come.
> In numerical terms, it will be of American proportions long before
> the end of the century (Enoch Powell in 1968 speech, (1969)).

Reflecting on the possible future developments in Britain with
regard to white racism and its political expression and effects, the
chapters in this book suggest that the following points need to be taken
into account. First, there is a need to consider the international context
and, in particular, the validity of comparisons between one country and
another. The chapters by John Rex, Christopher Husbands and Michael
Banton all indicate that it is not easy to draw parallels between the
British and American experience. Other parallels are not considered
here, but are nevertheless worthy of attention, particularly that of
Germany between 1918 and 1933 (the years of socio-economic crisis
and the rise of the NSDAP) and Britain in the 1970s. Comparative work
would, in this case, need to weigh up the relative importance to the
rise of fascism in Germany of at least the following factors: defeat of
Germany in the First World War, the political weakness of the German
right-wing bourgeois nationalist party, the nature and extent of the
German economic crisis and the size and political actions and reactions
of the German *petit-bourgeoisie* in the 1920s. The extent to which
similar conditions apply in Britain is debatable although the situation
is not static: neither the ongoing unity of the Conservative Party, nor
the long-term recovery of British capitalism, are inevitable.

Second, the presence and strength of the National Front, as well as
the nature and extent of racist voting, must be put into perspective.
The ability of the National Front to obtain media coverage may have
given the appearance of strength and a high level of support, but this
must stand the test of time and of the facts. The facts of membership
and election results suggest a relatively low and unstable level of
support and ongoing media interest cannot be guaranteed because, as
with Alsatian dogs, to use Peter Evans' (1976) analogy, the NF cannot
be news *all* the time. At the same time, one must bear in mind that the

NF may have had, and still be having, effects which are more difficult to measure than votes, that is to legitimate white racism and, as Michael Banton (chapter 10) points out, to influence the debate about 'race/immigration' within and between the Labour and Conservative parties.

Third, there is the question of the passage of time. It is only thirty years since the arrival of SS *Empire Windrush* and eighteen years since the peak of New Commonwealth immigration was stimulated by the first attempt at control in 1962. In that time the lives of whites and blacks in Britain have been lived, accommodations have been made, and learning has occurred. It is not that 'bad race relations' are balanced by 'good race relations' but that, as in Moss Side in Manchester, people have come to live and work together *without reference to race.* A similar point is made by Sandra Wallman when talking of the action of residents of a multi-ethnic street in contesting a compulsory purchase order: 'But Pearman Street could not have pulled itself together to contest the CPO except with the ties forged by years of continuous and viable neighbouring' (1975/6, p.520).

Nevertheless, white racism, nurtured by *inter alia* socio-economic decline, the words of Enoch Powell and the activities of the NF, remains and, given the historical context, is likely to remain a reality. Certainly, if one accepts the argument that British culture contains elements which makes racist ideas the norm, then one must be sceptical about the possibility of any short-term elimination of racism. However, in so far as our argument that working-class racism in the inner city is, at least in part, a product of the socio-economic decline of such areas, then there is scope for eliminating aspects of it by reversing that decline. But this, even if it is possible, will by itself have only limited value if there is not also a serious attack on the extent of racial disadvantage. If the current pattern of disadvantage is reproduced in the second and subsequent generations, the black British, then, it is not only confining to a subordinate economic position a section of the population which is not willing to be so confined, with all that that implies, but it may also have the function of confirming in the eyes of sections of the white population that the black worker is destined to be confined to such a role. The assumption of the inferiority of the black worker needs to be challenged not only at the level of ideas but in practice: here it is worth reflecting on Smith's finding that employers who ignored employees' objections to the employment of blacks were not later confronted with outward conflict between black and white workers (1974, pp.57–63).

Whether any of this is possible within the limitations and demands of a capitalist economy such as the British, requiring as it so obviously does, a 'reserve army' of labour and, in spite of technological advance, a semi- and unskilled sector of the workforce on low pay, is a moot point. What one can be fairly certain about is that the low paid, semi- and unskilled jobs currently occupied by blacks cannot be filled by another migrant labour force (Böhning, 1972) if at least a proportion of black workers are not able to move up the occupational hierarchy. One must be sceptical about this happening since the available evidence shows that discrimination remains widespread, particularly in the area of promotion, and that blacks are more likely to be unemployed than whites in an economic crisis (Smith, 1976, pp.56–63, 68, 112–14). Such a conclusion is reinforced by predictions about a level of unemployment exceeding one million for the forseeable future.

Furthermore, eliminating racism is difficult not only because of economic, but also because of political factors. It is possible to argue that so much of the running in the political debate about race has been by the right and the racists. Government is therefore compromised by its record, and this applies not only to Conservative, but also to Labour governments; in the 1950s one might have expected the latter to have opposed this trend, but the legislative history of the Labour Government shattered such expectations. As others have observed before us, the Labour Government's Race Relations Acts of 1965 and 1968 were sops to black interests following racist immigration legislation. This record makes it even more necessary for government to adopt a high profile with regard to white racism and the structure of racial disadvantage.

Perhaps the only other potential institutional opposition to these developments is the labour movement. But as we have shown elsewhere (Miles and Phizacklea, 1977b, 1978), the Trades Union Congress, although regularly confirming its principled opposition to racial discrimination, came to accept government policy by the mid-1960s and defined as the main issue, not white racism and racial discrimination, but the failure of the immigrants to 'integrate'. Since 1974 this policy has shifted towards a clearer opposition to racism in the light of the apparent 'rise' of the NF, but since its propaganda campaign against racism in the autumn of 1976 it has, at the time of writing (early 1978), lapsed into apparent silence.

In the context of all these factors, racism must continue to carry with it the potential for racist political action. It now seems likely that such action will produce a defensive response on the part of sections of the black communities which are threatened, and therein lies the potential for amplification of conflict. With regard to the future, much therefore depends upon confronting and containing those forces whose intervention serves as the motor to translate racism into political action, the most important of which recently have been the National Front, the news media and certain national politicians.

Notes

1 These events include the political storm following the housing of two Asian families in a four-star hotel, the arrival of Asians from Malawi, the Hawley Report 'scandal' unleashed by Enoch Powell, MP, and the murder of a Sikh in Southall.
2 We would like to thank our colleagues at the SSRC Research Unit on Ethnic Relations for their comments on an earlier draft of this essay.

Bibliography

Banton, M. and Harwood, J. (1975), *The Race Concept*, David & Charles, Newton Abbot.

Banton, M. (1976), 'The Adjective "Black": a Discussion Note', *Network*, no. 6, pp.2–3.

Banton, M. (1977), *The Idea of Race*, Tavistock, London.

Benewick, R. (1972), *The Fascist Movement in Britain*, Allen Lane, London.

Böhning, W.R. (1972), *The Migration of Workers in the United Kingdom and the European Community*, Oxford University Press, London.

Bristow, M. (1976), 'Britain's Response to the Ugandan Asian Crisis: Government Myths v. Political and Resettlement Realities', *New Community*, vol. v, no. 13, pp.265–79.

Bulmer, M. (ed.) (1975), *Working-Class Images of Society*, Routledge & Kegan Paul, London.

Butler, D. and Stokes, D. (1974), *Political Change in Britain*, Macmillan, London.

Deakin, N. (ed.) (1965), *Colour and the British Electorate 1964*, Pall Mall Press, London.

Engels, F. (1972), *The Condition of the Working Class in England*, Panther, London.

Evans, P. (1976), *Publish and Be Damned?*, Runnymede Trust, London.

Gainer, B. (1972), *The Alien Invasion*, Heinemann, London.

Gartner, L.P. (1973), *The Jewish Immigrant in England 1870–1914*, Simon Publications, London.

Hartmann, P. and Husbands, C. (1974), *Racism and the Mass Media*, Davis-Poynter, London.

Hebdige, D. (1975), 'Reggae, Rastas and Rudies', *Cultural Studies*, no. 7/8, pp.135–54.

Heineman, B.W. (1972), *The Politics of the Powerless*, Oxford University Press, London.

Horobin, A. (1972), ' "Paki-Bashing" in Coventry', *Police Journal*, vol. 45, pp.184–97.

Humphry, D. and Ward, M. (1974), *Passports and Control*, Penguin, Harmondsworth.

Kahn, V.S. (1976), 'Pakistanis in Britain: Perceptions of a Population', *New Community*, vol. v, pp.222–9.

Katznelson, I. (1973), *Black Men, White Cities*, Oxford University Press, London.

Lester, A. and Bindman, G. (1972), *Race and the Law*, Penguin, Harmondsworth.

Lyon, M. (1972), 'Race and Ethnicity in Pluralistic Societies', *New Community*, vol. 1, no. 4, pp.256–62.

Marx, K. and Engels, F. (1965), *Selected Correspondence*, Progress Publishers, Moscow.

Mason, P. (1969), 'Ten Years of the Institute', *Race*, vol. 10, no. 2, pp.193–202.

Miles, R. and Phizacklea, A. (1977a), 'Class, Race, Ethnicity and Political Action', *Political Studies*, vol. xxv, no. 4, pp.491–507.

Miles, R. and Phizacklea, A. (1977b), 'The TUC, Black Workers and New Commonwealth Immigration 1954–1973', *SSRC, Research Unit on Ethnic Relations Working Paper*, no. 6.

Miles, R. and Phizacklea, A. (1978), 'The TUC and Black Workers 1974–1976', *British Journal of Industrial Relations*, vol. xvi, no. 2, pp.195–207.

Nugent, N. (1976), 'The Anti-Immigration Groups', *New Community*, vol. v, no. 3, pp.302–10.

Pannell, N. and Brockway, F. (1965), *Immigration: What is the Answer?*, Routledge & Kegan Paul, London.

Parkin, F. (1972), *Class Inequality and Political Order*, Paladin, London.

Pearson, G. (1976), ' "Paki-Bashing" in a North-East Lancashire Cotton Town: A Case Study and its History' in G. Mungham and G. Pearson (eds), *Working-Class Youth Culture*, Routledge & Kegan Paul, London.

Phizacklea, A. (1975), 'A Sense of Political Efficacy: a Comparison of Black and White Adolescents', in I. Crewe (ed.), *British Political Sociology Yearbook*, vol. 2, *The Politics of Race*, Croom Helm, London.

Powell, E. (1969), *Freedom and Reality*, Elliot Right Way Books, Kingswood, Surrey.

Reaney, G.S. (1892), 'The Moral Aspect' in A. White (ed.), *The Destitute Alien in Great Britain*, London.

Sivanandan, A. (1976), 'Race, Class and the State: the Black Experience in Britain', *Race and Class*, vol. xvii, pp.347—68.

Smith, D. (1974), *Racial Disadvantage in Employment*, Political and Economic Planning, London.

Smith, D. (1976), *The Facts of Racial Disadvantage*, Political and Economic Planning, London.

Smith, M.G., Augier, R. and Nettleford, R. (1960), *The Rastafari Movement in Kingston, Jamaica*, Institute of Social and Economic Research, Jamaica.

Walker, M. (1977), *The National Front*, Fontana, London.

Wallman, S. (1975/6), 'A Street in Waterloo', *New Community*, vol. iv, pp.517—23.

Watson, J.L. (ed.) (1977), *Between Two Cultures: Migrants and Minorities in Britain*, Blackwell, Oxford.

Westergaard, J. and Resler, H. (1975), *Class in a Capitalist Society*, Heinemann, London.

Wicker, A. (1969), 'Attitudes Versus Actions', *Journal of Social Issues*, vol. 25.

Wilkins, W.H. (1892), *The Alien Invasion*, Methuen, London.

CHAPTER 2

Ethnic minorities, scapegoating and the extreme right

Neill Nugent and Roger King

Stereotyping and scapegoating

A frequent theme in the literature on right-wing politics is the abuse organizations level at minority sections of their native populations. Examples vary in kind, from the ruthless exploitation of Jews by the Nazis in Germany in the 1920s and 1930s, to the attack made upon Masons by the radical right in America for much of the nineteenth century. But though the campaigns may take very different forms the central message is always the same: the minority is responsible, directly or indirectly, for many of the nation's ills.

In many circumstances of course the actions of a minority – e.g. financiers, politicians, industrialists – are the cause of unwanted events and they can then become justifiable targets of criticism. But to identify and to attack minorities in these circumstances is different from, say, the National Front's assault upon Britain's black population. The distinction, which in practice is often a very fine one, lies in the closely related concepts of stereotyping and scapegoating.

Stereotyping involves three processes (Secord and Backman, 1974, p.21):

1　the identification of a category – such as policemen, hippies, or blacks;
2　the attribution of traits to the category;
3　the application of the traits to anyone belonging to the category.

In so far as it involves generalizations about groups of people, stereotyping may thus be regarded as an aspect of the common process of typification. But there is also, in stereotyping, the suggestion that the traits being ascribed are false. They are not necessarily wholly inaccurate, although in some cases they may be, but they are at least an exaggeration. Thus the commonly held picture of Jews as being particularly mercenary, talkative and religious is a stereotype in that, although it may have an element of truth, it is a gross over-generalization.

For the detached observer considerable problems are of course raised in ascertaining valid criteria for identifying stereotypes. But for many 'participants' the degree of factual accuracy is less important than the manner in which the traits are portrayed and the consequences which flow from believing them to be true. For, as psychologists in particular have long argued, stereotypes perform a key psychological role in substituting simplicity and order for complexity. This can result in a remarkable capacity for rationalizing selfish behaviour, in not being sensitive to contrary evidence, and also frequently ascribing to racial inheritance that which may be a cultural acquisition. Ethnic groups are indeed especially prone to being stereotyped for, as Tajfel has shown, the learning and assimilation of socially sanctioned values is made even easier through the existence of obvious visual clues which place each individual firmly and instantly in the category to which he belongs (1969, pp.79–98).

When stereotypes are used in the attribution of blame or evil, one can talk of scapegoating. Black immigrants, for example, are not only identified as a category, but their alleged traits, as well as being characteristic of all black immigrants, are seen as the cause of problems affecting the 'accusing group'. As with stereotyping there is the implication of factual error, scapegoating carrying with it the suggestion that it is a substitute for the analysis of the real causes of a problem – poor housing, unemployment, social crime rates or whatever. Scapegoating is then an aspect of prejudice and as such has tended to be viewed from two different perspectives: the psychological and the sociological.

The first links scapegoating with feelings of frustration and aggression that arise when individual needs are not satisfied. Almost any outlet for the frustration may be sought and so, if the real cause is impersonal or too powerful to be attacked, attention will be directed towards objects which are more suitable – those which are easily identifiable and which cannot, or will not, strike back.

The second approach, the sociological, whilst still emphasizing the importance of motives and inner drives, has widened the scope of study to stress the role of socio-economic conditions and cultural traditions. So Lipset and Raab (1971), and Allport (1958), have emphasized the consequences of social mobility for maintaining prejudiced stereotypes. Others, notably Rex and Moore (1967), have suggested that prejudiced attitudes are the outcome of the objective situation of housing competition or deprivation, while others still have taken the view that feelings of deprivation and deterioration are more important as the wellsprings of prejudice and scapegoating than actual hardship (see Richmond *et al.*, 1973; Robb, 1954).

Our concern here, however, is not to evaluate and assess these various approaches. Rather do they constitute an interesting backdrop to our interest which is the portrayal of the scapegoat by right-wing political organizations in Britain, a subject which, despite the increasing literature on right-wing extremism, has received surprisingly scant attention. A comparison will be made of the attempted exploitation of the favourite scapegoat of the British extreme right - ethnic minorities - by examining the campaigns of the major extremist group of three different periods in the twentieth century.

Pre First World War: the British Brothers League

No systematic attempt to scapegoat an ethnic minority was made by the right until the campaign of the British Brothers League (BBL) in the first years of the century.[1] At first sight it is surprising that no earlier attempt was made, for though Britain did not have an anti-Semitic tradition such as sustained many extremist groups in Europe, Irish immigration, which reached a peak between 1850 and 1880, had resulted in considerable tensions, resentments, and ill feeling. In addition, the Irish, if not as conspicuous as later arrivals, were identifiable - by virtue of their brogue, manners, customs and, frequently, dress - and their presence was widely believed to pose a threat, not only to the level of wages but to the moral standards of the population and the British way of life (see Jackson, 1963; Curtis, 1968). In attracting economic, religious, social, as well as ethnic prejudice they acted in many ways as forerunners of the later Jewish and black immigrants and though not subject to such widespread scapegoating they were quickly identified as a major problem and stereotyped. As Jackson has noted:

> The fact that Irish areas were singled out for special mention by the numerous commissions concerned to inquire into conditions in the large industrial towns led to the assumption that the Irish were

responsible for these conditions. . . . It was perhaps easier for contemporaries to lay the blame at the point that the evil was most evident rather than at its source (1963, p. 41).

But though anti-Irish prejudice gave rise to widespread disturbances and riots, particularly in Lancashire where concentrations were heavy, where itinerant preachers and Orange Lodges fanned the embers and where economic conditions, particularly in textiles, were precarious, no extremist political organization attempted to exploit the situation by, for example, calling for controls on Irish entry. There are three main reasons for this. First, the restricted franchise meant that those who had, or thought they had, most cause for complaint had little political weight. Even after the 1867 Reform Act approximately 40 per cent of the population in the boroughs, where the Irish were concentrated, did not have the vote. Second, though abuse could be laid upon the ever-hardening stereotype of 'Paddy' – he was 'childish, emotionally unstable, ignorant, indolent, superstitious, primitive or semi-civilised, dirty, vengeful and violent' (Curtis, 1968, p.53) – it was difficult, since Ireland was part of the United Kingdom, to translate this into concrete proposals. While many MPs might draw on the stereotype to imply that the Irish were unfit to govern themselves, they could hardly use it in an 'anti-foreigner' campaign. This was especially the case on the right of the political spectrum where imperialist and unionist sentiments were strongest. Third, the mid nineteenth century was, in general terms, a period of rising prosperity. There were periods of high unemployment and in some areas, such as Lancashire during the cotton famine, it was severe, but by and large social and economic distress was restricted to those with little influence. By the time of the onset of the Great Depression, which covered the last quarter of the century, when scapegoating appeals might have had a greater potency, the Irish, in terms of both numbers and life-style, were much less conspicuous. (As compared with a peak census figure of 3.0 per cent in 1861 the number of Irish born in England and Wales had dropped to 1.6 per cent of the total population in 1891.)

In any event, as the century drew to a close, there was a much more conspicuous, and therefore attractive, ethnic minority 'available' for exploitation. The exodus of the Jews from persecution in eastern Europe from the mid-1880s, although only resulting in about 2500 immigrants entering Britain each year, quickly attracted the attention of a powerful group of Conservative MPs and as early as 1892 the Party announced its intention of introducing controls. By the turn of the century, with numbers increasing as a result of famines and pogroms in Russia, Poland and Rumania, Britain had taken in more east European immigrants than any country except the United States. Many settled in the East End of London since it offered employment to the immigrants, who were mainly townsfolk but without industrial skills or accumulated capital and with a background of small trading rather than factory work.

It was in these circumstances that the British Brothers League was founded in 1902 in the East End by a Captain William Shaw, working in close association with the Tory member for Stepney, Major William Evans Gordan (see Gainer, 1972; Garrard, 1971). Campaigning under the slogan 'England for the English' it was the first English-based organization to systematically wage a campaign based on popular support against an ethnic minority.[2] Nationalism and anti-Semitism were the main ingredients of its appeal, though like many subsequent anti-immigration organizations its leaders strongly denied racialist prejudice and usually avoided the word 'Jew'.

In the campaign the classic scapegoating techniques were all to the fore. Increasingly the immigrants were an undifferentiated mass: 'rubbish', 'contents of dustbins', 'savages' and 'scum of humanity'. Wild exaggerations of the number of settlers were made amidst allegations of falsification of census returns. Britain was being 'flooded' and 'invaded' by 'alien swarms'. In areas of urban decay it was said to be 'like a foreign country', 'It is Jerusalem', 'There is a nation within a nation'.

As for the economic and social position of the native population, the main objections of the BBL were that immigration was creating over-crowding, was bringing about excessive rates and rents, and was causing unemployment. In an area where there was a considerable degree of economic uncertainty, these charges – that the alien was driving the Englishmen from 'hearth and home' – were potent, all the more so when allied with more general allegations, such as the claimed priority given to immigrants by the authorities and the supposed ultimate aim of the aliens to take over the country. The BBL warned, amidst prophecies of impending doom and racial conflict, that patience had its limits. Englishmen would not forever stand aside as 'many thousands of pauper aliens' entered every month (Royal Commission, 1903).

Undoubtedly immigration did exacerbate problems in the East End, but the BBL was quite wrong to present the aliens as the source of the difficulties. As with the black population of Britain today, it was nearer

the truth to say that the immigrants were, along with the native population, victims of changing economic conditions and inadequate social
planning. Thus, as Gainer has shown, the Jews were blamed for the
unemployment of dockers, when the real problem was recurrent
depressions; the unemployment of tailors, when they were being
replaced more by automation and provincial competition; and the
unemployment of shoemakers, when the industry was already in rapid
decline (1972, p.19ff). As for overcrowding, that was a long-standing
problem in East London, and in any event the increased pressure on
accommodation and rents at the turn of the century was occasioned as
much by an influx of provincials as by aliens.

But the Jews were conspicuous, convenient and available. Their
linguistic, cultural and occupational characteristics were all more
distinct than those of the Irish and they were, as Jones has shown,
further reinforced by immigrant religious leaders who fought to
preserve 'fundamental Judaism and the speaking of Yiddish, which
helped set them apart from Anglo-Jewry as well as English society'
(1977, p.71).

The political map, too, had begun to change rapidly. Increasingly
the state was expected to be responsive to the demands of a widening
electorate, which was probably less sympathetic to the immigrant than
were the 'educated' classes. Governments were visible and intervention-
ist, and had difficulty in ignoring calls for immigration controls by
groups which were concerned at the apparent increase in competition
for housing and education. Thus, it was poor immigrants, rather than
native, better off, Jewry who were the main target of abuse. They were
forced to be the 'whipping boys' and continued to be so even after the
Royal Commission on Alien Immigrants, which reported in 1903,
'cleared' the immigrants of most of the charges laid against them. As
Garrard has observed 'into areas particularly in need of a scapegoat,
came groups of people particularly suited for that role' (1971, p.49).
They provided a ready explanation for a number of social problems
which existed before they came and which would not have been substantially alleviated had they been prevented from coming. Evidence
refuting the charges could thus never satisfy BBL sympathizers and it
was only with the eventual passage of an Aliens Act, in 1905, that its
activities declined.

Inter-war: the British Union of Fascists

The British Union of Fascists (BUF) was by far the largest and most influential of the ultra-right-wing organizations in the inter-war period. Formed by Sir Oswald Mosley in 1932, and dominated by him until its activities were suspended by the government in 1940, it achieved a notoriety, particularly for its anti-Semitic campaign, which has scarcely been surpassed before or since.

Unquestionably there were anti-Semites active in the BUF from the outset, and many of them were close to Mosley, but there is little suggestion in the early period of an organized campaign against the Jews. Rather Mosley's proposals emphasized fundamental political and economic reforms which, it was claimed, were necessary in the face of the inability of the major political parties to reconcile 'the prerequisites of good government: progress and stability'. References are certainly to be found to the role of the Jews. Thus, in the autumn of 1933 leading headlines in the weekly newspaper *Blackshirt* included, 'Small Jews Drag Britain to War', 'The Jewish World Challenge', 'Too Many Aliens' (4 and 18 November, 2 December). But generally speaking, in the early stages, particularly for Mosley himself, the Jewish issue was a minor adjunct to the main thrust of the campaign. Then, from the autumn of 1934 an open full-scale attack was launched against the Jews. Why?

Most observers are agreed that the main explanation is to be sought in Mosley's opportunism and in his need to rationalize the declining fortunes of his movement. The initial momentum had fallen off and the BUF was not expanding as had been anticipated. Nor was there much prospect of an advance, for the worst of Britain's economic crisis was over, whilst at the same time the much publicized violence at the Olympia meeting in June 1934 had resulted in a withdrawal of support by most of what remained of the BUF's 'respectable' sympathizers. An issue to stimulate interest was therefore vital and a rationale to explain personal failure was perhaps also required. The projection of Britain's ills onto the Jews, a much more immediate and identifiable enemy than archaic economic systems or bankrupt politicians, must have been an attractive proposition. Certainly, the suddenness with which Mosley took up the question of the Jews (after a career in which there is no trace of anti-Semitism), comments from some of his intimates at the time, and his lack of concern with specific remedies for 'the Jewish problem' all suggest that, irrespective of whether he later came to believe in an all-pervasive Jewish conspiracy, his initial motives were primarily opportunistic. Doubtless the example of the Nazis' success, and pressure for a 'harder line' which was building up from the committed anti-Semites in the BUF, assisted in the decision.

The campaign had a number of elements, the most important of which was a conspiracy theory (see Mandle, 1968; Benewick, 1969; Skidelsky, 1975; Nugent and King, 1977). Increasingly the major institutions of state, the politicians, and the mass media were accused of being controlled by Jewry, either directly or via its money power. Thus, *Blackshirt*, on 5 October 1934, under a headline 'Alien Yiddish Finance is Running British Industry - the Leader Challenges the International Capitalists', reported Mosley as having said at Belle Vue, Manchester:

> It is international finance which dominates every party in the state today. The Conservative Party says we cannot get on 'without international trade'; the Socialists say, 'without international brotherhood'. They both mean they support the international finance market. Tory calls it business - Socialist calls it brotherhood. But they mean the same thing. They both sell the interests of this country to the interests of alien finance . . . . It is alien Yiddish finance, more than any other single factor, which is undermining the prosperity of Britain today.

Alternatively we may quote Mosley addressing a rally at the Royal Albert Hall in March 1935:

> We see at last the enemy and foe, sweating the East to ruin the West, destroying the Indians to fill the unemployment queues of Lancashire, grasping British Governments and Parliaments, grasping the puppets of Westminster - that is the enemy that fascism challenges, Jewish international finance (*The Times*, 25 March 1935).

Some members were even more pointed. William Joyce, Director of Propaganda and Deputy Leader wrote:

> The little Jew in the gutter who insults the Crown and the Flag is an impertinent anomaly to be removed as soon as possible, but the great Jewish financier who dictates to Government and Industry alike, constitutes by far the greatest danger to our land. . . . In Britain the danger is more insidious because the operations of Jewry are so carefully masked (1936, p.5).

As the campaign unfurled, so did initial distinctions between categories of Jews - big/small, bad/good - become increasingly indistinct. They were simply 'the Jews'. So too did the scope of the conspiracy become ever wider. Alien Jewish financiers - who were always vague and rather shadowy figures - were at the root not only of Britain's problems but those of the Western world. Based principally in New York (as evidenced by 'The Jew Deal') and Moscow, they propagated a system of international finance and trade from which the world, and Britain in particular, lost, but from which they gained.

The 'war mongerers' also fell within this same global view. Hostilities were in the interest only of international finance which wished to smash the challenge posed to it by Germany and Italy. 'A million Britons shall not die in your Jews' quarrel' (*The Times*, 17 July 1939), and 'It is only the Money Power that is not prepared to negotiate' (*Action*, 2 September 1939) were Mosley's main themes before the outbreak of war. After it had begun the message was the same: 'This is no quarrel of the British people; this is the quarrel of Jewish finance' (Mosley, 1939).

The main thrust of the BUF's campaign against the Jews, with its increasing emphasis on a world conspiracy, was thus very different from that of the British Brothers League which had emphasized a much more immediate and proximate threat. Whereas the BUF tended to portray Jews as manipulators, pulling the strings which control the world order, the League was more concerned with 'pauper' Jews, swelling the job market and forcing the Englishmen from their homes.

This is not, however, to say that the BUF neglected completely to indulge in scapegoating poor Jews. In the East End in particular, there were familiar suggestions of Gentiles suffering as a result of Jewish price-cutting, unfair practices, and exploitation of the housing situation. Often it was accompanied by the most virulent racism. Taking a lead perhaps from the more embittered racists in the upper echelons of the BUF, and also from the denunciations, caricatures and cartoons of the Fascist press - *Blackshirt* from 1935 ran a particularly scurrilous weekly column entitled at first 'The Jews Again' and later 'Jolly Judah - I Sketch Their World' - local speakers were often even more prone than had been the League to ascribe to the Jews undesirable racial characteristics.

As to why the campaign was unsuccessful, and the BUF probably never numbered more than 10,000 - paltry by comparison with most fascist movements on the continent of Europe - it may briefly be said that a key precondition for fascist success in the inter-war years was the weakness and instability of political systems. The legitimacy of the British political system was well established and a relatively moderate Conservative Party - absent in Germany and Italy - was able to assimilate much of the discontent on the far right. Working-class loyalties to the trade unions and the Labour Party also proved a successful bulwark against the blandishments of the BUF. Additionally there is evidence that the economic depression was never so severe in Britain as it was in Germany. Britain was almost alone in guarding consumers' expenditure from the depression, whilst unemployment mainly affected the working class, and then principally in those regions which had a strong trade union base (see Glynn and Oxborrow, 1976, p.13).

Post war: the National Front

The National Front (NF), by far the largest of the multitude of extreme right-wing groups that have emerged since the war, has developed and gained support during a period of economic uncertainty. Persisting unemployment and inflation, and consequent rescue loans from abroad, have testified to an increasing dependence of the British economy on the richer, more powerful nations. Economic decline has been accompanied by the loss of Empire and a world political role, by threats to internal authority, and by rapid social change in sexual and cultural codes. All these have occurred alongside continuing problems of poor housing, overcrowding, and urban decay.

For those who are concerned about or demoralized by such changes, National Front ideology, with its aggressive use of scapegoats, is potentially attractive. Even if the permissive society is exaggerated and the majority do remain cushioned against inflationary and unemployment pressures it is the perception of change that may be most important. As we noted earlier, some observers, for example Robb (1954) in his study of anti-Semitism in Bethnal Green, have argued that *beliefs* that conditions and prospects had deteriorated were a more potent force for prejudice than *actual* deterioration and deprivation.

The National Front's scapegoats - those groups to whom undesirable characteristics and blame for existing problems are continually attributed - fall into two separate categories: a 'higher level', who may be called the 'conspirators', and a 'lower level', who are the black population. 'Higher level' refers to those scapegoating processes where groups are blamed for their powerful, purposeful and dominating activity as a force for evil. Usually to be found high in the class structure they are, as well as being condemned, frequently regarded with a sneaking admiration for their 'wily ways'. 'Lower level' scapegoats on the other hand have little social prestige, are relatively powerless, and are often portrayed as the pawns of influential manipulators. As Edgar says, they are frequently viewed 'in a politically or socially inactive way: as the carriers of disease, as creatures of blind instinct (muggers and rapists) or as "innocent" victims of forces of which they are unaware' (1977, p.128).

Above all else the National Front prides itself on being a nationalist movement, a party which puts 'Britain First'. It boldly asserts an aggressive, authoritarian nationalism which is based on grandiose conceptions of the will and the strength of the nation state. Its leader John Tyndall argues:

> throughout the last hundred years Britain has lacked any truly national state authority to give disinterested and responsible direction to national affairs. We must undertake a revolution of ideas within the British people which will lead to the abandonment of liberal softness and to the recapture of National Pride, Willpower, Sense of Destiny and awareness of race (*Spearhead*, March 1977).

As in most stridently nationalist parties such beliefs are associated with a vehement opposition to the forces of internationalism, be it by the 'intellectuals', 'Marxists', 'financiers' or 'Zionists'. Britain's social and economic ills are the consequence 'of those forces operating in the world today that are behind the remorseless drive towards Internationalism, that is, towards a total monopoly of political power' (*Spearhead*, March 1977).

The international financial élite, who are held to be behind this world conspiracy, are 'dominated by persons of a Jewish or pro-Zionist background' - the Rockefellers, the Vanderbilts, the Rothschilds - who plan their shadowy schemes through organizations such as the Bilderberg group, the Council on Foreign Relations, and the Institute of International Affairs. 'Orders' for future world government, which will be under the control of the 'money power', are given to influential sympathizers, and are sustained by the influence and propaganda of 'media Zionists'. The establishment of international bodies such as the EEC, the IMF, and the UN, are all viewed as calculated steps along the road to world government. Even communism is part of the conspiracy, the suspension of belief occasioned by this claim being explained in terms of the communist search for world power and its consequent attraction for Zionist international bankers who sustain it with massive aid and technological support.

This all-embracing conspiracy theory serves two main purposes. On the one hand, by explaining the alleged decline of 'white civilization' in terms of alien forces it preserves intact the possibility of national regeneration. On the other hand, it provides a ready explanation for almost any event, as is illustrated by reference to the Front's perception of a number of recent developments. The 'sell out' of the white Rhodesians is viewed as having been 'imposed by world usury's Satanic reptile, Henry Kissinger' who, it is argued, has been 'groomed by the hereditary princes of this conspiracy to do their bidding' (*Spearhead*, October 1976). Similarly the Helsinki Agreement and general moves towards *détente* are seized upon as proof of the essential rapprochement of the Capitalist/Communist alliance. And the 1976 American election was seen as offering the electorate a choice between 'either Nelson Rockefeller's man, Ford, or David Rockefeller's man, Carter' (*Spearhead*, November 1976).

The conspiratorial element of the Front's scapegoating thus provides not only a simple and understandable explanation for both private and national ills, but it also may be used as a salve for nationalists who wish to continue believing in Britain's greatness but who need also to explain her decline. Personalized explanations, laying blame on the actions of evil and manipulating individuals, give an opportunity for venting spleen and attributing responsibility which is not provided by more theoretical explanations based upon structural historical forces. At the same time, international bodies such as the UN, the IMF, and the EEC, are particularly attractive targets since they are associated by the National Front with Britain's declining prestige and the increased external constraints on her world relationships.

But although Jews are alleged to play a key role in the 'international conspiracy', the NF nevertheless maintains a certain ambivalence on the 'Jewish question', for although anti-Semitism is never far from the surface, there is less emphasis, when compared with its opposition to black immigrants, on racial inferiority. Jews are attacked rather for their manipulative activities, for their clannishness, and for their support of Israel – 'the Jews' nation. It has first command on their loyalties.' Occasionally grudging admiration of their talents is offered. The National Front's Activities Organizer, Martin Webster, has written:

It is because the Jewish people have such a high per capita proportion of talent compared to many other ethnic groups, and because their special talents are linked to a remarkable will-to-power which in turn has resulted in Jewry being able to exert an undeniably massive influence in the field of politics, culture and finance both nationally and internationally, that the attitude of the Jewish establishment to such questions as race relations is important (*Spearhead*, June 1972).

Doubtless this 'moderation' - moderate, that is, by comparison with the British Union of Fascists' campaign in the 1930s and the policies of some of the Front's precursors in the early 1960s - is partly because of the greater post-war sensitivity to anti-Semitism and the likelihood that its use would be electorally counter-productive. In part too it may be because, as Edgar has suggested, the socio-economic circumstances are no longer so conducive to an anti-Semitic campaign, there having been a numerical decline in those groups, such as small businessmen, who are most likely to be worried by Jewish monopoly capitalism: 'This has created the need for the National-Socialists to penetrate much more deeply into the working class, and, consequently, for the concentration of their propaganda on an out-group which can be seen as directly threatening workers' (1977, p.120).

The Front thus judges it to be more opportune - with references to 'financiers', 'money-lenders', and 'usurers' - to leave cues for those who wish to pick them up, than to be continually referring to Jews. So, in the propaganda designed for mass circulation - leaflets and fly-stickers - the word 'Jew' virtually never appears, and even in the publications directed more towards sympathizers - *National Front News* and *Spearhead* - a distinction between Zionism and Jewry is usually attempted. An openly anti-Semitic campaign is then resisted. In any event it is no longer so necessary since the NF, unlike the British Brothers League and the British Union of Fascists, has 'available' an alternative scapegoat - the black immigrants. Further, opposition to blacks, as opposed to Jews, seems capable of generating greater popular support.

For all the hostility directed against 'conspirators' it is the National Front's attitude towards the black population (or 'immigrants' as it still insists on calling them, despite the rising number who have been born in Britain) that falls most clearly into the classic scapegoating pattern. These relatively powerless and clearly identifiable groups are blamed for a variety of problems, despite the existence of evidence which clearly refutes most of the charges (see Rose, 1969; Jones and Smith, 1970).

The scapegoating, which is frequently presented in explicitly racialist language and which is designed to create an atmosphere of resentment and fear amongst the white population, is related to the conspiratorial theory in that 'the immigrants' are viewed as agents and pawns of the 'international manipulators'. Thus one leaflet proclaims:

> If the British people have to worry about fighting for a job in the face of a tide of cheap immigrant labour, and are occupied in trying to get decent housing in competition with teeming millions of immigrants, then they will not have time to think about how the international Big Business Establishment is robbing them with such gigantic swindles as the Common Market (*The Asian Invasion*, 1975).

The main thrust of the campaign, however, focuses on four areas: unemployment, housing, crime and disease.

Although the Front's official position is that the main cause of unemployment is the financial policies of Zionist conspirators, and that black immigrants merely exacerbate the problem, the distinction is often blurred, particularly in the more popular propaganda. Immigrants are blamed simply for having jobs when there is 'white' unemployment. They are further accused of being a financial imposition on Britain's welfare state, thus diverting resources that could more profitably be used to counter unemployment.

Additionally, immigrants are accused of being favoured in the job market because 'the Race Relations industry is ensuring that preferential treatment is given to blacks'. Such claims multiply at times of rising unemployment. In April 1970, as unemployment rose to 1 million, *Spearhead*'s cover story asked: 'Blacks Hired, Whites Fired. Is this Employment Policy as Jobless Multiply?' Inside it maintains that: 'Patriots have known for some time that the Department of Employment has been extending special treatment to unemployed coloured immigrants; that is, going to extra pains to secure jobs for immigrants that would otherwise go to Britons.'

Unemployment is also blamed on black foreigners, so that African and Asian goods are alleged to receive special preferences on the home market, thus jeopardizing home production. Cheaper foreign production costs are explained with racialist overtones such as, 'The product of cheap, sweated foreign labour' while 'coolie labour, which does not mind drudgery, will work for a fraction of the pay of workers in developed countries' (*Spearhead*, August 1972).

With regard to housing, although the Front refers continually to the squalid condition of immigrant areas, their major objection is aimed at the presence of black people, and the positive discrimination in their favour allegedly shown by housing authorities. It is claimed that Asian families in particular aggravate the situation by swamping local authority waiting lists. In May 1976 *National Front News* reported that:

ninety-one Asian families have jumped ahead of thousands of British families on council house waiting lists in the London boroughs of Wandsworth and Hillingdon. They are just a fraction of the thousands of Asian immigrants pouring into Britain who have been given immediate priority over homeless British families.

Similarly, stories have been recounted of Asians living in £150,000 mock-Tudor mansions ('preventing a plan to house more than seventy British old folk'), and of 'screaming black squatters seizing white property'. In the summer of 1976, the report of East African Asians, newly arrived, being temporarily housed in 'luxury 4-star accommodation at a cost of £600 per week' also provided grist to the mill. *National Front News* in May alleged: 'Hundreds of Asians pouring into Gatwick and Heathrow airports have already gone straight onto social security and into hotels that could have been used for homeless British families.'

But, perhaps the most strident scapegoating of the black population centres on the blame they receive for the rising crime rate. An image of specifically 'alien' or 'black' crimes, in particular 'mugging', is deliberately propagated as evidence of the social dislocation brought by immigration. Frequently, this is explicitly related to other 'problems':

Britain is storing up for itself a nightmare future in the form of a growing army of young blacks leaving school with little prospect of useful employment. The appalling outbreaks of mugging in some overcrowded urban areas have highlighted this problem (*National Front News*, May 1976).

Immigrants are also blamed for racial disturbances, which in turn are used to conjure a sense of environmental deterioration. In December 1969, 'the peaceful old city of Gloucester saw gangs of West Indians on a rampage of destruction'. Typically the colour of the actors in the situation was stressed: 'Nearly every car belonging to a white person in the surrounding streets was severely damaged', while 'terrified white people watched from bedroom windows' (*Spearhead*, December 1969).

Reports of incidents emphasize, wherever possible, the defenceless-ness or infirmity of the victims. *National Front News* in May 1976 referred to 'marauding savages seeking out white women to assault and rob. Even our white old folk are not safe.' Another favourite slant is to suggest that community identities are being threatened and that mugging is spreading to hitherto 'safe' middle-class areas. In October 1976 it was reported by *National Front News* that 'black muggers are stepping up their war on white communities. They have sensed there are richer pickings in the suburbs.' Finally, the mugging imagery is made more lurid if sex and drugs can be used in the story. The headline 'Black Junkie rapes crippled widow of 73' (*National Front News*, October 1976) shows how an accumulation of undesirable charac-teristics may be suggested in a mere half dozen words.

The Front deliberately fosters the beliefs that immigrants introduce disease and epidemics and are a burden on the medical and social welfare services. It claims there is substantial evidence to show that diseases such as TB, leprosy, cholera and typhus are 'being introduced by infected immigrants – much to the detriment of the established community and at considerable cost to the National Health Service'. The increase in venereal disease is also traced to the immigrants because many 'come from societies where promiscuous sexual intercourse is extremely common' (*Spearhead*, June/July 1969).

As with other issues the incidence of disease is linked, wherever possible, with other 'immigrant problems'. Illegal immigration provides an example:

> Again there is the question of countless thousands of illegal immi-grants living in Britain. There is no reason for believing that a pro-portion of them are not lepers, and as they tend to live in squalid hide-outs for many months until they feel they can be absorbed into the 'legal' immigration community, they pose a serious con-tagion hazard (*Spearhead*, June/July 1969).

Scapegoating by the National Front thus attempts to concentrate its imagery. Black people are rarely blamed for one ill without at least indirect reference to several others. Diseased black muggers who rape defenceless white widows may well come from promiscuous, unstable family backgrounds, be unemployed, high on drugs, and have illegally entered the country to live in squalid housing.

It is a highly emotive and essentially provocative appeal. The following headlines from a recent *National Front News* (June 1977) are typical:

> 'Immigration: Whites face horrific disease risk'; ' "Deep Throat" gives NF secret report on "Blacks first" housing scandal'; 'In the Ghettos . . . "Blacks Now Better Off Than Whites" - Official'; 'Black Population: Immigration and birth rate zoom'; 'Make Whites Clean Toilets Say Asians'.

The message which the Front seeks to advance is thus clear: Britons are increasingly becoming 'second-class citizens in their own country'. The 'immigrants' are 'taking over' and the white population must quickly respond with firm action. Only the National Front - which 'proves' it will not be deflected in its course by deliberately contesting elections and holding rallies in 'sensitive' areas - is defending the interests of native Britons. Amidst prophecies of an impending racial explosion it argues that repatriation will greatly alleviate problems such as unemployment, rising crime and urban decay, and it will also avoid a race war in Britain. In so presenting its message it thus deliberately seeks to create prejudice, whilst tapping real fears and problems.

The extent to which support for the National Front is explained in terms of its attempt to feed on such fears is of course beyond the scope of this chapter (see Nugent and King, 1977). Nevertheless some brief comments on the appeal of its scapegoating may be made. Social scientific literature suggests that scapegoating is an irrational displacement of frustration onto any available object. The causal processes lie deep in the individual and find an outlet in aggressive behaviour towards groups often only tenuously related to the source of the anxiety. Evidence showing this to be a basis of Front support is naturally difficult to come by for it can hardly be suggested that individuals are acting for reasons that are obscurely located in upbringing and family biography without in-depth psychological analyses. There are, however, some indications, that for members at least, 'psychological' factors are a major determinant. Thus Scott (1975), in his study of a local National Front group, has argued that many members achieve satisfaction through marches, demonstrations and heckling, rather than through the normal indicators of political success, and further that many joined 'Not at the end of a long ideological equation which concluded with "National Front", but because of a single issue in society or in their personal lives, *and* because the local branch was active'.

As for a relationship between the National Front's electoral support and structural and social circumstances, Husbands has argued that the NF has

> developed electorally as part of a reaction by some voters *within a specific urban context* either to a real or perceived encroachment upon their own neighbourhood by an ethnic group that is regarded as a competitor in some sense or else merely to the apparently increasing local presence of this other group (1977, p.4).

He also suggests that these reactions may be linked to at least two types of circumstances. In expanding industrial areas the need for labour has attracted both 'white' and 'black' workers and has created fierce competition in the housing market. In declining industrial areas, on the other hand, 'competition for remaining traditional jobs . . . has become more intense or is seen by certain white residents to have done so' (1977, p.27).

This does not of course exhaust the motivational sources of National Front support and there is, for example, evidence to suggest that much of it is merely a general protest against the government of the day, and as such is little different from Liberal support (Husbands, 1975; Nugent and King, 1977). Further significant differences may well exist between the Front's electorate, membership, and leadership. It is quite possible that the 'inner core' are far more calculating in their pursuit of votes and power than the bulk of the party's supporters whose allegiance is more diffuse. The differing motivations that Newton suggests are at work within the British Communist Party (1969, pp.26–7) may well also apply to the National Front. If this is the case then, for some at least, the scapegoating of ethnic minorities is not simply a blind lashing out at a convenient object but is, in part, a more 'rational', if no less unfounded, response to circumstances. Scapegoating may, in other words, be deliberately tailored to the actual or perceived grievances of potential supporters and the content of the scapegoating, with its emphasis on the causes of unemployment, crime, disease etc., may be presented not simply because of tenuous links with the fears of neurotic individuals, but because it is rooted in the cultural and social conditions in which people find themselves.

Conclusions

Perhaps the most striking point to emerge from our analysis is the 'development' of Jews from 'low level' to 'high level' scapegoats, and their replacement, in the former role, by black immigrants. Thus, whilst the British Brothers League saw their main target as 'pauper' Jews, because of the alleged deleterious effects they had on housing, employment and health, the British Union of Fascists attacked the Jews on two levels, adding the 'international conspirator' to the 'scum of the earth'. With the National Front the transition has been completed since it focuses almost exclusively on the 'manipulative' role and uses black immigrants for its 'lower level' scapegoating.

These differences reflect changing social and economic circumstances. The Jews at the turn of the century were often poor *émigrés* and their concentration in an area of economic uncertainty inevitably resulted in them becoming associated with working-class and lower middle-class deprivations. As geographical and social mobility has assisted their assimilation, and as a more physically identifiable alternative has become available, so have Jews been transformed into more powerful scapegoats.

In National Front propaganda both scapegoats thus have a role to play with the emphasis varying according to the context. So the conspiratorial role is most emphasized in the more discursive and 'analytical' *Spearhead* while the blacks are the main target in the more popular *National Front News* as well as at marches, demonstrations and local meetings.

Moving to more general points, scapegoating has been considered here as part of an explicit political programme, for whilst it may feed on irrational responses to perceived deprivations it is also frequently a quite conscious political tactic. Its presence and emphasis may depend as much on questions of political calculation as feelings of frustration. This was seen most clearly in the case of the British Union of Fascists where the 'Jewish card' was cynically employed as a means of resurrecting a flagging campaign. In the National Front, too, there is evidence that scapegoating reflects political opportunism, waxing strongest, as with the arrival of Ugandan Asians, when the media is focusing on racial questions. At other times, when it is deemed appropriate to emphasize the 'breadth' of the programme, issues such as the EEC, capital punishment, and communist infiltration of public life may also become prominent.

Similarly, scapegoating, where it is an essential part of a party's programme, also has an internal function in that it gives an element of cohesion to ideology. On the extreme right there is not an intellectually coherent tradition or a corpus of central tenets that can match Marxism on the left. On the contrary, the emphasis is anti-intellectual and anti-theoretical, with the emphasis rather being on 'Action' and 'Will'. The scapegoating of ethnic minorities thus provides a way of linking diverse and often contradictory issues. If the blame is laid upon the Machiavellian activities of small groups virtually everything which is abhorrent or confusing can be explained. Thus *détente* becomes part of the Capitalist/Communist/Zionist alliance whilst its apparent opposite – the build-up of NATO and the Warsaw Pact – can also be attributed to the same conspiracy's determination to undermine nationalism and promote world integration.

Similarly, subversive conspiracies which have among their major targets the British Union of Fascists or the National Front are useful in maintaining internal solidarity. To blame 'the Establishment', 'the Race-Mixers' or 'the Zionists' for refusing facilities – for example, town halls – bolsters a sense of self-importance. It allows the boast that 'no political party operating in Britain today can claim to have more enemies than the NF'. It proves that it is a 'genuine British Nationalist party', while 'blows that do not knock you down make you stronger' (*Spearhead*, March 1977).

Finally, the increased support in the mid-1970s for the National Front – at least in local elections and parliamentary by-elections – may be an indication that scapegoating of ethnic minorities is becoming more potent in Britain as traditional political alignments waver and economic problems persist. Certainly those studies, such as Lipset and Raab (1971, chapter 11) and Benewick (1969) which suggest that Britain is in some way 'immune' from extremism and 'irrational appeals' – because of her alleged tolerant political culture and defer-ential working class – must be viewed with considerable caution. For there are strong grounds for believing that the tolerance has been exaggerated and the deference is actually conducive to extremism (Nugent and King, 1977). This being the case the only safe bulwark against the scapegoating policies of the extreme right is a more concerted attack by governments on the social and economic malaise on which they breed.

Notes

1 Although the BBL is being regarded here as an extreme right-wing group, it must be conceded that its general lack of interest in questions other than immigration does raise the question as to whether it should be classified on the conventional left/right spectrum. We would argue that although opposition to immigration does not in itself justify placing a group on the far right, such a labelling is reasonable if the policy is justified, as it frequently was by the League, in eugenic, nationalistic, and imperialistic terms.

2 The League's exact following is a matter of dispute. It claimed, in 1903, to have 45,000 members but as membership only required a signature, and no subscription, the level of commitment is clearly suspect. Certainly, however, a number of very successful rallies, with gatherings of over 4000, were held.

Bibliography

Allport, G. (1958), *The Nature of Prejudice*, Doubleday, New York.

Benewick, R. (1969), *Political Violence and Public Order*, Allen Lane, London.

Curtis, L.P. (1968), *Anglo-Saxons and Celts: A Study of Anti-Irish Prejudice in Victorian England*, University of Bridgeport.

Edgar, D. (1977), 'Racism, Fascism and the Politics of the National Front', *Race and Class*, vol. xix, no. 2, Autumn, 1977.

Gainer, B. (1972), *The Alien Invasion*, Heinemann, London.

Garrard, J.A. (1971), *The English and Immigration*, Oxford University Press, London.

Glynn, S. and Oxborrow, J.C. (1976), *Inter-War Britain: A Social and Economic History*, Allen & Unwin, London.

Husbands, C.T. (1975), 'The National Front: a Response to Crisis?', *New Society*, 15 May.

Husbands, C.T. (1977), 'The Political Economy of Contemporary Cities and the Genesis of Right-Wing Movements', British Sociological Association Conference Paper, presented at University of Sheffield.

Jackson, J.A. (1963), *The Irish in Britain*, Routledge & Kegan Paul, London.

Jones, K. and Smith, A. (1970), *The Economic Impact of Commonwealth Immigration*, Cambridge University Press.

Jones, C. (1977), *Immigration and Social Policy in Britain*, Tavistock, London.

Joyce, W. (1936), *Fascism and Jewry*, BUF Publications, London.

Lipset, S. and Raab, E. (1971), *The Politics of Unreason: Right-Wing Extremism in America 1790–1970*, Heinemann, London.

Mandle, W.F. (1968), *Anti-Semitism and the British Union of Fascists*, Longman, London.

Mosley, O. (1939), *The British Peace – How to Get It*, Greater Britain Publications, London.

Newton, K. (1969), *The Sociology of British Communism*, Allen Lane, London.

Nugent, N. and King, R. (1977), *The British Right: Conservative and Right-Wing Politics in Britain*, Saxon House, London.

Rex, J. and Moore, R. (1967), *Race, Community and Conflict*, Oxford University Press, London.

Richmond, A. *et al.* (1973), *Migration and Race Relations in an English City*, Oxford University Press, London.

Robb, J. (1954), *Working-Class Anti-Semitism*, Tavistock, London.

Rose, J. *et al.* (1969), *Colour and Citizenship*, Oxford University Press, London.

Royal Commission on Alien Immigration 1903. Evidence by J.W. Johnson, the Chairman of the British Brothers League.

Scott, D. (1975), 'The National Front in Local Politics: Some Interpretations', in *British Political Sociology Yearbook*, vol. 2, *The Politics of Race*, Croom Helm, London.

Secord, P. and Backman, C. (1974), *Social Psychology*, McGraw-Hill, New York.

Skidelsky, R. (1975), *Oswald Mosley*, Macmillan, London.

Tajfel, H. (1969), 'Cognitive Aspects of Prejudice', *Journal of Social Issues*, vol. 25.

CHAPTER 3

Labour and anti-Semitism:

An account of the political discourse surrounding the Labour Party's involvement with anti-Semitism in East London, 1934-6

Caroline Knowles

This chapter aims to show how the Labour Party, which claimed to represent the interests of the working class, opposed anti-Semitism in East London between 1934 and 1936 and, thereby, how the Labour Party functions as a federation of ideological perspectives which are arbitrated into specific positions in the arena of parliamentary politics.[1] It also forms a study of the way in which an anti-racist political strategy is formulated in a working-class organization. Through the analysis features of the specific political conjuncture of 1934 to 1936 will become apparent.

Anti-Semitism, when viewed as an ideology, can be seen as being synonymous with racism,[2] even if their objects are quite distinct. This is because, as systems of ideas, they have common characteristics, such as a concern for racial (conceived in terms of national) purity, and a fear of contamination of the racial stock and a desecration of 'England's green and pleasant land' as a result of the importation of 'alien elements'. The precise content of anti-Semitism is historically specific and in the 1930s the feudal concept of Jewish usury had been replaced by the plot of 'communist financiers' from the Protocols of Zion, to which were added more contemporary elements articulated by the British Union of Fascists.

The extent to which an anti-Semitic ideology was rooted in the consciousness of the working class in East London[3] is difficult to establish. There is some evidence to suggest that anti-Semitism was firmly established in parts of East London because newspaper reports, which show the place of residence and occupation of those charged with anti-Jewish activities, indicate that many of the offenders did live and work in this area. Moreover, although the politics and activities of the BUF were not the only expression of anti-Semitism, this organization did provide its most cohesive and active formulation and, as Benewick (1969) shows, it was particularly active in Stepney and Bethnal Green. However, in order to demonstrate a link between the working-class and an anti-Semitic ideology, it would be necessary to examine the institutions in which such an ideology might be articulated rather than by examining the attitudes of individual members of a class.

During the 1930s East London was a Labour Party stronghold: Labour MPs, Labour councils and Labour mayors were returned continually in most areas. The Labour Party had an extensive influence on the lives of the people of East London, it being concerned with the interests and welfare of the 'worker' not only as trade union member, but in all aspects of social life including dances, socials, sports activities and Sunday schools. It is within this context that the Labour Party's campaign against anti-Semitism must be considered. Because of its base in the area it was able to utilize demonstrations, rallies, marches, meetings, propaganda campaigns and speeches and activities in parliament to oppose anti-Semitism. Through these diverse activities, it is possible to identify a coherent political philosophy, a philosophy which this paper aims to elucidate.

This may seem to be an impossible task because not only is the Labour Party a federation of diverse institutions, but it also encompasses a number of ideological positions which can only be broadly categorized as 'socialist'. These ideological positions cut across the institutions of which the Labour Party is composed yet, in certain circumstances, do become identified with particular ones, if only temporarily. It follows from this diversity of ideological positions that, in relation to any specific issue, there will be competing analyses and different strategies proposed to respond to it. There follows what can be called a process of arbitration whereby the differing analyses are resolved into a single policy decision. This may involve a process of modification and compromise or simply the imposition of a policy by the party leadership, but it must usually involve concessions to numerically strong lobbies within the party. Below I will show how this process operated with regard to the opposition to anti-Semitism.

In the 1930s the Labour Party was proud of what it saw as its democratic and pluralistic nature, its ability to assimilate diverse political elements into its structure and allow their free political expression with certain limits. The limit to eclecticism was the unity of the party. There were codes of discipline used to ensure party loyalty and there is evidence that the unity of the party was a sensitive issue in this period.[4] Because party loyalty was given priority over sectional interests, the Labour Party was able to give the appearance of pursuing a single policy on its opposition to anti-Semitism and therefore to remain a coherent political organization in competition with others.

The Labour Party was not alone in the struggle against anti-Semitism in East London in this period. The various political groups active in the area represented distinct ideological positions and these became apparent in the ways in which anti-Semitism was posed as a 'problem' and the strategies which were proposed to deal with it. The most important of these other groups were the Communist Party (CP) and the Board of Deputies of Anglo-Jewry, both of which had to adopt a particular relationship to the Labour Party. The mode of this relationship and the consequences will be considered in the succeeding analysis.

Finally, it is worth commenting that some of the debates which took place between 1934 and 1936 have re-occurred in the 1970s in relation to the National Front. However, the political conjuncture of the former period is historically specific and therefore direct parallels with the 1970s are not easily drawn, as I will suggest in my conclusion. But an examination of the political discourse which took place in the mid-1930s may promote the development of the kind of conceptual apparatus which can be used to examine the Labour Party's contemporary opposition to racism.

Jew and anti-Jew

The way in which the different and ideologically distinct sections of the Labour Party regarded the category of 'Jew' was contingent on the way in which anti-Semitism in its various manifestations was regarded. It is possible to distinguish two main political positions on this issue, that which was associated with the Labour Party leadership and that which was associated with the left wing of the party. Alignments with these two positions at trade union and constituency level is difficult to determine, but at a parliamentary level it is possible to identify the alignment of certain personalities with the two institutions, the leadership and the left wing, although this is not intended to imply that these two major political positions were produced or generated by particular notable personalities, only that they took them up and articulated them at a parliamentary level. The prime minister and the majority of the Cabinet represented the official policy of the Labour Party and adopted what may be referred to as a 'centrist' position. Bevan and Lansbury were the two key personalities associated with a 'leftist' position.

The official Labour Party position, i.e. that which appears in party policy statements, suggests that Jews were a separate category of the working class. Jews were seen as an immigrant, rather than indigenous, part of the population of East London, even though Jewish immigration had largely ceased by this time. The poor immigrant Jew, the working Jew, was seen as a sub-section of the working class as a whole.[5] This probably reflects the fact that sections of the Jewish population in East London emphasized their separateness and distinct cultural identity which was lived out in their own forms of social organization. The religious sections of the Jewish community went to a separate 'church', and in some cases to Jewish schools. They spoke a different language, followed distinct cultural practices related to their religion and tended to be found in certain industries in East London.

The analysis by the Labour Party leadership reveals a pluralistic view of the population of East London in which Jews, as a 'visitor' group, were to be treated with human dignity. As it was put by one MP: 'What right has one section of the community to point the finger to a section to which we have given hospitality for years?' (*Daily Herald*, 15 October 1936). The Jews were conceived as a part, though a separate part, of the population of East London and as such it was thought that they should be treated with a certain deference. Thus, the Labour Party leadership set the terms of the debate. The issue of anti-Semitism was opposed as part of a humanitarian concern about inequality and social justice. This was illustrated by the outrage expressed by certain sections of the Labour Party at the persistence of 'Jew baiting' activities in the East End of London and the world-wide persecution of Jews.

Moreover, official Labour Party policy had consistently taken a pro-Jewish stand on the issue of Palestine and the need for a Jewish homeland and had demanded social justice for Jews in Britain (see Levenberg, 1938; *Daily Herald*, 25 March 1936). Although the Jewish 'problem' was an acknowledged part of the British political scene, it was ultimately seen to be resolvable through Zionism and thus removed from the British political conjuncture.

Reflecting this conception of Jewish separateness was the organization of Jewish workers in the Poale Zion, the Jewish Labour Party, which was affiliated to the Labour Party as an autonomous body. The interests of this group of workers were therefore not represented simply as labour, but as Jewish labour. This arrangement may have been based on the belief that, in many cases, Jews suffered far worse conditions than most of the labour that was indigenous to Britain, with the related concern that Jewish labour may serve to cheapen labour as a whole. Thus the British workers would need to be protected from the conditions in which many Jews worked.

The left-wing of the Labour Party treated the category 'Jew' in a quite different way. Their theoretical analysis, to some extent influenced by that of the Communist Party, divided the population into classes: Jews were thus members of a particular class and had no status as an independent ethnic category outside a class analysis. The category 'Jew' was subsumed beneath the category 'class' or more specifically 'worker' as the *Daily Herald* and *Daily Worker* put it (see also Gallacher, 1937). It follows from this kind of analysis that the defence of the working-class Jew was seen as part of the defence of the working class in general. The protection of the working class against fascism, the political movement which embodied anti-Semitism, and social justice and protection of the Jewish community were a single issue. This was in opposition to the official analysis of the Labour Party which kept the issue of social justice for Jews separate from that of the protection of the working class from fascism.

The Labour Party's approach to the question of Jewishness and anti-Semitism was part of a wider ideological perspective. Historically, the kind of socialism which was ingrained in the very fabric of East London was a curious marriage of Christianity and social reform. Labour Party paternalism, which was evident in East London during the 1930s, was a part of this tradition. The Labour Party in East London was both ideologically and institutionally linked with the church[6] which had provided many important and prominent Labour Party figures. There were also strong links between the League of Labour Youth and the Sunday schools. Human inequality, race being seen as an aspect of inequality, was a religious as well as a socialist theme. The church taught that all men were equal and socialism provided the practical means of attaining equality. A socialist creed such as that represented in sections of the Labour Party, held that social equality could be brought about by the correct form of social organization, and it was thought that this could be achieved by a process of nationalization. In this sense, socialism was practical religion.

It was therefore no accident that a paternalistic social-work concern for the working class is found to be an essential part of the Labour Party's operation in East London. Moreover, the East End had, traditionally, been the forcing housing for social reform. Throughout the nineteenth century its working-class population had been carefully watched and studied, not least because it had been seen as a potential threat to social stability in the late nineteenth century (Jones, 1976). Hence, the Labour Party in the 1930s was the current embodiment, albeit in the form of socialism, of paternalism, following in the footsteps of predecessors, the Liberals and the Fabians, and the Oxford and Cambridge missions. The strategy of the Labour Party was therefore to take hold of the machinery of local government, and to wield it in the interests of the working class. In the case of Poplar, the council managed to fix a minimum wage in the borough, to the annoyance of Bevin and the Transport and General Workers Union. Mayor Tate of Bethnal Green distributed cards to the citizens of that borough which bore the message: 'When you want any advice on any matter, housing, pensions, compensation, etc., come to the Labour Party office.'

It was also no accident that East London became a centre of anti-Semitic activity in the period 1934 to 1936. As well as being a locus of social reform and early socialism, East London was also the centre of the agitation which led to the Aliens Act of 1905 (Garrard, 1971). Concern over the influx of alien paupers (who were mainly Jews) was tied up with the moves towards social reform at the turn of the century, because it was into East London that the alien paupers were moving and it was believed that the interests of indigenous labour were threatened by the influx of these immigrants.

The terms of the debate: anti-Semitism or fascism?

During the mid-1930s a discourse was established between the major institutions involved in the opposition to racism, the purpose of which was to establish the principal object to be opposed: anti-Semitism or fascism? The political positions involved in this issue aligned themselves to three major institutions. First, there was the Labour Party leadership which upheld the official policy of the party as was reproduced in policy statements. Second, there was the Labour Party's left wing which expressed the views of different sections of all the institutions of the Party and was, in turn, influenced by the Communist Party.

Third, there was the Board of Deputies of Anglo-Jewry, an institution which represented the official voice of the Jewish community.

The official policy of the Labour Party on the issues of anti-Semitism and fascism in Britain in the period 1934–6 bears little resemblance to its pre-1934 analysis. The latter, as set out in party policy statements (see, for example, the National Executive Committee policy statement, *Fascism at home and abroad*, 1934) gives the impression that fascism and anti-Semitism were linked in the sense that the latter was a manifestation of a fascist political creed. The nature of this relation was not clearly explained, but there was an implication that the two were linked at some level. There was an analysis of the political situation in Europe in which fascist groups were gaining political credibility and warnings were given about the possibility of Britain being subject to similar influences. Particular note was taken of the way in which organized labour was being treated by fascist governments in Europe. From this it would appear that the possibility of fascism taking root in Britain was taken fairly seriously.

In 1934 the Labour Party drew up a document which examined the various attempts to establish fascism in Britain. It noted that successive attempts had failed to gain support on the mass basis required for success. The document also noted that the programme of the British Union of Fascists was anti-socialist and anti-Jewish, but concluded that it was not coherent. It was also officially recognized by the Labour Party that the BUF had fairly extensive funds and support from the Rothermere press, and was therefore likely to receive positive propaganda. Official policy statements up to 1934 also acknowledge the potential of the BUF to spread its ideas to all sections of society, including the working class. As early as 1933 there was a special Labour Party Conference which recorded a protest against 'anti-Semitic demagogy' and called attention to the close connection between the growing fascist movement and anti-Semitism and officially recognized that the two were represented in the same political movement (see Labour Party's *Annual Report*, 1933).

In 1934 an active and campaigning form of anti-Semitism appeared on the British political scene. This was also the year in which the Labour Party changed its analysis and separated the issues of fascism and anti-Semitism, as evidenced in the fact that Labour Party official records and policy documents no longer suggested that anti-Semitism and fascism were represented in the same political movement in Britain. There were, after 1934, a number of analyses of European fascism, and the dangers of a British counterpart were spelled out in terms of the danger to organized labour. It was this kind of thinking which led the Labour Party into a position of opposing fascism because it was seen as a political creed which attacked the very basis of what the Labour Party represented, the organized working class. The Labour Party was thus necessarily drawn into an opposition to fascism in defence of the class whose interests it expressly represented. There were a number of warnings in the *Daily Herald* (which on this issue represented the official view of the Labour Party), warning that fascism and socialism, to which the Labour Party was committed, were totally opposed creeds. Such warnings also outlined the consequences for the Labour and trade union movement should fascism take hold in Britain (*Daily Herald*, 8 July, 9 July, 10 July, 14 July 1936).

Anti-Semitism, although recognized as a feature of a fascist political creed was treated as a separate issue. The protection of the working class from fascism and the Jews from anti-Semitism were thus seen as two separate issues with different solutions. Jewish workers would thus suffer doubly as Jews and as workers under fascism. This kind of analysis was endorsed by the Poale Zion who stressed that the plight of the Jewish worker was different from the indigenous worker. In the 1935 General Election, a policy statement put out by the Central Committee of Poale Zion emphasized the need for the Labour Party and the Poale Zion to unite to fight their common enemy, fascism, but for different reasons. The Poale Zion was committed to the struggle against anti-Semitism, the Labour Party to the protection of the worker against fascism.

The political positions and debates on the left of the Labour Party on the question of an opposition to anti-Semitism or fascism presented a different perspective. Fascism was thought to be the main danger to the working class, while anti-Semitism was seen as an integral part of the fascist movement. Anti-Semitism was seen as the mechanism by which the ruling class sought to weaken the working class by dividing it internally. This kind of political thinking linked the position of the working class in general with Jews in particular in terms of the forces and interests which would benefit from their destruction as a political force (i.e. industrialists and bankers, etc.), and follows from the analysis of the Jews as being an integral part of the working class, with the result that an attack on the Jews was seen as a direct attack on the working class. This is the position set out in the left-wing press, notably the *Daily Worker*, which analysed the events of 1936, referred to as the 'Battle of Cable Street', in terms of the solidarity of the East London community defeating the Mosley marches (*Daily Worker*, 13 July, 2 October, 11 October 1936). Those who turned out to oppose racism on the streets were referred to as the 'people' or the 'workers' and their actions have gone down in Labour Movement mythology as an instance of united action on the part of all East Londoners in opposing fascism. In reality the opposition to fascism in East London was neither united, nor did it stop fascist activity in East London.

The position which the Board of Deputies adopted on this issue incorporated a variety of opinion, reflecting the fact that the Jewish community, which the Board of Deputies sought to represent, comprised a multiplicity of views. Its position appears to represent the views of community leaders, but it was influenced by the various pressure groups in the Jewish community which included socialists and trade unionists. The Board of Deputies also had to take account of its close connections with the synagogues and various social-work agencies, notably Toynbee Hall whose warden was on the board.

Initially the Board of Deputies refused to be drawn into the debate on fascism or anti-Semitism. It considered its work to be restricted to matters of religion rather than politics (Salomon, 1937; also *Jewish Weekly*, 27 November 1936; *Jewish Chronicle*, 3 July and 10 July 1936). It was only drawn into the discourse in the late summer of 1936 after a campaign for the defence of the Jewish community was conducted by the *Jewish Chronicle*. The Board of Deputies was thus forced to change its position under the threat that if the leaders of the community did not defend its members they would organize their own defence with those political groups already engaged in the struggle against fascism and to which the Labour Party and the Communist Party were giving ideological backing (*Jewish Chronicle*, 3 July, 10 July, 31 July 1936).

The Board of Deputies were therefore pressured into taking a position which can be summarized in the following words: 'Let us stand together as Jews, the employer, the worker, the Rabbi and the Youth' (*Jewish Weekly*, 16 October, 23 October, 20 November 1936). The issue for them, therefore, was anti-Semitism and not fascism, and this position led to a particular kind of action. The leaders of the Jewish community were concerned that the opposition to anti-Semitism should not involve any political affiliation or activities on behalf of the Jewish community by those who were not sanctioned to act for the community. It is relevant to recall that the Board of Deputies in this period was opposed to the organization of Jews as workers in the Poale Zion and Jewish trade unions and was, on the whole, opposed to communism and disapproved of communists taking up the cause of anti-Semitism. It claimed that its interests were Judaism and not 'half-baked political dogmas from Moscow'. The board was therefore arguing for a community-based opposition to anti-Semitism in the defence of their interests as a homogeneous ethnic group; the class divisions within the community were not seen to be relevant to this defence.

The fight against fascism and anti-Semitism: what form did it take?

It should therefore be clear that the Labour Party leadership, the left of the Labour Party and the Board of Deputies were all opposed to the ideology and activities of the British Union of Fascists, even though they disagreed about the nature of that organization and the nature of the issue at stake. They were, therefore, able to agree on the need for a campaign against the BUF, although not on the form that it should take. Opposition to the BUF in East London was of two kinds, one favouring direct confrontation, the other rejecting it. These two conflicting strategies followed from distinct political ideologies. The strategy of confrontation was aligned with certain institutions, notably the Communist Party, the left of the Labour Party and the Association of Jewish Ex-Servicemen, while the opposition to direct confrontation was associated with the official policy of the Labour Party and the Board of Deputies. These two ideologies were in conflict with each other as well as with the BUF and were reflected throughout the institutions of the labour movement. However, attempts were made within the labour movement to unite opposition to the BUF and anti-Semitism: the Communist Party instigated the movement for a United Front of all progressive forces. The Labour Party, given that it was concerned to ensure its ideological and political distinctiveness *vis-à-vis* the Communist Party, was reluctant to enter into a United Front and was therefore forced to tread a delicate political tight-rope between its opposition to anti-Semitism on the one hand and to the United Front on the other.

Confrontation

The confrontations which took place in East London were a direct response to the actions of the BUF. They took the form of counter-demonstrations, disruption of BUF meetings and assemblies, and usually involved physical confrontation and violence on the streets. It was the intention of those active in the institutions associated with this kind of opposition that the BUF should be seen to be resisted publicly. The ideology which corresponded to this kind of activity emphasized its legitimacy and orderliness with which the left-wing demonstrators conducted themselves, contrasting this with the methods employed by the BUF. Pollit, a leading member of the Communist Party, made a revealing statement of this position in 1936 when he said that the labour movement, of which the Communist Party was an integral part, 'conducted normal peaceful political agitation and propaganda within the normal democratic forms, and on the basis of a political democracy'. The basis of this evaluation was the view that the Communist Party and the Labour left operated within the parliamentary tradition whilst the BUF stood outside of it. In the view of the left, extra-parliamentary activity did not detract from the fact that the Labour Party's and the Communist Party's primary orientations were towards the maintenance of a system of parliamentary democracy, while the activities of the BUF were defined as being illegitimate in a democratic system.

The kind of confrontation which took place in East London between the BUF and those aligned to the left of the Labour Party was essentially defensive. Even where there was an active confrontation on the streets, the BUF set the venue and the terms of the debate ('We've got to get rid of the Yids'). The forces of the left went along to protect the Jews from their attackers.

The ideological confrontation which took place between the BUF and the left was also defensive and closely aligned to official Labour Party policy. The accusations levelled against the Jews by the BUF (that they were foreigners who put their sectarian interests above the interests of the nation, that they were unpatriotic international financiers, controllers of the press and communists) were taken up by the left and shown to be empirically incorrect. This kind of response implicitly accepted that the Jews were a homogeneous racial category and therefore contradicted the theoretical position adopted by the left in this discourse. It is also relevant to recall that the left side-stepped the issue of the origins of anti-Semitism. It simply assumed that anti-Semitism was alien to working-class consciousness, an instance of 'false consciousness', with the consequence that there was no need to analyse anti-Semitism as an ideology generated, at least in part, from within the working class.

The politics of non-confrontation

The kind of anti-fascist activity sponsored officially by the Labour Party was also of two kinds, first, public demonstrations (which did not take place in proximity to the BUF and therefore avoided clashes), and second, a response to the BUF's case against the Jews.

The political ideology implicit in the official Labour Party policy isolated two issues which were considered to be of primary importance. The first was that in opposing anti-Semitism, public order and social peace should be maintained at all times: well-organized demonstrations which did not cause civil disruption were seen as the democratic right of all citizens in the state. It was believed that free political expression should be allowed to all interest groups. In the case of the most famous conflict situation, the incidents which took place around Cable Street in the autumn of 1936, the official voice of the Labour Party articulated through the *Daily Herald* warned people to stay away, to avoid civil strife. At the beginning of October Mr Wall of the London Trades Council, who was part of a deputation organized by the Jewish People's Council, expressed a similar view when he said that the labour and trade union movement would do everything in its power to keep people off the streets (*Daily Herald*, 3 October 1936). It was reasoned in the *Daily Herald* that if people kept off the streets, then the police could be left to deal with those from either side who were in breach of the peace. Similar warnings were printed from Labour Party and trade union leaders.

Second, it was believed by many throughout the labour movement, and this became the official position of the Labour Party, that physical opposition to the BUF had made it into a credible political force. Again this was articulated through the *Daily Herald* (e.g. 15 October 1936) which claimed that if people stayed off the streets and refused to be provoked, fascism in Britain would die away. The *Daily Herald* carried a report (15 October 1936) of a Mosley march which had taken place in East London the previous day, at which there had been no organized opposition, stating that Mosley had spoken 'Hitler style' denouncing the Jews, but that the Jews refused to be 'baited'. The incident was simply labelled as a 'pathetic show of heel clicking'.

The battle on the ideological level as taken up officially by the Labour Party involved an appeal to 'facts' in order to inform public opinion about the part played by Jews in British society. Rather like its left wing, the Labour Party took up the accusations of the BUF and demonstrated them to be empirically incorrect. The Labour Party also stressed that the politics of the BUF exhibited a complete disregard for human equality and tolerance.

The position taken by the Board of Deputies on the issue of confrontation was broadly similar to that adopted by the Labour Party leadership. It responded at the ideological level by paying researchers to investigate the facts concerning the contribution which the Jews had made to humanity in order to 'dispel fascist lies'. The board also warned all Jews through the synagogues and the *Jewish Chronicle* to stay away from confrontations with the BUF on the streets. For example, on 30 August 1936, the *Jewish Chronicle* published this:

> It is understood that a large Black Shirt demonstration is to take place in East London next Sunday afternoon (Cable St.). Jews are urgently warned to keep away from the route of the Black Shirt march and from their meetings. Jews who, however, innocently become involved in any possible disorders will be actively helping anti-Semitism and Jew baiting. Unless you want to help the Jew baiters - keep away.

The United Front negotiations

Throughout the brief history of the Labour Party the Communist Party had attempted on a number of occasions to create closer links between the two and the events of 1934 to 1936 reopened the issue of collaboration. It was generally considered in the Communist Party that the Labour Party, although in many respects ideologically distinct from the Communist Party, was an effective political instrument by virtue of the extensive support which it received from the working class. In 1936 it was suggested that the Labour Party form part of a broad anti-fascist alliance with the Communist Party in the light of the events in Europe where similar political alliances had been formed to the same purpose. This was thought necessary in order to respond adequately to the demands of the political situation in Britain at that time. The Socialist League was to be the institution in which this political alliance was to be contained. A letter from the Secretary of the Socialist League to the Labour Party, dated 5 February 1936, stated that the present national and international situation was one which called for the unity of all working-class forces at home and abroad and demanded that the 'Differences and difficulties which have occurred over the years, should in the light of new circumstances be brought into proper perspective.' It was suggested that an effective defence of the working class against the forces of fascism required united activity under the leadership of the Labour Party.

It is difficult to estimate the degree of support received from the various sections of the Labour Party for a United Front. It is known that some prominent figures in the parliamentary party (for example, Bevin, Lansbury and Citrine) had campaigned and spoken on joint platforms with the Communist Party in the campaign against fascism. The documentation of some of the East London constituency parties also indicates that united action with the Communist Party did take place unofficially at a rank-and-file level on local issues. For example, a telegram was sent from Springhall Communist Party on 1 October 1936 to Mayor Tate of Bethnal Green, a locally well-known Labour Party member, which read 'Earnestly urge your Party rally all members and sympathisers for great anti fascist protest against Mosley march through the Jewish quarter. Assemble Aldgate, Cable St., Minories, London St., Commercial Rd. 2 o'clock Sunday 4th.' The possibility of large-scale physical violence occurring between the marchers and counter-demonstrators was widely publicized in the press and, contrary to the position officially adopted by the Labour Party and publicized in the *Daily Herald*, Mayor Tate replied in the affirmative.

The activities of what is estimated as a sizeable section of the East End Labour Party were thus in direct conflict with official party policy. This breach of discipline was dealt with in two, apparently contradictory, ways. First, prominent Labour Party members who had spoken on joint platforms with the Communist Party were reprimanded and ordered to discontinue their activities on threat of expulsion. They obeyed this direct challenge and stopped supporting joint activities. The Labour Party's aim was to disentangle itself from, and re-establish its ideological differences with, the Communist Party. Second, official party policy nevertheless tended to capitalize on the activities of its left wing in the struggle against anti-Semitism, at least by implication.

The actions of the left of the Labour Party in obstructing on a number of occasions the Mosley marchers became part of the Labour Party image and became officially accepted on a practical level as part of the Labour Party's record in the struggle against racism, although ideologically this was directly opposed to official policy on the issue. For example, the *Daily Herald* of 5 October 1936, reporting the incidents at Cable Street, stated that the crowd was raised to fury by the fascist's constant 'Jew-baiting' and their marches into Jewish districts. They were met with thousands of anti-fascists: 'Socialists, Jews and Communists of the East End were determined that Mosley should not pass.' It should be noted that the anti-fascists were organized by the Communist Party and the Independent Labour Party.

The opposition to the notion of the United Front pre-dated the events of 1936. In 1934, the National Executive Committee of the Labour Party issued a statement commenting on the movement for a United Front which concluded: 'There are no new circumstances which justify the Trade Union, Political Party and Co-operative movement departing from policy on this issue.' In January 1936, the *Daily Herald* still carried this same message: 'No circumstance has arisen to change the 1922 Conference in Edinburgh which rejected any such suggestion.' The Party also issued a document on this issue in 1937 entitled *Labour and the so-called Unity Campaign* claiming that the real United Front was that of the socialist, trade union and Co-operative Movement. The Labour Party, the document went on to explain, was the party of the working class, and held this position because, 'No Party has given greater attention to the devising of practical socialist policies that are of primary interest to the organised working class.' The Labour Party therefore saw itself as the only legitimate representative of the interests of the working class in the struggle against fascism. The Labour Party was proud of its pluralistic structure which allowed a federation of socialists as long as they worked within the limits of party discipline, and preserved the autonomy of the party from the ideology of the Communist Party and others in the parliamentary arena. It believed that, again to quote from the Executive Committee's statement of January 1937, its

> policy and programme are wide enough in scope to have enabled
> and still enable hundreds of thousands of men and women to express
> their socialist faith clearly and without reservation, and to work
> actively, happily and loyally within its ranks.

Totalitarianism and democracy

In opposing the United Front, the Labour Party typified the struggle in East London as an encounter between two extreme political creeds, communism and fascism, which were seen as totalitarian evils threatening the fabric of a political democracy. The distinction between totalitarianism and democracy corresponded to the way in which the official policy of the Labour Party aligned fascism and communism at the opposite end of the political spectrum from the democratic politics which it considered itself to represent. The distinction between totalitarian and democratic politics set the terms of the debate in which the Labour Party outlined its major ideological differences with the Communist Party. MacDonald represented this view when he stated that as far as political principles were concerned fascists and communists were born of the same parents (*Jewish Chronicle*, 16 October 1936). This analysis of the political situation in East London was related to two specific philosophical positions. The first was an overriding concern for the maintenance of civil peace and social order, the second what can broadly be termed a nationalist conception of politics.

A political position which, in the course of opposing a racist politics, asserts that the maintenance of the social order is a primary consideration, does two things. First, it assumes that the state is a force which is above the interests of the factions in dispute (a point to which I shall return) and, second, it asserts that the important factor in an opposition to racism is the method by which it is opposed, or more precisely, the method by which it is seen to be opposed. There were two kinds of civil peace at issue in East London in the period in question. The most publicized was the large-scale clashes which occurred with the British Union of Fascists on the streets, but there was also a campaign on the part of the BUF to terrorize individual Jews and destroy Jewish property. Official Labour Party policy on the issue of civil peace concentrated on the former and ignored the latter. The Communist Party on the other hand organized local vigilante groups to protect the Jewish community. Moreover, the counter-demonstrations organized by the Communist Party served to create an opposing presence as BUF demonstrations broke up which could serve as a deterrent to the BUF members who had a habit of rampaging through Jewish districts at the conclusion of a march. If the official policy of the Labour Party was concerned about civil peace, it was concerned about only one aspect of civil peace.

In the light of the above analysis it would appear that as far as official policy of the Labour Party was concerned, the clashes which took place in East London were not between the workers of East London and fascism, but between the state in the form of the forces of law and order and those at the extremities of the political spectrum whether on the right or left who threatened the order which the state represented. Herbert Morrison emphasized this position when he said of the Cable Street incidents: 'I have no more sympathy with those who desire to stimulate disorder from one side than those who provoke it from the other' (*Daily Herald*, 6 October 1936). This position is contrary to that which was printed by the *Daily Herald* on the previous day which had talked about a clash beween fascists and anti-fascists in the form of 'Socialists, Jews and Communists of the East End'. So it would appear that official Labour Party policy saw the struggle in East London as one which had been diverted from the real issue of an opposition between fascists and anti-fascists, to a street brawl between police and extremists.

To pose an opposition to fascism in terms of a conflict between the forces of the state and extreme totalitarian political creeds which were identified as a threat to that state, implies a nationalistic conception of politics. The totalitarian politics referred to are spoken of in terms of their foreignness to the British political tradition. Duff Cooper, the Secretary of State for War, expressed this view when he claimed that the conflict in East London was between the supporters of two foreign creeds: 'The majority of English men have no sympathy with red Communism or black Fascism, and we resent it deeply that the supporters of foreign creeds should make our city hideous' (*Daily Herald*, 15 October 1936). This implies that totalitarianism was alien to the British tradition of political sophistication or to a way of conducting things to which Britain was committed as a parliamentary democracy. These foreign political creeds were, by implication, suited to other, lower forms of social organization. Moreover, 'foreign' implies that totalitarianism was not 'home grown', that it was an element imported into British politics and, as such, alien to the British tradition.

Free speech, civil liberties and police activity

The activity of the British Union of Fascists and of those opposed to anti-Semitism and fascism in East London also raised the issues of free speech, civil liberty and the activities of the police which, when debated, raised two broader problems. The first was the nature of the class structure and its relationship to the state, and the second, the extent of British civil liberties and the limitations imposed on them in the interests of maintaining the state. Officially the Labour Party took up a different position to that of its left wing on these issues.

The position of the left on these issues was that the state was not, in its present form, neutral, although it was potentially so. It was seen to represent big business and to be unable or unwilling to effectively protect the Jews while exhibiting partiality towards the British Union of Fascists. As far as the rights of free speech and political liberty were concerned, the left argued that they were not universal principles, but should be maintained selectively in order to ensure social justice. It was argued that it was unfair to give one section of the community licence to persecute another, and that fascist provocation should be distinguished from the legitimate public expression of a political belief. On this issue the left was walking a political tight-rope because it was anxious that there should be no general restriction on the right of peaceful democratic assembly to express a political view but it wished there to be limits to this freedom. These limits were the activities of groups which sought to stimulate racial strife and which stood for the destruction of free speech for a certain section of the community (*Daily Worker*, 2 October, 14 October 1936; *Daily Herald*, 6 October 1936).

The official policy of the Labour Party posed this question in different terms. The basis of this position was a belief in the neutrality of the state as the protector of a sovereign entity of which it was a legitimate expression. It was the state which upheld the British social order. Free speech and civil liberties were not seen as things which could be bestowed selectively, given to one political group and not another, but were seen as qualities which provided the very fabric of a political democracy. The Home Secretary expressed this view when he said that his job, as he saw it, was to protect the extent of British liberties: 'The essence of British life is tolerance, and if this is to be changed it will be changed all round to effect demonstrations of the left as well as the right' (*Daily Worker*, 8 October 1936). Officially the Labour Party believed that all political groups should be afforded freedom of expression, as this was an integral part of the British political fabric, but it also believed in its ability to stifle fascism, not by banning the British Union of Fascists but by countering it with its own politics which it considered to be of a higher order of rationality than that of fascism, not least because it was the natural representative of the working class.

Conclusion

It now remains to indicate the ways in which a study of the opposition to anti-Semitism in the 1930s has a bearing on the current political conjuncture. The clashes between the National Front and the Socialist Workers' Party in Lewisham, London, and Ladywood, Birmingham, in 1977 and their political repercussions within the labour movement may seem familiar to the student of the 1930s. However, to pose the events in East London in the mid-1930s as completely analogous would be to ignore forty years of political development.

It may be that, as I suggested at the outset, the anti-Semitism of the 1930s and white racism in the 1970s are, as ideologies, identical phenomena, but the expression of these ideologies has to be considered in their full historical context. I would argue that the contemporary hostility towards black people in Britain should not be seen as part of a continuum, stretching from 'Jew-baiting' through to 'Paki-bashing', because this could imply the existence of an ideology which floated above institutions. Both anti-Semitism in the 1930s and white racism in the 1970s are products of particular economic and political conditions, and there are obvious differences in the conditions of the two periods. Contemporary racism exists against the background of a succession of increasingly restrictive immigration acts which aimed to prevent black people from settling in Britain and what has been called a 'race relations industry'. By way of contrast, the only piece of immigration legislation on the statute books in the 1930s was the Aliens Act 1905, and there was no bi-partisan agreement in parliament over what is now termed 'race relations' which has had the effect of sanctioning and legitimizing white, English hostility.

However, in arguing that the political situation of the 1930s is in many respects different from that of the 1970s, it should be noted that some of the issues and debates articulated in the earlier period are pertinent to the 1970s. These are principally concerned with the fact that opposition to racism has, in both periods, involved violent confrontations between racists and anti-racists on the streets. This necessarily raises questions of social order and the activity of the police force. It also raises the conflict between, on the one hand, the need to preserve the British style of political liberty and tolerance, the idea of 'free speech' and, on the other, the need to preserve a particular style of political activity which regards political violence as illegitimate in a liberal democratic state. In the final analysis, this conflict hinges on the question of the role of the state in a capitalist society.

The Public Order Act 1936, was designed to tread this delicate path between the principle of political liberty and the need to maintain a particular political style when it increased police powers to deal with marches which might make it impossible for the police to maintain social order. In so doing, responsibility was passed from the Home Office to the Commissioner of Police without actually resolving the issue, as demonstrated by the infrequent and hesitant use of the Act and the controversy which ensues whenever it is suggested that it should be used. This was very evident in the controversy over the National Front's decision to organize a march through Lewisham in London in 1977.

Some of the issues raised in the mid-1930s are therefore relevant to an analysis of contemporary racism and the way in which it is opposed, but these issues have to be understood in relation to the different circumstances of the two periods in question. This raises the issue of the relevance of the study of history. As far as this paper is concerned, history is not a recounting of past events for their own sake but a living process in which certain issues are highlighted at certain times and, through analysis, one can come to see how those issues were produced, maintained and resolved in contrast with other issues in the political arena. Seen in these terms, this study of the opposition to anti-Semitism in the 1930s can provide some of the conceptual tools and theoretical insights with which to analyse the current political conjuncture. More specifically, an analysis of the way in which the Labour Party dealt with racism in the 1930s contributes to our understanding of the way in which it operates more generally, both in the past and today. The way in which the Labour Party in the 1930s adopted and maintained an 'anti-racist' position which did not challenge the terms of the debate established by the racists says something very revealing about the nature of its ideology, a point which is very relevant to considerations of the recent 'socialist' opposition to racism on the part of the Labour Party.

Notes

1 I would like to offer my thanks to Dr S. Feuchtwang, Dr Levenberg, Mr J. Benningfield, David Carrington and the archivist at the National Museum of Labour History for their assistance.
2 It would appear from the literature of this period that the word 'racism' was not generally used so its usage here reflects its contemporary meaning in political discourse. However, the word 'racial' was used in Labour Party and Communist Party newspapers. For example, Herbert Morrison wrote, 'It [the fascist march] was deliberately organized not to give the expression to economic ideas but . . . was consciously organized to stimulate civil disorder and racial strife' (*Daily Herald*, 6 October 1936). Nevertheless, it was generally acknowledged within the labour movement that anti-Semitism, or what was more commonly referred to as 'Jew-baiting' was a problem pertaining to race.
3 The reference here is to what is often called the old East End, that is the area between the west bank of the River Lea and the City of London. This area includes Whitechapel, Bethnal Green, Shoreditch, Mile End, Limehouse and Poplar.
4 The Standing Orders of the Labour Party was a contentious issue in the 1930s as is shown by the number of times that they were revised.
5 The position was argued by the Jewish National Labour Council which was affiliated to the Labour Party and which had been established to deal with problems peculiar to Jewish workers, whose conditions it believed to be far worse than those of British labour in general. The Council was composed of Jewish unions and aimed to combat the sweated system and improve conditions in the lowest paid industries.
6 In a personal interview in 1977, Mr J. Benningfield, of Bow and Bromley Labour Party, recalled Labour Party Sunday school meetings at Lansbury's house where Lansbury would give sermons. Mr Benningfield said that this was common throughout the East End and that leading members of local Labour Party branches were also prominent church members. See also Postgate (1951).

Bibliography

Benewick, R. (1969), *Political Violence and Public Order*, Allen Lane, London.
Gallacher, W. (1937), *Anti-Semitism: What it Means to You*, Communist Party of Great Britain, London.
Garrard, J.A. (1971), *The English and Immigration*, Oxford University Press, London.
Jones, G.S. (1976), *Outcast London*, Penguin, Harmondsworth.

Levenberg, S. (1938), *British Labour Policy on Palestine: A Collection of Documents, Speeches and Articles 1917–1938*, London.
Postgate, R. (1951), *The Life of George Lansbury*, Longman, London.
Salomon, M.A. (1937), *Board of Deputies of Anglo-Jewry: A Short Historical Survey*, Board of Deputies of Anglo-Jewry, London.

CHAPTER 4

Black militancy and class conflict

John Rex

I want to suggest in this chapter that there are two contradictory or apparently contradictory tendencies at work in Britain today in the developing relationship between immigrant ethnic minorities and the class structure.[1] On the one hand there appears to be some statistical evidence that black immigrants and black Britons are slowly being absorbed into the British working class, albeit into its least privileged sectors. On the other there appears to be a tendency towards growing militancy among blacks which leads, given the fact of overt racist agitation and implicitly racialist policies being pursued by members of the white majority and the white government, to a situation of defensive confrontation. I am concerned with the interpretation both of the apparent absorption and the increasing militancy in the particular socio-political circumstances which prevail in Britain.

My first task is to make clear what the peculiarly British socio-political situation is. I propose to do this by drawing two contrasting ideal types designed to pin-point some of the sociologically significant differences between British and North American society, because there is a growing and mistaken tendency both in government and sociological circles to read American lessons into British experience. Like all ideal types, the schematic accounts of American and British social and political structure given here artificially accentuate certain elements of reality. Their purpose, however, is to emphasize the specificity of the British situation and to prevent its being confused with the American one. For this purpose I hope that they have value.

Ethnic minorities and the American political system

The major difference between American social and political structure and that which prevails in Britain is that, in the former, class structure and class conflict play a less significant role. The self-image of American society is that it is a society of equal opportunity for all. Individuals are thought of as competing as individuals rather than in fighting for justice as groups and the most humbly born child is thought of as being capable of rising from rags to riches or from log cabin to White House. In fact, however, the widely used concept of 'the American Dream' serves to mark the fact that this is more myth than reality. As Parsons noted in his essay, 'A Revised Analytic Approach to Social Stratification', in the lower reaches of the stratification system there is a tendency for the competitive striving on which the system is posited to be replaced by a quest for individual and group security (1954, p.434).

Obviously trade unionism plays some part in this quest for security in a competitive system but the notion of business unionism marks the fact that unions tend to be specialized organizations largely concerned with negotiating the price of labour and lacking in the communal qualities which the labour movement in Britain has had. On the other hand in a nation of immigrants the newest and weakest immigrants have tended to rely upon ethnic associations for protection in a threatening environment and these associations have had a great deal of significance in building up the American political system. Typically immigrant associations ranging from cultural groups and friendly societies to extra-legal organizations have produced leaders who could 'deliver the vote' and so buy for their members a degree of political protection. While organized labour does act as a political lobby, especially on a national scale, ethnic associations have an independent influence as well as exercising some control over the union organizations themselves.

Strikingly, however, the one group which until recently had not been able to buy its way into the system was that constituted by one of the two earliest groups of immigrants, the American blacks. They did have a period of influence after the civil war but their condemnation to a lower and, indeed, permanently inferior position in the status hierarchy was eventually sealed by the *Plessy* v *Ferguson* decision legalizing segregated facilities. For a long time then it was thought that although the society as a whole could be conceived as being built out of graded immigrant groups with individuals breaking free from these groups and following their own mobility paths, neither the blacks as a group nor black individuals could join the main system. As Lloyd Warner (1936) put it, there was a caste line between blacks and whites and even if some blacks became rich and educated the caste line would tilt rather than be breached. Subsequently the poverty programme, the civil rights programme and affirmative employment all sought to change this situation when it was challenged in the 1950s and 1960s by the Civil Rights Movement and by violent riots. As a result of this there seems to be some evidence that black leaders are now in a better position to compete on behalf of their groups and to buy the blacks into the competitive system. Indeed positive discrimination has launched a considerable minority of American blacks into middle-class positions.

A common over-simplification of the British situation is one which suggests that British blacks should now follow the Americans and buy their way in. As we shall show later this implied analogy is misleading, but first and in order to do it better we should draw attention to the structural peculiarities of the British socio-political system.

Ethnic minorities and class politics in Britain

Compared with the USA Britain obviously does not allow individual competition nearly such a free rein. On the one hand, its very capitalism has been taken over by a relatively closed ruling class or stratum so that there is considerable restriction of mobility arising from that source. On the other, capitalism itself has been prevented from completely determining the class system by a labour movement based upon the industrial struggles of the trade unions. This labour movement has both communal and political features which are lacking in the American situation and, aided by the ethnic homogeneity of the population, has been able to give to the working class an importance in the social structure which it has not had and may never have in the USA. It is desirable that this importance should be specified and the structure of the British working class made clear.

Karl Marx suggested that just as the bourgeoisie had moved from being a band of outlaws through being an armed and independent estate to imposing their social and political hegemony, so the working class, at first organized by the bourgeoisie to fight against the enemies of their own enemies, would then organize themselves industrially, go on to pursue their conflicts in the political sphere and, when they reached the fulfilment of being a class-for-itself, would go on to impose their hegemony and so usher in a new post-bourgeois society.

It is familiar enough ground to say that the working class has not gone fully through these stages. But, with this said, it should still be pointed out that, far from the trade unions simply providing a base for business unionism, they have provided the core and the focus of both communal and political organization. Working-class culture both regionally and nationally divides the working class from upper-class society and 'being working class' in a cultural and social sense has a meaning which it could not ever have in America. Far more important, though, is the fact that a political movement and, more narrowly, a political party based upon the unions has come into existence which, through its exercise of political power, acts to protect its members in whatever markets they find themselves and wherever their rights are at stake. Even though we may take the Weberian point that there is an identity between market situations and class situations, and hence, as many class situations as there are markets, as a matter of history and empirical fact the way in which the underprivileged and the weak have protected themselves or increased their rights in such fields as housing, education, medicine and social insurance is through the actions of the Labour Party which is based above all on the trade unions.

I have suggested elsewhere (Rex, 1961) that it is neither true that the British labour movement will become more revolutionary, nor that, given the achievement of the welfare state, it will become redundant. I suggest that what we have is a truce in the class war within which welfare rights are guaranteed by the continuing solidarity and mobilized power of the working class. But, so long as the truce lasts, there will be some set of agreed principles between the parties and, within these agreed principles, a set of mobility rules. It becomes part of working-class thinking that working-class children should have all rights, including the right to mobility, and that even adult workers should seek and be permitted to seek mobility in their own lifetime to such privileges as suburban semi-detached housing and white-collar employment.

There is in this situation no way into the British social system other than through entry into its class system. Some few may simply enter it nearer the top through setting up private businesses or gaining entry into the professions. The vast majority of incoming immigrants, however, will seek to enter the society by joining the working class and by sharing in the benefits which it enjoys including the right of their children to mobility. There is no equivalent for poor immigrants to the ethnic association which buys its way in, because the labour movement cannot be by-passed. The question which faces us in trying to describe the political relationship of incoming immigrant minorities to British society is mainly that of how far they can gain acceptance in the working class, joining its organizations and gaining the full and equal protection which British workers enjoy.

Now the immediate evidence which we encounter when we turn to any careful quantitative study of immigrant rights and immigrant achievement is that Asian and West Indian immigrants suffer disadvantage even if they are not subject to overt and wilful discrimination in the fields of employment, housing and education. Morever, as the PEP surveys show, far from it being the case that West Indian and Asian immigrants have chips on their shoulders, the fact is that they under-report discrimination, because they are either unaware of it or they accept it as inevitable (Daniel, 1968; Smith, 1977). The technique of employing English, black immigrant and European immigrant actors as applicants for houses and jobs shows clearly enough that there is a great deal of discrimination which is never tested by immigrant pressure.

Despite this, however, it is possible if one looks at settled populations of immigrants who have been in England for more than ten years to find considerable numbers who either own their own homes or have council tenancies, who have been stably employed for long periods and who have children in schools with which they as parents are fully satisfied. It is when one meets people like these, as we have done in Handsworth, Birmingham, in recent years that one can fairly readily be persuaded that Britain's blacks are becoming normal members of the working class and that the working class is becoming partially black. Mixing of black and white teenagers seems to be beginning and black faces as well as white are now to be seen amongst the professional footballers who are the working-class folk heroes.

One should, in fact, admit that some partial assimilation is taking place here and one should note that, the Grunwick case notwithstanding, immigrant workers do overwhelmingly join their appropriate trade union. But does this mean that there is simply a gradation of advantage/disadvantage and that there is no structural break between immigrants and the main body of the working class? I think that there is some evidence against this and that there are highly dramatic situations as well as incipient organizations which seem to suggest that there is such a structural break.

Immigrants and the labour market

In the field of employment, even if one looks at those who are stably employed, one should also notice that the jobs in which immigrants find themselves have low initial skill requirements or require only skills learned on the job, that they are jobs which young white men do not want but which were previously held by white people who have now reached retirement, that the jobs are often dirty and boring, that they involve a lot of shiftwork and also often involve longer hours than equivalently paid work amongst whites. What seems to have happened on closer analysis is that there has been a process of invasion and succession in certain types of jobs and that blacks have moved in where whites have moved out. It may also be the case that the distribution of jobs is partially explained in terms of dual labour market theory, but generally the relationship between immigrant workers and the native born in the labour market does not completely coincide with that which is posited in this market theory. There are some traditional jobs, which in a way one would say were protected from the forces of market competition, which immigrants enter. There are also others, particularly those taken up by female immigrants, which have all the features which are usually mentioned in this theory, such as frequent part-time employment, relatively short tenure of a particular job, low pay and lack of union protection.

One very important question for all immigrants, however, is that of their relationship to the union. In our experience a high proportion of our long-employed immigrants were in trade unions, particularly in the Transport and General Workers Union (TGWU) and the Amalgamated Union of Engineering Workers (AUEW) and expressed themselves satisfied with what the union did. This did not mean, however, that the unions had necessarily been tested in terms of their service to immigrant members. Only a study of the actual disposal of cases would show how well the unions were serving the immigrants. There is, moreover, quite a lot of case-study evidence such as that collected from European countries by Castles and Kosack (1973) which suggests that while immigrants are loyal to the unions on all trade union and what one might call class matters, where grievances specific to the immigrants are at issue the union does not act effectively to protect them. The evidence of the Wolf, Mansfield Hosiery and Imperial Typewriter disputes all confirm this. In the long run the picture which may emerge is that, despite their trade union membership and their loyalty to the unions, the immigrants may confront unions which at best ignore their grievances and at worst positively support more privileged native workers in preventing the immigrants from breaking out of replacement employment into the main parts of the labour market.

Immigrants in the housing market

If the present position of immigrants in the labour market is one in which a process of invasion and succession has occurred, that is to say that immigrants move quietly into positions which have been vacated by whites, this is even more true in the housing market. We should not be deceived by the fact that so many immigrants crop up in our statistics as owner-occupiers into believing that immigrants enjoy a privileged position in the housing market. My theory of housing classes is relevant here (Rex, 1973). I never did claim, as Roy Haddon (1970) has suggested, that a man's housing class depended upon the sort of housing which he occupied. In fact, I agree entirely with Haddon that the important point of differentiation concerns access rather than occupation. The point which I would now make is that the housing situation is now far too complex for us to be misled into thinking that owner-occupation represents a more privileged housing position than being a tenant of a council house or of private furnished and unfurnished accommodation. The crucial point is that we should distinguish between those who can benefit from the normal sorts of housing provision through building society mortgages and council tenancies and those who cannot.

When we look at the immigrant population some ten to twenty years after their first arrival, we find that they do indeed have roofs over their heads and that they often own those roofs. But it is still the case that they are where they are primarily because of disadvantage arising out of the system of housing allocation. As the process of redevelopment and of rehousing the urban population has gone on, more and more of the slum-dwellers, particularly amongst the native-born, have found themselves rehoused, not through the list but through slum clearance programmes. Immigrants, however, were not represented in these slums proportionately to the white working class. Unable to get council houses either through redevelopment schemes or through the list because of residential qualifications during their early years, they bought houses which were slightly better than the slums but were often leasehold properties in housing improvement areas. Thus, although they were the beneficiaries of the council's own mortgage scheme they were getting the sort of finance and going into the sort of areas which whites no longer wanted. Similarly those who obtained flats in the same areas rented from housing associations were turning to a special source of housing for the underprivileged. It is not necessary to the argument here to maintain that immigrants had actually wanted to apply for council houses and were prevented by some set of rules from doing so. In fact many of those whom we interviewed in Birmingham said that they actually preferred to house themselves. What does matter, however, is the system of constraints within which they made their decision and that the kind of housing finance and tenancy they chose was an under-privileged one. What had happened was that in redrawing the city map the planners had decided to clear the slums and move some slum-dwellers to better housing, leaving behind areas of housing which were now the most dilapidated, and tell a section of the population that they could have these houses improved, rather than being allowed access to the newer and better housing in the suburbs or in council flats.

At an earlier period, I dwelt upon the question of multi-occupied houses as representing the bottom of the housing hierarchy. There are still many houses of this kind and I would rank the tenants and the owners of these houses as amongst the least advantaged of all in the system of housing allocation. What we are now discussing, however, is a population which is better off in that it includes many who live in single family occupation, but which is still none the less disadvantaged. It is not yet a ghetto population but interestingly enough the white neighbours who remain are characteristically retired people whose roots are so deep in the area that they do not want to move. The black residents of the area complain that their housing is poor and some of them would like the chance of better housing to buy or to rent. The retired whites paradoxically want their houses to stand and blame the low status of the area not on the quality of the housing so much as on the character of their neighbours.

Of course many blacks have now passed through a long period of waiting and qualified for council housing. But just as we must distinguish between different kinds of owner-occupiers in terms of their strength in the housing allocation system, so we must distinguish between different groups of council tenants. It would seem that it is easier for blacks to get on some council estates than others and that in the better areas some councils have adopted a forced dispersal policy. Thus, whether an immigrant tends to be offered a house on a less desired estate or a house on a better estate provided that he does not have black neighbours, he clearly is in a position of weakness and disadvantage in the housing system.

It would seem then that even more clearly than in the sphere of employment, in the field of housing the immigrant is not merely quantitatively at a disadvantage compared with whites; he is actually in a qualitatively different and inferior position. Moreover, the political parties have housing policies which are responsive to the needs of precisely the groups from which immigrants are excluded. The Labour Party has traditionally defended the interests of the council house tenantry and those in the slums who might become council house tenants. The Conservative Party has on the whole defended the rights of the building society's mortgagee. Thus the main debates about housing policy, about the level of council rents, about the subsidization of rents versus mortgages, or about the sale of council houses go on over the heads of immigrants. In this the most important area of their deprivation they lack effective political defenders.

Immigrants and the education system

In the field of education the arrival of immigrants has produced two distinct sorts of complaint. One is a complaint from the white native parents that there are too many immigrants in the schools. The other is a complaint from the immigrant populations, particularly from the West Indians, that too many of their children are placed in special schools for the sub-normal and in lower streams. These complaints reflect some of the tensions which result from immigrants entering into the complex class system of British society. Indeed, it is perhaps in the sphere of education, more than in any other sphere that the more subtle tensions and problems of the class system are reflected.

The problems posed for parents by the English educational system are in fact already complex enough quite apart from the arrival of immigrants and are even more complex at the present time because the system is undergoing reform and change. Until the recent reforms based upon the idea of comprehensive non-selective secondary education, the following types of secondary education were available: fee-paying schools, the best of which ensured fairly ready entry into Oxford and

Cambridge as well as other universities; state secondary schools, including grammar schools which prepared some children for university; technical schools which prepared some children for further technical education, and modern schools which did occasionally allow children to stay on to take Higher Certificate examinations, but normally let their pupils leave at the age of fifteen; and, between the private fee-paying and the state free schools, other so-called direct-grant schools, which had some fee-paying and some scholarship students, the latter being paid for by local authorities. Through this system, working-class children could hope to get to even the prestigious universities even though they were excluded from the privileged private sector.

Present plans being implemented under a Labour Government are for the elimination of selection in the state sector without abolishing the private sector. This means that the former ladders to mobility which were a clearly distinguishable element in the old system (i.e. the direct-grant and grammar) schools are being eliminated, leaving only the fee-paying schools on the one hand and the upper streams of comprehensives on the other as avenues to higher education and privilege. There is currently a boom in fee-paying education and much uncertainty about the comprehensive system.

The concern about comprehensive education lies in the fact it is uncertain whether selection and social advancement will be available in all of them. Some schools may be based upon mixed-ability teaching and others on streaming but it is very difficult for parents to find out what will actually occur. Moreover, since the change-over to comprehensive education will need a period of about fifty years because of shortage of buildings, many children will not go to a purpose-built comprehensive school but into a campus or consortium combining schools of different quality. Many working-class parents are worried by this situation but send their children to what they believe to be the best school and hope that, if they are not academically successful they will, none the less, through their local contacts be able to get apprenticeships or jobs.

Immigrants seeking to enter the British class system are even more dependant than native working-class people on the educational system. On the whole, other avenues of entry to working life, such as an apprenticeship or jobs found through local contacts, are closed to them. Thus, it is not surprising that in some modern schools which allowed children to stay on for an extra year, a high proportion of those who stayed were immigrants. All immigrants, however, are concerned that, within the school system, their children should have the same chance as the average English child. They are probably more in the dark than English parents about what the options are, but once their children are in school they want to be sure that they get the best opportunities possible. What West Indian parents seem to find, however, is that their children do badly in nearly all the selective processes. At worst they end up in schools for the educationally sub-normal.

There does seem to be some difference between the performance of West Indian and Asian children and also in the degree of satisfaction of their parents. Asian children do better at school and their parents are more satisfied. Paradoxically this goes along with a lack of commitment to English society and a largely instrumental attitude towards education. West Indian parents therefore may make the obvious connection and come to believe that it is the Asian's maintenance of his own distinct cultural identity which helps. The problem then is not to push children into forced assimilation but to help them to believe in their own distinct culture and themselves. Black studies in school may then be proposed not as a means of withdrawing from competition within English society but as a precondition of success in that competition.

Black studies, however, may also be seen in a different light. It may well be that for many assertion of a black cultural identity appeals simply because competition in white schools on white terms seems to be unfair. In any case, since black studies programmes draw heavily upon a culture of revolt, their initiation is bound to mean the focusing of moral and political ideas about a centre distinct from that which is to be found in working-class culture. Thus the growth of black consciousness and black power movements is a sign not merely of withdrawal from approved forms of middle-class mobility seeking but from the working-class values which have arisen both in conflict with this mobility striving and as an adjustment to it.

Militant black ideologies make their appearance even more frequently amongst unemployed school-leavers who live a large part of their lives on the streets in the black quarters of English towns and are hence often in trouble with the police. Thus a highly articulate black leader, whom we met shortly after we had visited a rather good primary school, much interested in raising the reading age of West Indian children, commented 'The reality for us is not passing the 11+ examination. Too many of our people live in that middle-class dream. The reality for our people consists in the harassment of our young unemployed boys on the streets and in the violence which is used against them in police stations.'

Black organizations and the Labour movement

I now come to the central point of this paper. I suggested earlier that for most working-class people a political labour movement organized around the unions was their principal means of support and provided the focus for their lives. Immigrant leaders are also members of that movement at least as members of trade unions. But they do not receive the same service and support from it that white workers do. For the support that white workers get from the Labour movement and from working-class culture they look to militant black movements which are neighbourhood- rather than work-based and which deal centrally, not with work problems, but with the problems which the young unemployed and under-employed face in their conflicts with the forces of law and order. Black power groups constitute for the immigrants and the British blacks the functional equivalent of the working-class movement.

It should be recognized that I am not saying that the vast majority of black immigrants and black British are conscious supporters of black power. But then the vast majority of British workers are not Marxists either. The fact of the matter is that most respectable immigrant families do the best they can to get on and to help their children get on in British society. But at the same time they will know something of the militant groups and may quietly approve their activities just as passive and acquiescent British workers often silently approve reports of industrial militancy in other industries. It is also possible that we are only seeing the beginnings of these movements and that the present passive support which they receive may take a far more active form.

Types of black political movement

Three examples of different types of black movement can be given from our research in Birmingham. These are examples of issue-oriented movements, personality-oriented movements and ideologically oriented movements. Of the first kind is a movement started by a former Pentecostalist preacher and door-to-door man. After first building up a reputation as a man who could help the young boys at the police station, he then turned his attention to the second mortgage scandal which was associated with loans given to people who wished to join an apparently lucrative sales organization. His success in exposing this scandal and in helping individuals to get their debts reduced, led to his establishment of a large and national organization for immigrant self-defence and welfare.

The second type of organization centred around a young man who has a peculiar gift for seeking out trouble and appearing as a martyr to white supremacy. Having first become known for being shot up by another black man in a quarrel, he moved on to become president of the students' union at a local college of further education where he was taking his 'A' levels. After a brief period at this college he was expelled for keeping students away from classes and for alleged physical violence against members of staff. During the Relf demonstrations outside Winson Green prison he claims to have organized a black defence force to fight the police, at the same time claiming that the original shooting of which he had been the victim was the work of the British army. Since then he has visited those whom he calls 'the brothers' in Mozambique and Tanzania and most recently was gaoled for using threatening behaviour when forced to wait in a queue at the offices of the DHSS where he was drawing his dole.

A man such as this, who is regarded by most of those who meet him from positions of authority and responsibility as nothing more than a nuisance and a buffoon, might well be looked on in a different light by young militant West Indians on the street. Not merely are they prepared to give him the benefit of the doubt. They see his talent for defying white authority as a splendid encouragement to themselves and as something which can be used to give them all self-respect. He is said to be particularly popular amongst young boys who rove the streets wearing Rastafari hairstyles and little woollen hats with Rasta colours. He and people like him can fit quite easily into their Black Zionist ideology.

More intellectually serious are a group of educated young black social workers who started a hostel for unemployed West Indian youth at the same time as educating themselves in black political theories such as those of Garvey and Fanon. These more than any others consciously tried to use black studies education carried on in their hostel as a means of restoring the dignity and self-respect of young blacks. These men were fairly hostile to the white race-relations industry and to people like ourselves doing race-relations research. They did, however, talk to us whereas another group more radical in its black orientations than this one refused on principle to have a meeting with us. This other group also refused to let in the white organizer of the Free Angola Movement who brought round an Angolan speaker. The black speaker went in but the hapless young English communist girl was made to wait outside.

In many ways the Asian community's politics differ from those of the West Indian. On the one hand they centre around traditional national cultures. On the other they have a more anglicized mode of expression than the West Indian. The traditional national culture provides a leadership which fits easily into the paternalistic framework provided by the Community Relations Commission (now reorganized into the Commission for Racial Equality). Not wanting total acceptance into English society for their people these leaders are quite happy to sit on a body which helps to ensure that traditional culture is kept alive and which irons out any cultural misunderstandings which might arise. On the other hand most workers from the Indian sub-continent have some experience of politics of a kind which derives ultimately from Britain. Some will have been members of the Indian Congress Party or bodies like the Muslim League in Pakistan and some will have had experience of Marxist organizations both in industry and in politics.

Indian labour and Marxist organizations help in some ways to bring the Indian worker closer to the British and there are, indeed, some instances in which Indians have helped to establish or strengthen branches of British trade unions. In these cases the 'Marxism' of the Indian worker probably means no more than a recognition that trade unionism is an important field of political activity as well as being very effective in an instrumental sense as a means of getting the best price for one's labour while staying in an alien land.

Among Asians, then, it is no surprise that, along with some traditional cultural and welfare organizations, there are organizations which are primarily workers' organizations which, like the British trade unions, may provide a base for organizations outside the industrial field. In some cases these organizations have been able to make their political presence felt through negotiation with the Conservative as well as the Labour and Liberal parties. But the mere existence of labour-oriented organizations does not mean that they are necessarily militant defenders of Asian rights. There are two separate ways in which militancy may develop.

One way is through the development of temporary or permanent organizations of Asian workers which recognize that in order to defend themselves they might have to fight the white unions as well as employers, to ensure that they get adequate protection in 'black workshops' and to gain entry for their members to jobs protected by a *de facto* colour bar. Such organizations have difficult decisions to make and it is not possible to describe the decision to stay in or leave white unions as *ipso facto* militant or accommodating. The important question is whether the organizations concerned win or compromise. It is possible either to win or to compromise while staying out of the unions or joining them.

The other type of militancy is that which takes advantage of the militant-accommodating distinction within the British labour movement and within British Marxism. It does seem to be the case that more and more young Asians, often educated in Britain, are taking part in Trotskyist organizations like International Socialism (now the Socialist Workers' Party) and using the organizations which they provide both for industrial struggles and for street demonstrations. I do not think that we can conclude from this that what we are witnessing is the growing unity of the working class. Whenever British Trotskyists and Asian workers come together there is considerable uncertainty as to who is using whom. But in any case it has to be noted that the structural break between the main sections of the working class and the immigrant community is such that the most common form of connection between articulate immigrants and the working class is with minority organizations. The structural position of the immigrant community is such that it is not adequately served by orthodox trade unions or by Labour city councils.

What these separate accounts of West Indian and Asian militancy suggest is that, although there are differences between them they represent signs of the same underlying sociological and political phenomenon. What is being expressed in immigrant politics is not the politics of the simple and straightforward class struggle within capitalism either in its reformist or its Marxist version. What we are considering is the political formation of an immigrant under-class. It is that class which is cut off from the main class structure of the society not merely in quantitative but in structural or qualitative terms and for the moment at least cannot be construed as merely an underprivileged part of the British labour movement.

Some misleading views of immigrant politics

To some this may seem merely platitudinous, but it is worth noting that it is a view which conflicts with three others. One is the paternalistic view in terms of which immigrant matters are normally discussed in Britain. Another is the new view which treats the British situation as akin to that in the United States where there is a powerful civil rights movement and a Civil Rights Programme. The third is what I shall call the Plain Marxist view.

All the major institutions set up by the government to deal with problems of race relations have been paternalist in nature. They came into being together with the introduction of immigration control for Commonwealth citizens, and all of them bear the marks of that origin. The National Committee for Commonwealth Immigrants (NCCI) and the Race Relations Board (RRB) were the first bodies concerned and they were followed by the Community Relations Commission (CRC) with its local councils and, finally, through the amalgamation of the Race Relations Board and the Community Relations Commission, by the Commission for Racial Equality (CRE).

The National Committee for Commonwealth Immigrants was conceived in a mild way as a built-in political lobby for the immigrants. Several not wholly compromised members of immigrant élites were invited to join the committee and were backed by prestigious non-party political figures drawn from British élites. But the National Committee for Commonwealth Immigrants never won the support of the major immigrant organizations and had no way of affiliating them. If it represented a militant voice at all it was because there were some radical figures on its specialized panels. Even then, however, the main committee tamely acquiesced when the government failed to carry out its recommendations or allowed all its recommendations to be channelled into one, namely a plea for the extension of the powers of the Race Relations Board.

The Race Relations Board had been set up in 1965 at the same time as the Labour Government's attempt to further limit Commonwealth Immigration and had been little more than a sop. It could not deal with the key areas of housing and employment and could do nothing more fearsome, legally speaking, than to conciliate the contending parties when there was a dispute. The second Act, which was eventually passed in 1968, did deal with the areas of employment and housing but in such restricted ways that its effect was derisory. Crucially the board did not

assume judicial powers and could at most form an opinion of discrimination and, in doing this, it had no powers to call for papers or to sub-
poena witnesses.

The National Committee for Commonwealth Immigrants broke up
in confusion when a number of members resigned following the Home
Secretary's decision to restrict the immigration rights of British citizens
from East Africa. It was replaced by a body which did not even pretend
to be a political body, the Community Relations Commission. This
body from the start misdefined the problems of ethnic minorities
essentially as problems of cultural difference and set about co-opting
immigrant élites who were interested in these questions (see Hill and
Issacharoff, 1971). But it was not equipped to deal with political
questions which were increasingly being posed by the immigrant leaders
or even with problems of discrimination which were problems for the
Race Relations Board.

Dissatisfaction among members of the Community Relations Commission and its councils with their restricted powers was one of the
reasons why it was suggested that the quasi-judicial functions of the
Race Relations Board and the Community Relations Commission
should be merged in a single body. But, obviously, if the new Commission for Racial Equality feels that it is getting teeth through moving
into the new field, those concerned with its judicial role have grave
doubts about its being performed within a body whose prime purpose is
that of good community relations and social work.

Still less is the new body well equipped to play a political role. It
lacks any kind of representative base and has only the most slender
connection with the immigrant organizations mentioned above. The
one thing which it can do in the political sphere is to put a small number of black men into professional jobs within its own organization.
Thus, at the moment of the foundation of the Commission for Racial
Equality there was a dispute over the number of top jobs which would
go to black men. The media were quick to take this up and represent
it as a genuine political struggle in which black rights were at stake. Far
from this being the case, however, the only thing which was at stake
was the number of black men who would get jobs in an unrepresent-
ative and paternalistic organization. Whereas in the United States the
process of blacks buying themselves into the system had produced a
number of black mayors and other local officials elected by the whole
population and responsible for their government, what was happening
in Britain was quite different. The new professional black men had

not made it in the wider society. They simply found niches for themselves within the paternalistic apparatus.

Crucially missing in the British situation was any kind of effective civil rights movement. Martin Luther King had attempted to get one started in the form of the Campaign Against Racial Discrimination (CARD) but this failed in almost every way (see Heineman, 1972). It did not, until the last moment of its existence, obtain the support of most West Indian organizations; its leading members were characteristically either b'.ack men who had gained acceptance in white intellectual and political quarters and white liberals trying to make the race question politically manageable; and, finally, when it might perhaps have become at least like the American National Association for the Advancement of Coloured People (NAACP) as the body which would argue from an immigrant point of view before the Race Relations Board, its leaders set their sights on arguing the political case for legal machinery within the Labour Party. When these leaders withdrew from CARD they issued a remarkable manifesto saying that CARD had been taken over by Maoists, Trotskyists and West Indians. In view of what we have said above, this was precisely a disavowal of any connection with the militant groups I have discussed. As we saw, the more radical young Asian leaders were beginning to follow left Marxist leaders, while those who believed in West Indian community politics seemed *ipso facto* to be on a par with other extremists from the point of view of the liberal establishment.

The point which I am seeking to make here is that there was an obvious difference between the British situation and that prevailing in America when civil rights programmes were launched. In America there had been more than a decade of militant black activity before civil rights programmes were launched. The programmes represented at least a partial victory won by the black people for themselves. In Britain, such political action as occurred was the product of an uneasy white conscience following the passage of the legislation to control black immigration in 1962, 1965 and 1968. This guilty conscience was aptly expressed by Roy Hattersley, the MP for Sparkbrook, after he had accepted immigration control in defiance of the views of his immigrant constituents: 'Integration without control is impossible. Control without integration is morally indefensible.' Thus, whereas in the United States there were independent black leaders arguing civil rights cases before various tribunals, such advocacy as there was to be in Britain came from within the paternalistic bodies set up by the government. Still worse, a self-help programme for black groups was financed which could only have the effect of castrating the groups who took the money.

As we have seen, one of the consequences of the collapse of CARD was the dissociation of white liberals and highly placed intellectual blacks from the black political groups and a transfer of their activities into the Labour Party. This represented another important trend which made it possible for British social democrats and orthodox Marxists to evade the political problem posed by the presence of an immigrant under-class. From the point of view of Labour leaders the proper vehicles for civil rights activity were to be found in the Labour Party itself and in the trade unions. From the point of view of Marxists of an orthodox kind, the main point to be made about civil rights was that it was the working class as such which was deprived of rights in a capitalist society and that the proper thing for black workers to do therefore was to work within the working-class movement. Characteristically, therefore, Labour and Communist leaders throughout the 1960s and early 1970s avoided any serious involvement in issues which were specific to immigrants.

What I am trying to say here is that the British situation was not one in which immigrant rights could be preserved through paternalism; the incipient civil rights movement had collapsed in disarray; and the orthodox British forms felt themselves continually under attack from racists and unprotected by the law. Powell's speeches gave him a reputation with the British public as a somewhat deviant politician but also as a man of genius, and a series of judicial decisions and police comments seemed to suggest that, if anything, the judges and the police were more concerned with the threat of black action against white society than they were with the defence of black civil rights. I have in mind here the judge in Brixton who called for the establishment of white vigilante squads when he was faced with a number of young men charged with handbag snatching. I have in mind Sir Robert Mark commenting, after the Southall murder in 1976, that it was wrong to interpret this crime as racial. And I have in mind the extraordinary police operation which was set up to deal with 'pickpockets' at the 1976 Notting Hill carnival. In these circumstances the message which militant leaders put out to their members was that they must be prepared to defend themselves.

The politics of defensive confrontation

I hope that this account will not be thought to be exaggerated because, if anything, it understates the degree of militancy in the black communities today. Nearly all the black leaders I have met make references to war and violence and it is not sufficient merely to dismiss them as extremists. I think that street battles and riots provoked by blacks are unlikely and I do not, though I am less sure here, think there will be any literal application of the slogan 'Burn, baby burn' in British cities. While I think there may be some tendency for embattled immigrants to return home, I do not see a serious possibility in some sort of Rastafarian or Garveyan exodus to a Black Zion. But these notions do form a central myth for the black communities. They play the same role in uniting the community as Sorel saw the notion of the final cataclysmic general strike playing for working-class solidarity in Europe.

I do think, however, that the black political movements are moving toward a posture of defensive confrontation and that they are quite realistic in doing so. I have tried to show that though some blacks are slowly gaining acceptance in the lower strata of the working class in general, the situation of the blacks is structurally distinct from that of the majority of the working class. The working class is protected by a political movement based upon the unions but extending its protection into other social and cultural spheres. The blacks, while they formally belong to unions and affirm support for them, have had to develop communally organized groups based normally upon the place of residence and dealing above all with the problems which exist for and are posed by the unemployed young blacks. I expect these groups to use a violent rhetoric and one which talks of war with British society, but I also expect that in the long run their main effect will be to provide necessary protection for blacks in a hostile world. Such defensive confrontation, moreover, may not in the long run prevent the entry of blacks into the working class. It is simply the essential precondition of that entry, contrary to the view of those conservatives, liberals and Marxists who unite in imagining that justice can be given out to black men on a purely paternalistic basis. While the immediate effect of black militancy may be a white backlash in the labour movement as elsewhere, there is certainly more likely to be a place found for black workers in the labour movement if they are militant than if they rely upon the paternalism of labour leaders; it may take time before this is learned either by black leaders or trade unionists and Labour politicians.

Note

1 The conclusions of this paper are based on research currently being conducted in Birmingham by John Rex, Sally Tomlinson and David Hearnden on racial discrimination in employment, housing and education.

Bibliography

Castles, S. and Kosack G. (1973), *Immigrant Workers and the Class Structure*, Oxford University Press, London.

Daniel W.W. (1968), *Racial Discrimination in England*, Penguin, Harmondsworth.

Haddon, R.F. (1970), 'A Minority in a Welfare State Society: The Location of West Indians in the London Housing Market', *New Atlantis*, vol. 2, no. 1.

Heineman, B.W. (1972), *The Politics of the Powerless*, Oxford University Press, London.

Hill, M.J. and Issacharoff, R.M. (1971), *Community Action and Race Relations*, Oxford University Press, London.

Parsons, T. (1954), *Essays in Sociological Theory*, Free Press, Chicago.

Rex, J. (1961), *Key Problems of Sociological Theory*, Routledge & Kegan Paul, London.

Rex, J. (1973), *Race, Colonialism and the City*, Routledge & Kegan Paul, London.

Smith, D. (1977), *Racial Disadvantage in Britain*, Penguin, Harmondsworth.

Sorel, G. (1950), *Reflections on Violence*, Free Press, Chicago.

Warner, W.L. (1936), 'American Class and Caste', *American Journal of Sociology*, vol. xlii, pp.234–7.

CHAPTER 5

Working-class racist beliefs in the inner city

Annie Phizacklea and Robert Miles

They know instinctively, although a lot of them can't put it into words, that there is something rotten in this country, that there is something wrong, that in fifty years we have come from a nation that was one of the world's first powers to a nation that is now one of the standing jokes of the world. Immigration is the issue which exemplifies and brings to the fore this sense of dissatisfaction most readily and for the greatest number of people.

(Anthony Reed-Herbert, National Front Organizer in Leicester)

Introduction

Over the past twenty-five years New Commonwealth immigration and its political exploitation by Enoch Powell MP (see Foot, 1969; Roth, 1970; Schoen, 1977) and the National Front (see Walker, 1977) among others, have led to speculation about the nature and extent of racism in Britain. More recently, it has become apparent that the National Front, which views itself as a 'racialist' party, has increasingly drawn upon working-class electoral support. This development suggests that working-class racism may exist as a distinct phenomenon, although surprisingly little attention has been paid to it in the academic literature. A notable exception is Paul Foot's *Immigration and Race in British Politics* (1965) in which he identifies two somewhat contradictory tendencies in the reaction in working-class areas to New Commonwealth immigrants. He suggests that the reaction was 'kind, even helpful', but that there were expressions of 'resentment and xenophobia'. The latter reaction he links, as do most commentators on British racism, to imperialism and conquest: 'The subjects of this conquest were coloured. All great men, they were led to believe, were white men, and all uncivilised, weak, backward peoples were black' (1965, pp.232–5).

In the next section of this paper we will argue that negative and/or hostile references to black people can be labelled racist. If this is the case then, given the findings of a nation-wide survey of electors carried out by Butler and Stokes (1974), racism is widespread in Britain. They conclude that throughout the 1960s, 'strong and overwhelmingly hostile attitudes towards immigration were quite general in the country' (1974, p.306). They refer, of course, to coloured immigration, the two having become synonymous in public discussion over the last twenty years. A quarter of their sample went on to spontaneously elaborate on their reasons for such hostility, their comments focusing on competition for housing and jobs and the deterioration of health and living standards that the immigrants were thought to bring about.

Thus while hostility towards the presence of black people in Britain is evidently widespread, the findings of Butler and Stokes suggest that such hostility is strongest among unskilled manual workers. Mackenzie and Silver indicated that 83 per cent of their sample of manual workers questioned in 1960 were in favour of restrictions on black immigration (1968, p.152). It is the main argument of this paper that the pervasive nature of hostility expressed towards black people among the majority of male manual workers we interviewed in one inner-city area is best understood not simply in terms of the racial stereotypes inherited from an imperial past, but also in relation to the socio-economic decline of the area in which our interviewees reside and work. This decline has coincided with the arrival of New Commonwealth immigrants who provide for our respondents an obvious and immediate explanation for the decline of the area and its attendant problems and who reinforce the perception of disadvantage amongst 'us' who have been left behind and trapped in the decaying inner city. We are therefore suggesting that not only is it unwise to use one explanation for the existence of racist beliefs in British society as a whole, but that it is also unwise to view the working class as homogeneous and existing in static cultural and socio-economic circumstances. We believe that this does not hold in reality and hence the analysis in this paper refers only to the white, manual (predominantly unskilled) working class to be found in and around part of the inner city of London. Furthermore, we would suggest generalization from our analysis only if the part of the inner city we have studied can be shown to be similar to equivalent areas in other major conurbations.

A more obvious assumption which needs to be questioned in the debate over British racism is that there is agreement upon the meaning of racism. This is manifestly not the case at a theoretical level as the following section will indicate. We will then make a case for arguing that the negative references to black workers/black immigrants can be labelled racist. In referring to black workers we mean, collectively, persons who originate from the West Indies, India, Pakistan and Bangladesh, although where necessary we will separately identify the specific ethnic or national group.

The concept of racism

In considering the various definitions of racism that can be found in the literature, we are less interested in locating a correct position than in identifying a theoretical position which we believe is helpful in identifying and explaining the main features and content of working-class racism in Britain. Over ten years ago Michael Banton defined racism as 'the doctrine that a man's behaviour is determined by stable inherited characters deriving from separate racial stocks having distinctive attributes and usually considered to stand to one another in relations of superiority and inferiority' (1970, p.18). He concluded that arguments which in the past appealed to biological justifications have often in recent times relied upon observations in the field of social science, and asserted that the current arguments used to deny equal treatment to members of ethnic minorities might more accurately be described as expressions of ethnocentrism (Banton, 1970, p.31). More recently he has contended that the pre-Darwinian doctrine that used to be called 'scientific racism' would be better designated racial typology and he is no longer concerned with trying to find a use for 'racism' as a concept within social science (1977, pp.5, 156–62, 169).

Other writers, such as Van den Berghe (1967), Schermerhorn (1970) and Wilson (1973), define racism in a manner that relates it to what Banton now calls the doctrine of racial typology. For example, Schermerhorn describes racism as 'an ideology that sees an invariable connection between cultural behaviour and physical type. Hence it defines specific outgroups as having characteristic traits (usually detestable or in some way inferior) that are inherent outgrowths of their biological constructions' (1970, p.102). However, Wilson pushes the distinction between racism and ethnocentrism further than Banton did, and argues that both can refer to, or be based upon, physical and cultural criteria. He asserts that 'ethnocentrism is a principle of invidious group distinction, whereas racism is a philosophy or ideology of racial exploitation'. Ethnocentrism that is based upon physical criteria does not involve an ideology justifying racial domination in terms of biological arguments: 'rather, it denotes a general disdain or contempt for out-group physical features and nothing more'. Moreover, cultural racism, in contrast to physical racism, 'does not logically imply a rationale for subjugation of the minority because it is not assumed that the minority is biologically incapable of achieving equality'. The essence of Wilson's distinction between racism and ethnocentrism therefore concerns the presence or absence of, on the part of the dominant group, an ideology of exploitation of the identified out-group (1973, pp.31–3).

Are such distinctions necessary and helpful? John Rex has, for instance, argued that to use the concept of racism to refer to a deterministic theory which relates human behaviour to biology is to employ an unnecessarily restrictive definition, especially since other kinds of theory can serve the same social functions. He defines a racist theory as one which posits a deterministic relationship between membership of a specifically identified group (often, but not always, on the basis of colour) and possession of certain qualities; such a theory may be of a scientific, cultural, religious or historical kind. Rex suggests that the existence of such a theory is one of three conditions which define a 'race relations situation', the others being the existence of harsh oppression and exploitation, and the identification of groups involved in terms of signs which are regarded as unalterable (1970, pp.12, 144–60; 1973, pp.218–21).

We will show below that if the concept 'racism' is to be limited to theories/ideologies which maintain that the biological inferiority of a specific group justifies them being confined to an inferior socio-economic role, then the concept 'racist' can be applied only to a very small proportion of the British working class. But this does not alter the fact that a substantial proportion of our sample hold a negative evaluation of black people. We argue that it is useful to define the concept of racism in relation to the social process which creates what can be called a racial category. This has the advantage of both relating the concept of racism to recent theoretical developments concerning the distinction between the concepts of race and ethnicity (Lyon, 1972) and firmly locating racism in processes of social interaction. A racial category is *inter alia* the product of negative beliefs held by a majority group about a minority group which identify and set apart the latter on the basis of some observable physical and/or hereditary characteristic. The category is therefore externally defined, the boundary supported by those beliefs which allow processes of racial exclusion to operate, these taking the form of varying levels of discrimination and segregation (see Miles and Phizacklea, 1977b). These beliefs are racist in nature because implicit in the notions of 'them' and 'us' in Willesden (i.e., implicit in the creation of the boundary) are the notions of 'black' and 'white' and not because they necessarily appeal to pseudo-biological variation. The creation of the boundary and, hence, the racial category is dependant upon the identification of 'them' in terms of some physical feature, the possessors of which are also said to have some other (negatively evaluated) feature or to act in a certain (negatively evaluated) manner.

In explaining the source of this process, and the racism that is an integral part of the process, we cannot accept a crude, conspiracy theory which asserts that racist ideas are purposely fostered within a dominant ideology with the aim of dividing an otherwise united working class. For, as Williams as argued:

> if ideology were merely some abstract imposed notion, if our social
> and political and cultural ideas and assumptions and habits were
> merely the result of specified manipulation, of a kind of overt
> training which might be simply ended or withdrawn, then the
> society would be very much easier to change than in practice it has
> ever been or is (1973, p.8).

Moreover, although we believe that derogatory images from an imperial past can act as a basis for, or be a constituent part of, the negative evaluation of 'coloureds' by the white working class in Britain (Foot, 1965, pp.232–5; Hartmann and Husbands, 1974, p.29), we have not found widespread conscious articulation of such images in our research. However, such images have been used to justify racial exclusion and, as a consequence, 'the coloureds' are automatically cast as illegitimate competitors in any allocation of scarce resources, a competition which is particularly characteristic of life in the inner city. But cultural transmission alone cannot provide a full understanding of current working-class beliefs in the inner-city context. These beliefs should also be understood in relation to the material realities of working-class life in the major conurbations of contemporary British capitalism. 'The coloureds' provide an obvious immediate explanation for the decline of material production and housing stock which is a feature of the nature of capitalist production and with which has coincided the arrival of New Commonwealth immigrants. Working-class racism is less an aberration than a likely response in the current circumstances; it is based upon a perception of disadvantage among 'us' who are most vulnerable to the effects of inflation, the rise in unemployment, and the continuing housing shortage. It therefore stems, at least in part, from a competition for access to scarce resources, a competition that characterizes the old Borough of Willesden, the area in which we carried out our research.

The socio-economic structure of the old Borough of Willesden

The Borough of Willesden in north-west London ceased to exist in 1965 when it was amalgamated with Wembley to form the London Borough of Brent. Our discussion here concentrates upon the area which was designated as the Borough of Willesden and which now corresponds roughly to the present parliamentary constituency boundaries of Brent East and Brent South, the latter being the specific location of our research. In the past hundred years, Willesden has been transformed from a quiet, rural parish, through a period of substantial industrial expansion, into an area of socio-economic decline, showing many of the characteristics of what has become known as the 'inner city' (see CDP, 1977; Hall, 1977).

Willesden's rural character was first altered by the arrival of city bankers and financiers in the second half of the eighteenth century. They built large houses in rural seclusion and travelled to the City by a daily coach service. However, the arrival of the railway in 1842 made the first dramatic difference and by the end of the nineteenth century Willesden, in common with Kilburn and Cricklewood, had become a large dormitory suburb of London with a population of 115,000 (Potter, 1926, p.156; Coppock and Prince, 1964, pp.126, 143–4). Up until this point, industrial development had been virtually absent, but from the turn of the century the then suburban character of Willesden began to change again as light engineering and printing works and laundries were established (Morris, 1950, p.10).

The First World War stimulated this emergent industrial growth, with the government sponsoring factory development at Park Royal to meet the demands for ammunition, and at the end of the war these buildings passed into the hands of private enterprise. By 1925, concentrations of industry were found not only at Park Royal but throughout the borough and the demand for labour, including skilled labour, further increased. The population rose to 172,000 exacerbating an already acute housing shortage (Morris, 1950, p.10), but inter-war expansion continued, with new industries engaged in the production of cars, food and drink, chemicals and consumer durables becoming established (Smith, 1933). The industrial expansion and subsequent increase in population continued through the national economic crisis of the 1930s when a small outflow of population was more than compensated for by migrants, particularly Welsh and Scots, who came in search of work. The pattern of a transient population supplementing the movement of a proportion of the stable population, evident even before the First World War, has continued to characterize the area.

By 1938, the population had reached 198,000 yet private enterprise had failed to produce sufficient new housing stock for the influx of workers. Willesden Council reported in the late 1930s that 'overcrowding' was a substantial problem in the area, even according to the low standards of what constituted overcrowding (Leff and Blunden, n.d., p.31). The Second World War brought the exodus of 60,000 residents, but the immediate post-war period saw the inflow of a partial replacement population, some of whom were from eastern Europe and the Irish Republic. By 1948, the population of this now industrially developed borough stood at 180,000 of which about a quarter had not lived in the borough before 1940. Since then, the population has steadily declined, falling to 161,120 in 1966, even though immigration from the New Commonwealth, particularly the West Indies, had brought 16,000 new residents to the area (Weintraub, 1972, p.44).

While the population has steadily decreased, housing remains the most pressing problem in Willesden (see Lomas 1975, p.12; Greve *et al.*, 1971, pp.22–39; Daly, 1971, pp.21–2). Given the failure of private enterprise to produce sufficient new housing stock, the local authority began to meet the demand for more and better housing in the early 1960s through large redevelopment schemes while simultaneously encouraging both people and industry to move to New Towns (a policy that is now under review). Nevertheless, according to data supplied by Brent Housing Department, the housing waiting list still stood at 9417 for the borough as a whole in 1977, and the housing conditions of many in Willesden remains a depressing one. Part of the residential sample was selected from the district of Harlesden in South Brent. The district has a typical inner-city population: declining in size and ethnically mixed and, compared to Brent as a whole, relatively young, mobile and unskilled (London Borough of Brent, 1975, p.2). An indication of housing conditions in this district is given in Table 1: these conditions are appreciably worse than those found in the rest of the borough. In 1973, a GLC report identified the area as one of the more physically and socially deprived areas of London (GLC, 1973).

Among those fortunate enough to qualify for rehousing, there are many who find themselves in a new systems-built flat on an estate which they dislike intensely. This reaction has tended to characterize the attitude of the majority of respondents in the residential sample reported on later. The estate where these respondents live is on the edge of Harlesden, the oldest part having been built in the mid-1960s and the larger complex of high rise, medium rise and terrace-house units having been built during 1975 and 1976. The council finds letting difficult on this estate, despite the size of the housing waiting list. A large majority in Harlesden and on the new council estate work locally, the largest employers being on the adjacent Park Royal Estate.

The Park Royal Estate is a major part of the industrial belt which runs along the western boundary of the old Borough of Willesden. The development of this area was complete by the end of the 1940s and a survey of that time shows that the dominant industries were precision engineering, radio and electrical goods, food and drink manufacture, motor engineering and printing. In the late 1940s, only 4 of the 455 factories had more than 1000 employees, yet those four factories employed over 22 per cent of the total industrial labour force (Morris, 1950, p.42). Since the 1950s, Park Royal and the other industrial areas have gone into decline. Changes in the industrial structure of British capitalism, rationalization, lack of space for expansion and the increasingly high cost of production have all contributed to factory closures in the area, as throughout London. Thus, between 1966 and 1972, 217,000 people were made redundant in London, 77 per cent of whom were employed in the manufacturing sector, and the bulk of these redundancies have occurred in the traditional areas of manufacturing industry, which includes Willesden (Lomas, 1975, pp.1–6). The cyclical pattern of capitalist development, which brought Willesden into existence as an industrial area, is now on its downward turn.

Table 1 Housing conditions in the Harlesden district compared to Brent as a whole (percentages)

	Owner-occupiers	Council	Private unfurnished	Private furnished	Total
HARLESDEN					
Tenure groups	28	7	40	24	
% households over 1.5 person per room					11
% share or lack hot water	13	13	37	51	32
% share or lack bath	22	7	48	64	41
% share or lack inside WC	14	4	31	60	31
BRENT					
Tenure groups	48	13	22	17	
% households over 1.5 person per room					6
% share or lack hot water	6	5	28	44	10
% share or lack bath	8	10	36	64	32
% share or lack inside WC	6	5	23	60	28

Source: 1971 Census of Population as reproduced in *Harlesden: Report of Studies*, London Borough of Brent, 1975 (compiled from Appendices 2C, 2E and 2F).

The reduction of jobs in the manufacturing sector in Willesden has been substantial, and according to information supplied by the Borough of Brent, has been concentrated in the food and drink industry, mechanical and electrical engineering industry, and in vehicle manufacture. In Brent as a whole, 6000 manufacturing jobs were lost between 1971 and 1973, and a large proportion of these were in Willesden, with both large and small units being affected. When the resulting vacant premises have been reoccupied (and many have not), the replacement firms have been mainly engaged in storage and distribution, showrooms and car repairs, all of which are less labour-intensive than the manufacturing industries they have replaced.

The effect of this industrial decline on unemployment is not clear-cut. Throughout the 1960s and early 1970s, the level of unemployment in the Willesden Employment Exchange area followed the trend in Greater London as a whole, which was itself a reflection of the national trend, although proportionally lower. Since 1973, unemployment in Willesden has increased dramatically, the rate of increase between August 1974 and August 1975 being 14 per cent, among the highest in the UK. In July 1977, there were 5700 registered unemployed in the Willesden Employment Exchange Area, far in excess of the previous peaks of 2400 in January 1968 and 2800 in April 1972. It would there-fore seem that the loss of manufacturing jobs in the area has been, at least partially, matched by movement of population out of the area, but that the overall decline in manufacturing industry, and the problems that the remaining firms face in terms of profitability, makes the area increasingly susceptible to a national economic crisis.

The old Borough of Willesden is therefore characterized by a very serious housing problem, in the form of both a shortage of accommo-dation and a low standard of much of the existing stock, and a decline in the economic base of the area. The housing problem has existed for at least fifty years and the factors leading to the economic decline have their origin in the cycle of capitalist production. Coincidentally with these developments has been the movement into the area of black immigrants from the New Commonwealth in the 1950s and 1960s. An analysis of the 1971 census has shown that of all the London boroughs, Brent had the highest number who were born in the New Commonwealth (14 per cent) and of those 18,040 were born in the West Indies. This makes Brent the London borough with the largest overall number of individuals born in the West Indies (Field *et al.*, 1974, pp.16–17).

Race and politics in Willesden

The Labour Party has held office during the development of these processes since 1945. The old Willesden Council was Labour dominated, as befits an area that contains a predominantly manual working-class population, and pursued policies which were of benefit to the working class as a whole (e.g. an emphasis on the construction of council housing) but, with an eye on the newly arrived West Indian immigrants, it also pursued an independent race relations programme. The local Labour Party also remained critical of the party's growing support of immigration control (Weintraub, 1972, p.152) at least up until 1965. The merger of Wembley and Willesden in 1965 greatly reduced the Labour majority on the new council and the party became increasingly preoccupied with maintaining itself in office and, hence, pursued policies that were unlikely to lose white, working-class votes. This did not prevent the Conservative opposition from attacking policies, aimed at benefiting the working class as a whole, as particularly favouring the black population (Weintraub, 1972, p.194). The Labour Party lost their majority in 1968 but has since regained control of the council. Their policies have continued to err on the side of caution although this has not absolved them from criticism, particularly over the housing of Ugandan Asians and, since 1974, over lettings and the formation of black estates in the southern half of the borough.

At the parliamentary level, Brent is split into three constituencies, Brent North (held by Rhodes Boyson), Brent East (by Reg Freeson, Minister for Housing) and Brent South (Laurie Pavitt). Prior to selection as a parliamentary candidate, Freeson had been critical of national Labour Party policies on immigration but, during the 1964 election campaign, he indicated his acceptance of the policy of immigration control. Freeson won the seat (which was then Willesden East) from the Conservatives (who had won the seat only in 1959 after three Labour victories after the war) and has retained it ever since. By comparison, Brent South (formerly Willesden West) has been a safe seat for Labour who have lost it only once to the Conservatives since 1923.

The Labour Party has, therefore, dominated both parliamentary and council elections in Willesden since 1945 and, in the case of Willesden West, since the 1920s. Parliamentary elections have tended to be two-way fights although a Communist Party candidate has fought Willesden West (now Brent South) regularly since 1959, further emphasizing the working-class base of the area. The 1974 elections were also contested by the Liberal Party and the National Front with, in the October election, the Liberals running a poor third and the National Front fourth to Labour. The emergence of the National Front as an electoral force in 1974 was met by a council ban on it using any council-controlled property for their meetings, this following the formation

of an action committee by the local Trades Council to organize opposition to the National Front's activity in the area. The National Front
has continued to be electorally weak (compared to other parts of
London), capturing 6.3 per cent and 4.6 per cent of the votes cast in
Brent South and East respectively in the May 1977 GLC elections.

Race has continued to be an issue for the Labour Party in the area
since the Conservative criticisms of the mid-1960s. The arrival of both
the Kenyan and Ugandan Asians provoked increased concern about the
housing shortage and the Labour Party has been at great pains to justify
its policy. In 1976, racism became an issue and the Labour Party has
found itself in competition with the Socialist Workers Party (SWP) and
local young black activists for the leadership of opposition to racism,
the result of which has been two separate campaigns. The strike at
Grunwick then stimulated the active support of both the Labour Party
and the Trades Council and this has increased their credibility amongst
the local black population, seemingly without arousing the hostility of
the white working class.

In sum, the predominantly working-class nature of Willesden is
reflected in the Labour electoral domination while the arrival of New
Commonwealth immigrants has forced the Labour Party to respond
to white hostility, particularly on the issue of housing which, as the
previous section has shown, is in poor condition and in short supply.
The Labour Party has also had to adopt a position on racism and it is
the nature of this racism that we wish to investigate, following an
outline of the nature and methods of our own empirical research.

Location of research and data collection

The data we report on were collected as part of a larger study on
political conceptualization and action amongst the English and West
Indian manual working class. Thus, our data does not permit a comparison with non-manual workers because it was not designed to do so. We
chose as our method of data collection a combination of participant
observation and in-depth interviewing in preference to a large-scale
sample survey. One of the researchers lived in the area and worked in a
local advice centre, both to test the feasibility of carrying out the
research and to begin to develop a network of informants. The bulk of
our analysis in this paper refers to the in-depth interviews conducted
with English male respondents who fall into two samples.

1 The factory sample: this was obtained from a large food-processing firm employing approximately 2400 individuals, situated on an industrial estate on the southern edge of Brent South. Of the total number of employees, 2000 are hourly paid and are engaged in some form of manual job, either connected directly with production or with storage and distribution. The workforce is divided into a permanent day shift and a permanent night shift.

A small pilot sample from two production departments was interviewed in the autumn of 1975 for the dual purpose of developing and testing an interview schedule, and of establishing a presence in the factory which would permit observational techniques. The main sample was drawn using a listing supplied by the company of all hourly paid employees which identified each individual by sex, shift, date of birth, date of joining and department. As the skilled craftsmen were identified as belonging to separate departments, it was possible to exclude them from the sample. It was also possible to obtain information on self-reported 'nationality'. Using this information, a sample of eighty individuals was drawn randomly from the population of English and West Indian males, aged twenty-five to forty years. The sample of eighty was equally divided into English and West Indian respondents, and by shift. A reserve sample was also randomly selected, from which an individual was drawn if any person from the main sample refused to participate, had left the company's employ or had been promoted.

All interviews were conducted by one of the authors and were carried out in conjunction with ongoing observational work in the factory. Interviewing began in June 1976 and was completed in September 1976. In sum, seventy-two individuals were interviewed, equally divided between English and West Indians, but the analysis here refers only to the thirty-six English respondents (N=36).

2 The residential sample: this sample of eighty was divided according to both gender and ethnicity, resulting in forty men and women of English parentage and forty men and women of West Indian parentage being interviewed. For reasons of comparability with the factory sample, only the nineteen English male interviewees (N=19) will be referred to here. It was additionally decided to select half of the respondents from the private-housing sector and half from the public-housing sector. The areas to be sampled were not chosen randomly but were sought out on the basis of having fairly equal numbers of English and West Indian residents. Choosing these areas was simplified in the private sector by the availability of a relatively reliable, if dated, sampling

frame in the form of the 1971 census. Using the small area statistics as a base, two virtually identical enumeration districts were selected for the first forty interviews. Sampling in both the private and public sector was conducted in the same way. A full listing process of all eligibles in all households was carried out (English and West Indians aged between twenty-five and forty-five) and interviews continued until the quota in that sector was complete. While this was a satisfactory method in the council sector, an increasingly aging population of English parentage resulted in a shortfall of eligible male interviewees in the private sector.

Locating eligible interviewees of English parentage was much easier in the council sector. Even though no sampling frame existed for any of the new redevelopment estates, certain patterns are evident. For at least the last four years, it is estimated that 50 per cent of lettings in the council sector have gone to minority group families in Brent, the majority to tenants of West Indian parentage. The movement into the council sector of West Indian families has increased for two main reasons. First, in areas of housing stress and which also have large black populations throughout London and other large cities, the rate of movement into the council sector is now very fast (Working Party of Housing Directors, 1976, p.29). Second, most West Indians whom we interviewed had come to the UK in the early 1960s and had moved into council accommodation through the 'normal' channels, i.e. the waiting list.

Thus while the chosen estate contained a high proportion of West Indians, the latter were disproportionately located in the medium and high-rise flats on the estate, while the English were located more easily in the houses and maisonnettes. The housing department explains this differential allocation pattern as a function of the differing expectations of white and black tenants. We have already stated that there is difficulty in letting units on the estate, particularly in the medium and high-rise blocks. It is also suggested that while white tenants will repeatedly turn down offers until they get what they want (in most cases a house), the black tenants do not. This raises the question as to whether black tenants have as much information about letting procedures or whether other factors are at work?

It is only possible to speculate: whatever the answer we knew in advance where to locate interviewees of English parentage. Sixteen of the nineteen interviews in the residential sample were carried out on the estate by screening adjacent areas of houses and maisonnettes and continuing to interview where we located eligibles until our quota of

English males was complete. The estate is split into two parts by a busy main road. The most recent part, where we conducted the interviews, is viewed as not having as yet as 'bad a reputation' as the rest, but few tenants were happy with their situation whatever part of the estate they lived on. After a summer of daily visits the researcher was convinced that the density of units, the lack of imagination in design, playspace, shops and entertainment resulted in a thoroughly depressing place in which to live, even before the attendant problems of vandalism, noise and robbery which exist (though in a lesser degree than an outsider is led to believe) on the estate are considered.

Working-class racism in Willesden

In presenting our data we reiterate that our aim is to identify the main features and content of the hostility expressed by white workers towards blacks. We have suggested that, in the main, this hostility has little to do with notions of biological inferiority but has a great deal to do with competition over scarce resources with a physically and numerically obvious group – 'the coloureds' as they are usually described by our respondents. Our description of Willesden has shown that employment and, more particularly, housing are scarce resources and it now remains for us to explain how our white, working-class sample viewed these socio-economic realities.

Our data have to be understood in the context of two methodological procedures we rigidly adhered to. First, at no point did any of our respondents have any idea that we were employed at the Research Unit on Ethnic Relations, nor did we indicate any special interest in their views on race and/or ethnicity. None of our questions specifically asked about race and/or ethnicity, although where a respondent indicated, for example, that 'the coloureds cause problems' this was pursued, but in the same way that the response 'inflation causes the problems' was pursued. We therefore feel that the racist ideas expressed by our respondents were not articulated to meet perceived interviewer expectations. Second, when coding our data, we took great care to ensure that our respondents definitions were strictly adhered to. For example, in coding the responses to the question 'What would you say are the major problems facing ordinary working people in this area?' there were separate categories for 'coloureds/coloured immigrants', 'immigrants' and 'overpopulation'. Thus, unless the respondent clearly indicated that the 'immigrants' were black or that by 'too many people in the area' he meant 'too many blacks', his responses were coded into the separate categories as indicated. However, our long acquaintance with the area and its people convinces us that references to 'immigrants' and 'overpopulation' by whites are invariably references to blacks unless it is categorically stated otherwise, but we were also concerned not to 'over-interpret' our interview data. As a result, we believe that our analysis presents a minimal picture of white working-class racism or, to put it more strongly, it probably under-emphasizes the extent and depth of white working-class racism in the inner city.

The interview questions were designed to elicit information relating to political conceptualization and action among the West Indian and English working class. A broad range of questions were asked, covering employment history, trade union membership and activity, voting behaviour and political activity as well as a large number of general political attitude questions. But those questions which elicited the highest percentage of racist responses were those which asked the respondent to tell us what they saw the local problems facing ordinary people in the area to be, the causes of local and national unemployment, and the causes of the local housing problem. In Table 2, we show the proportion of our sample who believed that, in response to each of the specific questions, blacks were a problem in themselves or were a cause of unemployment or the housing problem. Thus, 38 per cent of our sample believed that blacks were a local problem in themselves, or caused local problems. A small proportion of the total sample were willing to be specific about what problems the blacks caused, i.e. unemployment (local and national) and housing, although 37 per cent of the residential sample believed that blacks caused the local housing problem.

This brings us to the interesting difference between the factory sample and the residential sample: a higher proportion of the residential sample were prepared to blame the blacks for causing unemployment (local and national) and the housing problem, the difference being greatest on the question concerning housing. We argue that for the residential sample, there is a more immediate and concrete conflict over scarce resources in the public sector of housing. The residential sample was drawn directly from the area of acute housing competition while the factory sample is not residentially concentrated (the respondents live in various parts of North West London) and comes from mixed housing tenure groups. Our argument is given additional support by the finding that 42 per cent of the residential sample, compared with 22 per cent of the factory sample, believed that blacks received preferential treatment in the allocation of council houses.

Thus far, we have established that almost two-fifths of our sample believe that black people are or cause local problems, with a smaller proportion believing that they cause specific problems. However, analysis of responses to single questions presents a limited picture. People's 'view of the world' is rarely, if ever, ordered and consistent: hence, any single individual may not believe that blacks are a local problem but may believe that they cause the local housing problem. So, when we examined responses to all four questions illustrated in Table 2, we found that 58 per cent of all respondents expressed the view that black people were responsible for at least one of these problems or were a problem in themselves. In other words, almost three-fifths of our sample were shown to hold at least some form of hostile belief about blacks in response to these four questions.

However, references to black people were not confined to responses to these four questions. As already stressed, our interview schedules were designed to elicit our respondents' political conceptualization and did not contain specific questions about black people in Britain, but almost all of our respondents made some reference to black people. These references ranged from positive evaluations, through fairly disinterested, factual statements, to negative references. In the light of the findings reported so far it should not be surprising to report that the majority of the references were negative and hostile, and we have summarized the most commonly mentioned themes in Table 3. What particularly interested us when considering the negative references to blacks was that they were often connected with, or related to,

Table 2 Percentage of respondents who expressed the belief that blacks were to blame for local problems, unemployment (local and national) and the local housing problem

% of respondents who believed that blacks are a cause of:	Factory (N = 36) %	Residential (N = 19) %	Total (N = 55) %
1 local problems	39 (14)	37 (7)	38 (21)
2 local unemployment	3 (1)	10.5 (2)	5 (3)
3 national unemployment	6 (2)	21 (4)	11 (6)
4 local housing problem	17 (6)	37 (7)	24 (13)

nationalist sentiment and hence the themes 'we/government don't take care of "our/their own" ', a point to which we shall return. The extent of hostility is indicated by the fact that only 7 (19 per cent) of the factory sample and 7 (37 per cent) of the residential sample made no negative reference to blacks, or in other words, 75 per cent of the total sample held some negative belief about black people in Britain.

A very common theme among the council tenants in the residential sample was that the whites were being 'forced out of the area' by the blacks. Given the residential concentration of, particularly, West Indians in the area as a whole, this reaction has some grounding in reality. However, that West Indians are living in the area is only problematic if their presence is perceived as undesirable by whites, hence the talk of being 'forced out'. In relation to this, it is interesting that, unlike the factory sample, very few of the residential sample suggested support for a complete halt to immigration but instead, speak either in terms of moving out themselves or moving the blacks out. For example, when asked if housing was a local problem, a skilled worker in his mid-forties, who had been a member of the National Front in the past, responded:

> 'It still is a major problem even if it's eased a good deal. It's a pet theory of mine that it's overpopulated with the wrong people, too many coloureds in inverse ratio to the white people, and I think whoever runs these things should spread them out a bit more. For instance, they could have taken a few thousand of these coloured people that we've got into areas like Hampstead, the nice élite areas, and let them see how we have to live amongst them. Politicians who bring them or allow them in never have to really mix with them: they don't see them in the way the working people do. And they don't have to work with them.'

Others in the residential sample felt that moving out themselves was the solution but were constrained from doing so for mainly financial reasons. In contrast, the factory sample did contain 'movers'. For example, one shop steward described his reasons for moving as follows:

> 'I think this place will become a coloured ghetto in years to come. People like myself just won't move into the area. This is why I moved to where I live now. I moved out to Harrow a couple, well about four years ago, when the Ugandan Asians started to move in and bought a couple of the local shops. I thought now is the time to

move and out I went. This place now I can't really afford: I'm up to my neck in debt but there are no coloureds around at all, although lots of Jews.'

These white workers resent the very presence of blacks, to the extent that they are prepared to leave the area even at great financial loss to themselves, leaving housing vacant for anyone wishing to move into the area. Where such movement does occur, it is the clear result of white hostility to black workers, but it is predicated on the actual presence of blacks in the area: as has been said, most blacks do not live 'in the élite areas'.

Table 3 Negative references to blacks suggested by English respondents

	Factory N	Residential N	Total % (N)
Whites being forced out/black take-over	9	10	34.5 (19)
Blacks receive preference for council houses	8	9	31 (17)
Want complete halt to immigration	14	2	29 (16)
Blacks cause a housing problem	7	7	25 (14)
Blacks cause unemployment	7	5	22 (12)
Blacks protected by the law	7	2	16 (9)
Dislike of blacks' style of life/habits	5	1	11 (6)
We/government don't take care of our/their own	4	2	11 (6)

The theme of preferential treatment in the allocation of council houses was also a deeply felt grievance of the residential sample, as illustrated by the following comments:

'In my opinion, I don't think the council are fair in the way they allocate the housing. I'm not colour prejudiced but there are a lot of immigrants that I know who have come from these foreign places and have gone straight into good housing. They say it's the points system but I don't agree with that because working on the council I see quite a few things. I reckon if you're black, you'll get a place. If you're not, you just have to wait until one comes along.'

'Look at some of the Asians coming into this country. As soon as they get here, they have a council house. It's not right, they should put people from this country first.'

Blaming the blacks for the housing problems in the area was a common theme in the interviews as a whole, and this reflects the picture already reported in relation to the specific questions on local problems etc. However, the importance of the 'blacks cause unemployment' theme shown in Table 3 (22 per cent of the total sample voiced this belief) is in contrast with the findings in Table 2, and this further confirms the importance of not basing conclusions about the nature and extent of working-class racism upon responses to single questions alone.

In the residential sample, the four men who were sympathetic to the policies of the National Front (two had voted for the National Front and two were convinced that the National Front was the only 'solution' for the future) all blamed the blacks for national unemployment. For instance:

A: The country is overpopulated, there are too many people and not enough jobs to go round.
Q: What would you like to see done about it?
A: Well, all the ones who haven't got passports, they should be sent back. We've taken the rubbish. They should put them in little towns like they are at the moment in Southall. All you need there is an elephant.

Q: What are the main reasons for the high level of unemployment?
A: Well the population is too big isn't it?
Q: What could be done to reduce the level of unemployment?
A: Voluntary repatriation of the immigrants. I know that's the National Front but even Enoch suggested that and he's a Conservative isn't he? The Government should look at the coloured people not working.

Q: What could be done to reduce the level of unemployment?
A: Well the first thing to do would be to stop immigration. Let's stop these foreign people coming over here and taking all these jobs. It really bugs me when I walk around this place and I know that 60 per cent or 70 per cent of them are coloured.

These beliefs were not limited to the residential sample, as the following quote from a respondent in the factory sample illustrates: 'It's obvious why it is. You can't have an influx of immigrants and expect to keep your own employed.'

A further point that needs to be made in relation to Table 3 is the prevalence of the view that blacks are protected by the law and thereby, occupy a privileged position in British society. A corollary of this belief is the view that 'we' are becoming second-class citizens in 'our own country'. The most common reference was to the Race Relations Acts which were seen to both prevent the English person's right to free speech and to not only protect the black persons, but also to allow them to take advantage. The following quotations from the factory sample are illustrative:

'Well I think the English people in this country are frightened of what they say to them because straight away they are in trouble with the courts. Even in court you have to be careful. They have this Race Relations Act and it's like an angel on the black man's back all the time so he can't do any wrong, which is wrong. In this factory there are some coloured chaps that shouldn't be here but they are. The reason they keep them in is because they can't do anything because of that Act. It's not as if they can work because they can't work.'

'Another thing is they have brought in this law saying that you can't really say anything to a coloured man because he could take you to court because of it. But he could say it to you because it doesn't work for the other way round. So we are living in fear and fear breeds hate.'

'Well the Sikhs have just had this helmet law reversed and they can now go about on bikes with their turbans. I think that's wrong. I don't think it could be called religious grounds. I think it's just a case of "Right we'll let them off this and perhaps they will be a bit more co-operative in other respects". In some cases they probably get an easier deal in the courts simply because they don't want to cause a riot.'

The belief that blacks are protected by the law is only one example of the more general belief that black people are privileged in comparison to 'us': we have already illustrated the theme that blacks receive preference in the allocation of council accommodation, and the notion of privilege is also found in the belief that the courts and/or the police treat blacks leniently.

Having documented these negative images of black people held by white manual workers, we wanted to know whether the frequency with which they were made was related to age, trade union membership, housing tenure and past voting behaviour. We found a slight tendency for those under thirty-five years of age to make fewer negative references to blacks than the older group. There was no relationship with trade union membership, but given that the factory sample was drawn from a firm which had what amounted to a post-entry closed shop (and this applied to some of those in the residential sample), this is not surprising. There was no relationship in the factory sample with housing tenure and there could be no relationship in the case of the residential sample because over 80 per cent lived in the public sector.

We were also interested in examining the possibility that varying levels of racism co-varied with the presence or absence of class-consciousness. On a preliminary analysis of our data we could not distinguish a negative relationship between the presence of racist beliefs and expressions of class consciousness. Rather, racist beliefs could happily co-exist with even high levels of class consciousness. The following examples taken from an interview with an unskilled council worker, aged in his late thirties, a trade unionist, and a Communist Party voter, illustrate this point.

Q: Do you sometimes feel that the Council takes notice of some people's needs and demands more than others?
A: Yes, I think they do. Look at some of the Asians coming into the country, as soon as they get here they have a council house.
Q: You think they get better treatment?
A: I think they do. It's not right, they should put people from this country first.

(Later in the interview)

A: There was one (an Asian) on the television that brought £1000 into the country and he said he wouldn't touch it because he was keeping it for a rainy day. He was relying on the welfare state and in my opinion that's all wrong. It's us, the working bloke who has to pay for them.

Hostility and resentment towards blacks co-exist with expressions of class consciousness, although in this case it is the latter which predominates in the interview taken as a whole:

Q: How do you think then that people should fight back against
rising prices?
A: Look at what happened in Poland when they put the prices up,
the people went on the streets and fought for their rights because
their prices were too high.
Q: Have you heard of the Community Land Bill?
A: Yes, I think it's a good thing because it's the people's land.
It shouldn't belong to anyone really. Why should one bloke own
acres and acres of land and the bloke who works on it own nothing?
Q: Do you think the government should take over the land and pay
compensation to the owners or not pay them compensation?
A: I don't think they should pay them compensation, I think they
should nationalize all the land because it's the people's land.
Q: What do you think are the main reasons for the current level of
unemployment?
A: Profit, the higher the unemployment is the more profit they
make.

One further interesting finding emerged. In the factory sample, not
one individual said that he had in the past or intended in the future to
vote for the National Front while in the residential sample there were
three open supporters of the party and one ex-member. All four lived in
the same block of houses, have been or still are Labour voters and made
similar negative references about blacks. Their reasons for having or
intending to vote National Front clearly invoke nationalist sentiment
which is, in turn, related to the presence of black people in 'our
country':

Q: Why did you vote National Front?
A: Because our dads fought to keep this country a white man's
country and because the way things are in the area at the moment.
I don't have anything against the coloureds, I even have a couple of
coloured friends and they agree with me about the way things are
going now. You've got to see to your own before you see to anyone
else and they'll have no chance, our kids. They are outnumbered
now, especially if they stay in this area. I'd go if I could tomorrow.

'When I first went in [i.e. joined the NF] I had visions of a united
England, you know, England for the English. I know it's racist, but
it appealed to me in itself.'

'I voted Labour last time and to be quite honest I am going to vote National Front next time. I don't think the Labour Party are doing as much for this country as they should. I think they are getting us into a lot of trouble. I think the National Front will be a major party in the future. They are anti-immigration for a start and this is one of the things I like. I think we have too many foreigners in this country.'

However, the relationship between negative references to blacks and the expression of nationalist sentiment is not limited to National Front supporters: as Table 3 shows, four members of the factory sample believed that 'We/government don't take care of our/their own' and a further four expressed opposition to foreign aid before 'looking after our own'. In addition, there were references to 'us' and 'our country' in relation to several of the other themes mentioned in Table 3. The following quotations are illustrative and suggest that, in comparison with the National Front supporters, the beliefs are expressed in a slightly less focused manner:

'I think this country's a bit stupid anyway because they don't take care of their own. They spend all the money on foreign aid before making sure things in this country's alright. You wouldn't believe that we won the war and Germany lost it.'

'They [i.e. the government] ought to think about their own people first and then the coloured people next.'

'When you think of it, we virtually used to rule the world. Now we don't even rule our own country: spades rule our country.'

Discussion

We earlier argued that the concept of racism should be understood as a set of beliefs which serve to create a racial category, and that what is crucial to labelling these beliefs as racist is that a reference is made to some physical feature in defining membership of the out-group which is also described in some negative and hostile way. We have analysed our data consistent with this definition, indeed so strictly, that we believe we have probably underestimated the extent of racism within our sample of white manual workers. Nevertheless, to reiterate, we found that 38 per cent of our sample reported that blacks were a local problem in themselves or caused local problems in response to a specific question, 58 per cent believed that blacks were responsible for the housing problem and unemployment or were a problem in themselves, and that 75 per cent made negative references to black people in the course of the interview. In sum, we are arguing that 75 per cent of our sample of white manual workers hold racist beliefs.

We believe that our preliminary analysis of the interviews with these English male workers throws some light on the current form of working-class racist beliefs in an inner-city context, but gives little guidance in explaining why some workers evaluate black people in Britain more negatively than others. As far as the latter is concerned, we can only state the obvious, which is that the interviewees with the most systematic set of negative assumptions and arguments either support, vote for or were once members of the National Front, although which came first is a matter for speculation. Whether they can be said to subscribe to a racist ideology depends upon how one wants to define ideology, but what is clear is that for these respondents, their view of local and national political and economic developments is consistently related to their negative views on the presence of black people in Britain.

Beyond this, we have identified a larger number of white workers whose negative references to black people are more piecemeal, although none the less deeply felt. We describe the racism of this group as piecemeal because, for example, not all those who believed that 'the coloureds' were the cause of the local housing problem also believed that 'they' cause unemployment. When we compared those workers who neither blamed the blacks for causing problems, nor expressed negative evaluations of black people (25 per cent of the total sample) with those workers who did both, we found that the former were most likely to be established Labour voters while the latter were 'Labour switchers' (i.e. reported voting Labour in the past but indicated that they either would not vote Labour again or would not vote at all in the future) and/or were highly critical of the way that the Labour Party had 'betrayed' the working class and/or the country. As far as the latter are concerned, their racism is fragmented yet materially based in the following sense.

A large proportion of the racist beliefs expressed in the interviews stem from a perceived conflict with black people over the allocation of scarce resources, particularly housing. In this conflict, black people are seen to be a privileged minority (not least because of the action of the authorities, whether they be the local council or the national government) which is seen to be 'taking over'. Moreover, those white workers who were born and brought up in north-west London have been caught up directly in the most recent stage of the socio-economic decline of the Willesden area. These workers have lived the consequences of this decline and its coincidence with the arrival of New Commonwealth immigrants is viewed as cause and effect. What we are arguing therefore is that the white working class in Willesden can immediately identify the cause of their problems in the very presence of black workers in the area: because *black* people live and work in Willesden, then they can be *seen* to live in houses in which white workers did and could have lived and to occupy jobs which white workers did and could have done. On many occasions, we were told forcefully, following a long catalogue of racist beliefs. that 'if you lived here, you'd know what I mean'. The working-class racist beliefs in the Willesden area are therefore an attempt to understand and explain *immediate daily experience*, while the real reasons for both the socio-economic decline and New Commonwealth immigration are to be found in much more abstract and long-standing social and economic processes which cannot be grasped in terms of daily experience.

We have also identified a tendency whereby the unfavourable categorization of black people strongly invokes nationalist sentiment. This tendency extends the boundary drawn between 'them' ('the coloureds') and 'us' (the English) in relation to housing and jobs, in conjunction with the notion of 'us' being 'taking over/pushed out', so that it takes on a meaning beyond the local reference point of Willesden. 'We' becomes more than the white working class of Willesden, the boundary being extended to encompass the 'English people'. Where the boundary distinguishes between 'the coloureds' and 'the English' (rather than 'the whites'), it can follow that the former can never in the eyes of the perceiver be English, even if they are legally British citizens by birth.

It is in relation to this process of boundary definition and creation of racial categories that the argument posited by Nairn assumes its significance. He believes English nationalism to be 'cryptic' or 'submerged' (1977, pp.79, 287) and to be inextricably linked to the structure of British imperialism. His argument, in sum, is that the British economic and political crisis, in the context of the loss of empire, the post Second World War economic boom of the 1950s, and the emergence of both the EEC and Scottish and Welsh nationalism, has forced the English to reconsider who they are, 'to reinvent an identity of some sort better than the battered cliché-ridden hulk which the retreating tide of imperialism has left them' (1977, p.259). In the last seventy years, he maintains, war has been the means of confirming and revalidating English nationalism, but with the advent of black immigration 'it has become possible to define Englishness *vis-à-vis* this internal "enemy", this "foreign body" in our own streets' (1977, p.274). Thus the English in identifying and setting apart 'the coloureds', i.e. in creating a racial category, are asserting a nationalism through the means of racism. It is the presence of black people in conjunction with seeing them as problems which brings to the surface the question of 'who are we?': the setting apart implies not only a definition of 'them', but also of 'us'. It is at this stage that it becomes necessary for those drawing such boundaries to fall back upon past folk heroes and myths upon the 'collective unconscious' (1977, pp.343–50).

It is here that we wish to return to the question of the relative importance of ideas and images derived from the imperial past. Lawrence (1974, pp.52–6), and Hartmann and Husbands (1974, pp.29–33), among others, suggest that racial stereotypes and feelings of (white) superiority, all of which are strongly related to British imperialism, are widespread in British culture and are culturally transmitted. With this we would not disagree, not least because it is to this 'collective unconscious' that the white worker, as indeed any English person, can be drawn when searching for explanations and justifications of his/her position.

Lawrence's argument can be supported by the findings of Butler and Stokes (1974) and Studlar (1977) who have shown that somewhere in excess of 75 per cent of the British population are moderately or strongly hostile to immigrants (who are assumed to be black), that this hostility is more or less constant over time (since 1963) and that, in the case of Studlar's data, this hostility does not correlate significantly with social context variables such as age, social class, job competition and so on. On the latter point, there is a difference with Butler and Stokes, although one should add that Studlar's analysis combines the responses to two questions, with the result that like is not being compared with like. Butler and Stokes found that the lower the occupational grade the greater the number of respondents who offered spontaneous elaborations of their hostility were more likely to live in areas of high concentration of black immigrants. Moreover, the objections centred on competition for housing and jobs and deteriorating health and living standards (1974, pp.303–8).

Butler and Stokes' findings are not inconsistent with our own but Studlar's argument seems more problematic. However, if one agrees that the high level of hostility towards black immigration is to be found equally amongst different sections of the white population, it does not follow that, for example, manual working-class hostility and dominant class hostility can be explained by the same set of factors, or to the same set of factors in the same proportion. Two and two do make four, but there are other ways of making four. In addition, and more importantly, racism can consist of more than just hostility to black immigration, as our data shows.

We therefore argue that although a racist culture may form the backdrop to the way in which large sections of the British population view black people (with the result that the working-class racism which we have identified in the inner city can share many ideas with, say, dominant class racism), for the white working class in the 'inner city' of Willesden, there is a very specific set of circumstances which both shapes the content of their racism and which can force them to draw upon myths about the past. In other words, it is not a question of posing cultural transmission against direct experience as alternative explanations. As Lawrence suggests, 'the prevalence of such stereotypes and feelings does at least constitute an underlying basis for hostility' (1974, p.56) and in the inner city, we argue, it is the immediate daily experience which leads a substantial proportion of white workers to have such firmly held negative views of black workers, in the context of a national culture which is in itself racist. One consequence of this is that they are very resistant to modification as a result of argument from 'outsiders'. It is on the basis of this that we would speculate about the reasons for Enoch Powell having achieved the prominence that he has amongst sections of the British working class: unlike so many other politicians he speaks as if he too 'knows' because he has listened to and understood people who have had 'the experience'. Moreover, in so far as we argue for the importance of the role of direct experience, we are also suggesting that, in at least this respect, there is a world of difference between the racist from Bournemouth and the racist from Willesden. The former may demonstrate as high a level of hostility to blacks as the latter, but it is likely to take a more abstract form.

The Bournemouth racist is likely to differ from the Willesden racist in at least one other dimension, that of having a consciousness of being working class. Although we are not yet able to state how widespread this is within our own sample, we have shown that a working-class consciousness can co-exist with racist ideas. There can be no single explanation for this, but we believe the following considerations are relevant. As with racism, a working-class consciousness (which can be expected to include a positive evaluation of trade unionism) is a product of both personal experience and cultural transmission. Beynon has shown how manual workers come to hold a factory-class consciousness which is 'rooted in the workplace where struggles are fought over the control of the job and the rights of managers and workers' (1973, p.98). Such a consciousness, when structured by the factory situation, is not automatically or easily extended to other areas of life, with the consequence that feelings of solidarity with 'fellow workers' elsewhere is not easily achieved. Such a fractured or constrained consciousness is encouraged by the ideological tradition of the working class. As Saville has argued (1973), the working-class self-help organizations (e.g. trade unions, friendly societies) established in the late nineteenth century implied a notion of defensiveness. In so far as this has continued to structure contemporary consciousness, trade unionism can demonstrate a narrow protectionism, as the argument about differentials clearly shows.

We have argued elsewhere that, given the defensive role of trade unionism in a capitalist economy, 'the abstract principles of the international brotherhood of the working class are more likely than not to be sacrificed in the defence of the *British* working class and, ultimately, British *capitalism*' (1977a, p.34). The point is, therefore, that for both sociological and historical reasons, English working-class consciousness is not a logical and coherent phenomenon, but it is necessarily ridden with limitations and contradictions (cf. Nichols and Armstrong, 1976). Thus, the English worker can accept at the general level that all workers are equal, but also believe that some are more equal than others (especially when they are white) when a specific interest is at stake.

Finally, we would like to record that the findings and arguments presented in this paper lead us to pessimistic conclusions about the effectiveness of the recent strategy of the British Labour Movement to combat racism. The campaign against racism, organized jointly by the Trades Union Congress and the Labour Party in 1976 (see Miles and Phizacklea, 1978) assumed that the way to eliminate working-class racism was to provide counter-arguments to common racist beliefs: in other words, the 'ideological baggage' constructed by the dominant class can be pushed out of workers' heads and be replaced by 'the truth'. However, if working-class racism in the inner city is grounded in the daily experience and the material realities of working-class life in the way we suggest it seems to us the moral and principle arguments are unlikely to have had the effect that the Labour leadership desired. A partial solution to 'the problem' of working-class racism in the inner city depends upon a strategy for eliminating the material disadvantage of the working class (although this would do little to counter the more general and deep-seated racist notions in British culture), and the adequacy of Labour Party policy to such a task is a matter of contention.

Bibliography

Banton, M. (1970), 'The Concept of Racism' in S. Zubaida (ed.), *Race and Racialism*, Tavistock, London.

Banton, M. (1977), *The Idea of Race*, Tavistock, London.

Beynon, H. (1973), *Working for Ford*, Penguin, Harmondsworth.

Butler, D. and Stokes, D. (1974), *Political Change in Britain*, Macmillan, London.

Community Development Project (1977), *The Costs of Industrial Change*, CDP.

Coppock, J.P. and Prince, H.C. (eds) (1964), *Greater London*, Faber & Faber, London.

Daly, M. (1971), *Characteristics of 12 Clusters of Wards in Greater London*, GLC Department of Planning and Transportation, Research Report no. 13.

Field, A.M. *et al.* (1974), *1971 Census Data on London's Overseas Born Population and their Children*, GLC Research Memorandum no. 425.

Foot, P. (1965), *Immigration and Race in British Politics*, Penguin, Harmondsworth.

Foot, P. (1969), *The Rise of Enoch Powell*, Penguin, Harmondsworth.

Greater London Council (1973), *London's Deprived Areas: A Comparative Appraisal*, Report by Controller of Planning and Transportation, 17 July.

Greve, J., Page, D. and Greve, S. (1971), *Homelessness in London*, Scottish Academic Press.

Hall, P. (1977), 'The Inner Cities Dilemma', *New Society*, 3 February 1977.

Hartmann, P. and Husbands, C. (1974), *Racism and the Mass Media*, Davis-Poynter, London.

Lawrence, D. (1974), *Black Migrants: White Natives*, Cambridge University Press.

Leff, V. and Blunden, G.H. (n.d.), *The Willesden Story*, Research Writers, London.

Lomas, G. (1975), *The Inner City*, London Council of Social Service.

London Borough of Brent (1975), *Harlesden: Report of Studies*, Borough of Brent.

Lyon, M. (1972), 'Race and Ethnicity in Pluralistic Societies', *New Community*, vol. 1, pp.256–62.

Mackenzie, R. and Silver, A. (1968), *Angels in Marble: Working-Class Conservatives in Urban England*, Heinemann, London.

Miles, R. and Phizacklea, A. (1977a), 'The TUC, Black Workers and Immigration 1954–1973', *SSRC, Research Unit on Ethnic Relations Working Paper*, no. 6.

Miles, R. and Phizacklea, A. (1977b), 'Class, Race, Ethnicity and Political Action', *Political Studies*, vol. xxv, no. 4, pp.491–507.

Miles, R. and Phizacklea, A. (1978), 'The TUC and Black Workers 1974–1976', *British Journal of Industrial Relations*, vol. xvi, no. 2, pp.195–207.

Morris, J.C. (1950), *The Willesden Survey*, Corporation of Willesden.

Nairn, T. (1977), *The Break-Up of Britain*, New Left Books, London.

Nichols, T. and Armstrong, P. (1976), *Workers Divided*, Fontana, London.

Potter, S. (1926), *The Story of Willesden*, Pitman.

Rex, J. (1970), *Race Relations in Sociological Theory*, Weidenfeld & Nicolson, London.

Rex, J. (1973), *Race, Colonialism and the City*, Routledge & Kegan Paul, London.

Roth, A. (1970), *Enoch Powell, Tory Tribune*, MacDonald, London.

Saville, J. (1973), 'The Ideology of Labourism' in R. Benewick *et al.* (eds), *Knowledge and Belief in Politics*, Allen & Unwin, London.

Schermerhorn, R.A. (1970), *Comparative Ethnic Relations*, Random House, London.

Schoen, D.S. (1977), *Enoch Powell and the Powellites*, Macmillan, London.

Smith, D.H. (1933), *The Industries of Greater London*, King & Son.

Studlar, D.T. (1977), 'Social Context and Attitudes toward Coloured Immigrants', *British Journal of Sociology*, vol. 28, no. 2, pp.168–84.

Van den Berghe, P. (1967), *Race and Racism*, Wiley, London.

Walker, M. (1977), *The National Front*, Fontana, London.

Weintraub, A.L. (1972), 'Race and Local Politics in England: A Case Study of Willesden', Columbia University, PhD thesis.

Williams, R. (1973), 'Base and Superstructure in Marxist Cultural Theory', *New Left Review*, no. 82, pp.3–16.

Wilson, W.J. (1973), *Power, Racism and Privilege*, Macmillan, London.

Working Party of Housing Directors (1976), *Housing in Multi-Racial Areas*, Community Relations Commission.

CHAPTER 6

The National Front:
Anatomy of a political movement

Stan Taylor

The formation of the National Front (NF) as a union of the British National Party and League of Empire Loyalists in February 1967, was almost totally ignored by the mass media and the public. Eleven years later the NF is regarded as a serious political movement and has won greater electoral support than any other far right party in British political history. An understanding of the party's structure (leadership, organization and finance), ideology, strategy and tactics, and popular support in terms of membership and votes, and an evaluation of why the movement has grown and how it may be expected to perform in the future, are essential both to the academic concerned to comprehend a new political phenomenon and to those who seek to combat racism in British society.

Party structure: leadership, organization and finance

The top leadership of the NF, the Executive Committee of the Directorate, has been drawn almost exclusively from the members of the various groups which came together to form the NF or which were disbanded just after the formation of the NF and members encouraged to transfer. The present executive committee, for example, includes John Tyndall and Martin Webster, formerly of the Greater Britain Movement, Andrew Fountaine, once of the British National Party, Peter Williams, a former Blackshirt, and Andrew Brons, a college lecturer who was allegedly a member of the National Socialist Movement (Walker, 1977, p.68; *Observer*, 11 September 1977; *Searchlight*,

September 1977). The first three have led the Front almost continuously in the 1970s, and survived two challenges from new recruits who have wished to remove the 'Nazi' stain on the leadership and broaden the party's ideological appeal (Walker, 1977, pp.189–95; Nugent, 1977, pp.171–2). The retention of this leadership has meant that the men in charge of the movement have considerable political experience. On the other hand the Nazi and neo-Nazi past of the leaders has been considerably exploited by the NF's opponents, as in the controversial Labour Party political broadcast of 7 December 1977, and this may have alienated some popular support, particularly among voters who fought in the war (Taylor, 1978, p.2). However, it is important to distinguish between the leadership, composed of what Lipset and Raab (1971, p.484) have termed 'evil-structured types', and the membership and electorate because their disposition towards the NF does not necessarily imply approval or perhaps, in the case of voters, even knowledge of the origins and biases of the leadership.

The formal structure of the NF is not significantly different from the extra-parliamentary organizations of other British political parties. At local level the NF has 231 branches (*Sunday Telegraph*, 2 October 1977) with more than twelve members, and an indeterminate number of groups with less than twelve. These elect representatives to regional

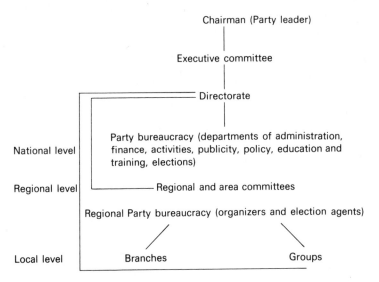

Figure 1   Formal structure of the National Front

or area committees, whose officers liaise with the (centrally-appointed and paid) regional bureaucrats. At national level the ruling body of the party is the directorate, composed of twenty members, one third of whom are required to submit to re-election by the mass membership each year. Sub-committees of this body oversee the various departments of the national bureaucracy. Each year the directorate elects a chairman, a deputy chairman and three other executive members, who are responsible for the day-to-day running of the party, subject to ratification of their decisions by the full directorate. The organization provides for a two-way flow of inputs and outputs between leaders and followers, although it may be hazarded that the flow is generally downwards rather than upwards. On the other hand, as successful attempts to challenge the leadership have shown, the party is by no means totally authoritarian.

The local party organizations of the NF have expanded greatly over the past decade. The NF began as an almost purely London-based organization and now has branches in almost all areas of England, and a few in Scotland and Wales. The wide spread does not appear, however, to represent membership in depth. Average branch size is around forty according to the NF (*Sunday Telegraph*, 2 October 1977) which, considering that branches outside London are based on whole towns, does not indicate great strength. In September 1977 the NF extended its organization with the formation of the 'Young National Front' for members between the ages of fourteen and twenty-five, and announced its intention to recruit in the schools. This has inevitably invited comparison with Nazi attempts to politicize the young. In assessing the probable impact of this movement, it must be remembered that the NF, unlike the Nazis, cannot rely upon encouragement within the schools themselves by sympathetic training staff. Moreover, the youth movement may be a temporary craze, although it may have a longer-term impact if the employment situation for school-leavers deteriorates further in the near future.

The NF gains most of its income from membership fees, donations and branch activities, all of which are sent to and controlled by NF headquarters. The party has not had access to business funds, although there were reports in late 1977 that a group of Conservative industrialists had approached the NF with an offer of financial support in return for a toning down of policies and the party not putting up candidates in seats where the Conservatives might be harmed (*Sunday Telegraph*, 2 October 1977; *Searchlight*, September 1977). This was apparently refused. If the NF does, as promised, substantially increase the number of parliamentary candidates, the burden of lost deposits and campaign expenses may place a very considerable strain on finances and the party may become less selective in sources of finance in the future.

Party ideology

The ideology and ideological appeal of the NF may be considered in terms of the distinction developed by Almond between an 'esoteric' appeal to 'intellectual' insiders, and a grossly simplified 'exoteric' appeal to the mass membership and the electorate (1954, pp.62–8). The core of the 'esoteric' appeal is, as Neill Nugent and Roger King suggest in chapter 2, the proposition that there exists and has existed for centuries a grand conspiracy by Jews or pro-Zionists to dominate the world. Success would involve the displacement from dominance of the white 'race', and the destruction of nations and nationalism. Such destruction would, given that it is held that the ultimate progress of mankind depends upon the white 'nations', entail a return to the 'Dark Ages'. The NF views itself as fighting the conspiracy, preserving the British 'race' or section of the white 'race' from extinction, and guaranteeing the survival of civilization. The conspiracy is seen to be trying to dilute the British 'race' by 'mongrelization' through the introduction of an 'immigrant' population (*Spearhead*, June 1977).

The NF believes that the conspiracy can be subverted by, firstly, compulsory repatriation of all 'coloured immigrants'. What is seen as the trend to 'internationalism' would be reversed by Britain leaving all international bodies where blacks are represented and negotiating a 'New Commonwealth' of white nations, led by Britain and including Canada, Australia, New Zealand, South Africa and Rhodesia (NF Statement of Policy, 1977). The 'chaos of capitalism and socialism' would be replaced by an economic system involving on the one hand state intervention in support of national objectives, on the other a highly competitive capitalist economy. The state would protect British industry by a siege economy, direct investment into Britain, control of the money supply to regulate wages and prices, and a reorganization of the unions to create industrial unions. Apart from this, there would be no intervention either in the form of subsidies for ailing firms or nationalization (*Spearhead*, June 1977). These proposals are similar in some respects to those advanced by Mosley in the early 1930s

(Benewick, 1969, pp.132–68), although the NF eschews the corporate state. In education, welfare and social policy, the NF would try and reverse the 'debilitating' effects of re-organization in the post-war period.

The key question concerning this 'insider' ideology would seem to be whether or not it can legitimately be termed 'fascist'. The answer depends to a large extent upon what is meant by fascism, a word which has been used to describe ideologies and political systems varying from the European movements of the inter-war years to some contemporary African societies (Hughes and Kolinsky, 1976, pp.371–2). NF ideology does have some of the features which have been associated with fascism in a general sense, in particular, intense nationalism, the aim of creating a self-sufficient industrial state, and some of the methods of economic regeneration outlined above. The racial dimension is closely allied to that present in the more specifically European fascist movements, with similar beliefs in racial and national hierarchies and of course the same 'high-level' scapegoats, to use Nugent and King's phrase, the Jews or Zionists. However, other features of fascism, such as the charismatic leader 'energizing' the masses, one-party or totalitarian control over political socialization, communication and aggregation, are absent from the ideological baggage of the movement. The NF claims to be a democratic movement, with no affinity for the Nazi or fascist parties:

> The . . . policy of the NF is and always has been to support British democracy and Parliamentary government. Every policy statement published by the NF, and indeed its party constitution, whole-heartedly supports British parliamentary democracy, and pledges the NF to achieve and retain political office solely by the way of the will and votes of the British people. In accordance with this commitment the NF fields hundreds of local and Parliamentary candidates every year in all parts of the Country. In spite of being challenged many times the opponents of the NF have not produced a single piece of evidence or statement by NF leaders supporting the allegation that the NF is anti-democratic. How can the National Front be 'Nazi' or 'fascist' when it is totally committed to parliamentary democracy? (*Why Are the British People Being Fed Communist Lies?*, 1977).

This claim may be judged in the light of the alleged violent activities of NF members catalogued each month in *Searchlight*, the anti-fascist magazine, as well as statements by NF leaders in earlier incarnations.

For example, Tyndall, in his National Socialist Movement days, wrote that:

> The Jew knows that only within a state governed according to
> his self-proclaimed theories of Liberalism and 'Freedom' will he be
> permitted to continue unhampered, the activities by which he has
> corrupted every nation that has opened its doors to him . . . in place
> of the Jew-inspired illusion of 'freedom' we must substitute the
> honest reality of freedom, i.e. freedom for those fit to use it and a
> curb on those who are not. Such a principle forms the basis of the
> authoritarian state which we seek to build in Britain. (From *The
> Authoritarian State*, 1961, quoted in Walker, 1977, pp.70–1).

Further the strategy and tactics of the NF, in particular the attempts to show that they 'control' the streets (see below), are not normal parts of the political weaponry of democratic parties, but associated with authoritarian, extremist ones. Doubts may therefore be expressed as to the validity of the NF's claim that the specifically political dimensions of fascism are totally absent from its ideology and behaviour.

The 'exoteric' ideological appeal of the NF to the mass membership and the electorate is rather different in emphasis from the 'insider' one. The weightier theories of conspiracies are abandoned for, as the editor of *Spearhead* (October 1977, p.4) has put it, 'to persuade the politically unaware that conspiracy is an active agent in the operation of international power politics is a difficult task'. The *National Front News* and election literature concentrate upon attacking the 'lower level' scapegoat of blacks relative to, as Nugent and King show in Chapter 2, the issues of unemployment, housing shortages, crime and the welfare state. The 'Communist menace' and the need for Britain to leave the Common Market are also frequently mentioned. These simple, negative themes are intended to appeal to the 'gut' feelings of people that, for example, there are 'too many' blacks, or that Britain has not gained from membership of the Common Market, or that the educational system and the unions have been infiltrated by the far left and used for nefarious ends.

Most parties have differentiated ideological appeals, as a glance at election manifestos compared to election literature will reveal. The 'insider' doctrine of the NF is, however, much more complex and far-reaching than the 'exoteric' appeal than is the case with other British parties. The Labour voter would not find too much discrepancy between an election leaflet and *Labour Weekly*: an NF voter or indeed member might get something of a shock if he delved too far into *Spearhead*. Given that one of the aims of the NF's strategy and tactics is to ensure that its appeal is seen as remaining within the corpus of the values and norms of the political culture of British society, many NF members or voters may not realize precisely what kind of wolf lies under the sheep's clothing, see that 'populism' conceals - at least arguably - a brand of fascism, or wonder how long the wolf would stay clothed if the NF gained power.

Strategy and tactics

The NF's strategy and tactics may be considered in terms of organization for electoral purposes, publicity to acquire support and create an image of inevitable success, and attempts to ensure that the movement is seen as legitimate by the mass population. For long-term electoral success, the NF has to build up, slowly and painfully, a party organization and mass electoral support which will help carry it to power. This must be long-term in so far as the 'first-past-the-post' electoral system has a relatively high threshold for the achievement of representation compared to others, there being no specific arrangements for the representation of small minorities (Rae, 1971, pp.77–9). As was seen earlier, some progress has been made along these lines, but not enough to suggest that the NF has an adequate infrastructure for achieving significant advances. In the shorter term, the NF has tried to boost its vote and membership by taking maximum advantage of every opportunity for publicity, or if none is available, 'manufacturing' headlines. The picketing to protest against the admission of the Ugandan Asians and the Malawi Asians (Walker, 1977, pp.137–9, 196–7), which was widely reported, comes into the former category; the holding of NF meetings and marches in areas where there is a significant black population - as in Lewisham and Ladywood in 1977 - in the expectation of provoking the far left to violence is an example of the latter (Layton-Henry and Taylor, 1977). The marches have not only provided publicity, but have also been intended to show the power of the NF to the public. The serried ranks of marching, flag-waving members are meant to indicate the strength of the movement, and its control over the streets, to invite comparison with a disciplined army marching to victory. This has, unsurprisingly, been equated with Nazi rallies in Germany. To counter such charges, the NF makes efforts to be seen by the public as within the pale of the British political culture, and not as an alien or violent movement. The selection of the Union flag as the movement's symbol, and the orders that members should not use violence against the left, at least in front of the cameras, may be understood in these terms. It may be noted that these tactics only have a substantial impact because they are widely, and on occasion somewhat sympathetically, reported in the mass media.

Party support: membership

The NF in late 1977 claimed to have over 13,000 members (*Observer*, 11 September 1977; *Spearhead*, October 1977, p.13). More impartial estimates put membership at between 4500 and 6000 (Nugent, 1977, pp.175–6; *Sunday Times*, 21 August 1977), although these do not take account of members who may have returned to the NF after the demise of the breakaway group, the National Party, in August 1977. While the current membership is perhaps three or four times larger than that in 1967, it does not represent the outcome of a continuous pattern of growth over the past decade. Nugent has suggested that the membership grew from a low level to a peak of around 14,000 during the Ugandan Asian affair in 1973, declined to 9000 in early 1975, and was further reduced by 2000 to 2500 after the formation of the National Party to reach its present level (1977, pp.196–7). Membership of the NF is then, in absolute terms, not very high and, depending upon whose figures are taken, has remained constant or declined since 1973.

The questions as to the type of people who join the NF, and why they do so, can only be adequately answered by conducting a large-scale survey, for which the NF is unlikely to provide the necessary co-operation. Analyses of the social backgrounds of NF members in a Lancashire town (Scott, 1975, pp.214–39) or of parliamentary candidates (Taylor, 1977, pp.283–4), suggest that it is difficult to generalize upon the social sources of NF membership. The NF draws members from both the middle class and the working class with, if anything, a slight predominance of the former. In terms of education, most NF candidates have only a secondary education, although the party is not unrepresented among those who have some higher education. The party has some appeal to trade union members who comprised nearly one in three candidates in 1974. Given that they were union activists, it would be wrong to suggest that such NF members were involuntary unionists.

The most striking social characteristic of NF candidates compared to those of other parties was their comparative youth, which experience suggests is also true of the membership at large. The composition of NF members does not fit neatly with explanations of support for extremist movements in terms of 'working-class authoritarianism' or 'middle-class backlash' (Lipset 1963, pp.97–130, 173–6), although one may begin to enquire as to why the NF should appeal to younger as opposed to older people. This may reflect the generally greater flexibility of the young to new movements and ideas (Abrams and Little, 1965, p.98; Butler and Stokes, 1974, pp.58–66), coupled with the unattractiveness of the major parties to the newest political generations (Crewe, Sarlvik and Alt 1977, pp.161–8), as well as perhaps the unsettling effects of very rapid educational change or high levels of unemployment among school-leavers.

The reasons why people join the NF cannot simply be inferred from the fact that it claims to be a 'racialist party'. This being said, the point may be made that in the few accounts of the attitudes of NF members available, the theme of 'race' does predominate, although not to the exclusion of other issues. One NF member, Derek Day, an unofficial organizer in the Hoxton area of Hackney and Shoreditch, described his support for the party as stemming from the following perceptions of what happened in Hoxton after some immigrants moved in:

> It was one of the most prosperous boroughs in London. It had every commodity and luxury. All of a sudden the immigrants come and it's a ghetto. It's crawling with rats . . . Hoxton was of course originally called 'Ogs' Den' of course. The Queen used to come through here on her way to hunt the wild boar. . . . It was a close-ties community. You could leave your purse on the counter and anyone what nicks it gets his hand chopped off. Bang.

> Now you can't walk the street at night without being mugged. If a young girl walked down here at night with a sovereign around her neck it's wallop. I put my borough before my wife and children. And its been destroyed, not only by the bombs what the Germans done, but by the councillors put in to represent the people (*Observer*, 11 September 1977).

The entry of 'immigrants' was equated causally with the decline of the inner-city area in terms of the environment and the dismemberment of a close-knit community, as well as the incidence of crime and violence.

It need not be said that there is no evidence to support such a causal connection. These reasons provided the background for Day's support of the NF: the 'final straw' which motivated him to become an activist was the belief that the council had given preference to blacks on the housing list, that blacks were given homes when whites were homeless. Again the point may be made that this has no factual basis: discrimination tends to operate in favour of whites (Daniel, 1968, pp.177–205; Lawrence, 1974, pp.69–100; Smith, 1977, pp.236–84). The same issue of alleged positive discrimination was raised by a NF member living on the fringes of an area similar to Hoxton in Birmingham in conversation with the author: 'Look at your council and your welfare. The blacks get everything they want – houses, social security, bleeding social workers – and we (the whites) are bleeding well paying for it.' Thus, as Annie Phizacklea and Robert Miles' analysis in chapter 5 implies, some membership of the NF could be explained in terms of a response to neglect of the plight of the inner-city areas, the problems of which are blamed upon local black populations, and perceptions of favouritism.

It is of some relevance that all of those quoted above were working class. The reasons given by a middle-class organizer in the Midlands to the author were rather different. This member had been a young Conservative delegate to the 1972 Conference where, after a prolonged tussle, a resolution moved by Powell to condemn the (Conservative) government for abandoning immigration control and allowing in the Asians from Uganda, was rejected by a small majority. In the member's opinion:

> 'This was a complete betrayal of the party by the leaders who
> manipulated the final vote by allowing Young Conservatives who
> were not accredited delegates to take part in the count. In fact they
> were bussed in from London and given seats in front of the cameras,
> seats which proper delegates had been asked to vacate. Heath's
> treason was the final straw.'

When asked his reasons for dislike of blacks in the first place, the member responded in terms of a 'Britain for the British' argument, a primarily intellectual, nationalist one, and then later in the conversation mentioned somewhat diffidently the conspiracy theory discussed earlier. The notable point was that his analysis was almost completely without the passionate 'gut' reaction of the workers in the inner-city areas, but proceeded from quite abstract views of nation and race.

It is tempting to conclude from this that the reasons why people join the NF may be neatly divided into working-class racism dependant upon proximity to a black population, the ideology being stimulated by 'immediate daily experience', to use Phizacklea and Miles' phrase in the conclusion of chapter 5, and middle-class racism dependant upon the more abstract view that the uniqueness of Britain as a nation or of the British 'race' or 'nation' is being suddenly and deliberately destroyed. However, more data would be needed to substantiate this. Moreover, there are other possible reasons why people join the NF, such as the appeal of an allegedly violent party to the same strata who spend Saturday afternoons attacking supporters of rival football teams (Panorama, 21 November 1977; Labour Party broadcast, 7 December 1977), or the satisfaction of socio-psychological needs by the more lurid kinds of NF activity.

Party support: the nature of electoral support

The NF, uniquely of any party, can point to a record of sustained growth in the number of votes gained in English elections in the 1970s. In England it won just over 12,000 votes in the General Election of 1970, 77,000 in the February 1974 election, 114,000 in October 1974, and over 200,000 in the County Elections of 1977. The significance of this depends upon whether it is taken 1 in absolute terms, 2 relative to the voting population as a whole or to the voting population in seats contested by the NF, or 3 in the context of the NF gaining representation in the short or longer term.

The absolute number of votes for the National Front

The most simple context in which this growth can be considered is that it represents a quite dramatic increase in the number of English electors who are prepared to vote for a self-confessed 'racialist', perhaps fascist, political party. This argument involves the assumption that the NF has tapped a new and growing source of electoral strength, one which could not have been mobilized by earlier far right parties. In order to assess this, the obvious method would be to examine the votes of other far right parties prior to the formation of the NF in constituencies which have comparable boundaries and populations to those fought more recently by the NF, and compare levels of votes. However, because of the relatively small number of seats contested by far right parties prior to the NF, changes in constituency boundaries and in the social characteristics of the population which make comparison difficult, adequate evaluation has not been possible. For London, where some comparisons may be made, Steed (*Guardian*, 20 August 1977) has suggested that the NF has only mobilized a vote which has always been available, although I have disputed the basis of his assertion elsewhere (1978, pp.16–17), arguing that the NF has carved out its own niche in London.

The National Front vote relative to the English electorate

In the context of the voting population as a whole, the NF's share has never risen above 1 per cent. It has grown somewhat since 1970, from 0.05 per cent in that year to around 0.8 per cent in 1977, but this is hardly the signal for those opposed to the NF to leave the country. It may, of course, be argued that this comparison is unfair, given that the NF has only put up candidates in a minority of English seats, and that its support should be considered relative to the share of the total vote in seats contested. The NF's performance is rather better when viewed in this context, but does not suggest, in the words of *The Economist* (20 August 1977, p.17) 'that Fascism is about to engulf the British'. In the 1970 General Election the NF gained an average of 3.8 per cent of the English vote (nine seats), in February 1974 3.2 per cent (fifty-four seats) and in October 1974 3.1 per cent (eighty-nine seats). In the District elections of 1976, the NF averaged 8.9 per cent of the vote in 168 seats, and in the 413 Metropolitan and County Council constituencies fought in 1977, 4.2 per cent. The NF's best in a general election is the support of around one in thirty voters in seats contested, in a local election about one in twelve. The latter figure, which is quite high, must be considered in the light of the facts that the NF does proportionately better in local elections than in national ones for reasons related to variations in turnout rather than greater NF strength (Taylor, 1978, p.20), and that the 1976 local elections occurred just after the wide, inaccurate and irresponsible press coverage of the entry of the Malawi Asians. This encouraged a 'flash' vote for the NF, particularly in areas where it was expected that the immigrants would settle, a vote which subsided in May 1977 to an overall level comparable to that gained in the 1974 elections. These data indicate that the NF is not making substantially greater inroads into the white electorate consistently over time, contrary to the beliefs of many observers.

The National Front vote and the chances of the party gaining representation

It is clear from the above analysis that the NF is a long way from gaining representation on a wide basis, as the present level of its votes is well below the threshold required to attain general representation under the British electoral system. In a 'first-past-the-post' system, a party with even one-fifth or more of the popular vote may gain no or very limited representation, as the Liberals demonstrated in the two 1974 elections. The NF would have to increase its general vote by a multiple of five or six before standing a chance of becoming a serious opposition party. This is unlikely given that the NF has not performed brilliantly during the period 1974—77 in which circumstances have been relatively favourable for its development, with economic recession, high inflation, a rapidly changing social structure, disintegrating political loyalties, and many people feeling threatened by 'big' capital and 'big' labour (Walker, 1977, pp.203—15).

If the mean NF vote is small and unlikely to develop into a major threat, it is possible that high votes in a few areas could provide a springboard for limited representation in a few seats. If a fairly broad definition of NF strength is taken – parliamentary constituencies, GLC seats or District or county areas where the NF has gained more than 10 per cent of the vote in the three general elections of the 1970s or the local elections of 1976 or 1977 – twenty-six areas of disproportionate strength may be identified (see Table 4). The electoral area is set out in column 1, and the NF percentages are rank-ordered in column 3, where the figures in brackets refer to the election in which the vote was achieved.

Several points may be made concerning these data. Firstly, the NF gained over 20 per cent (i.e. approached the critical threshold for representation) in only two areas, and broke the 15 per cent barrier in only eight. Thus even in the NF's best seats, it has some considerable way to go before it can begin to challenge for representation. Secondly, there is a question as to whether these high NF votes represent stable growth, the NF may gain representation at some point in the future: if it is unable to sustain them, then representation is less likely. To investigate this, comparison was attempted between shares in elections previous to the 'best' result and, where the 'best' result was prior to 1977, results in following elections. These comparisons were difficult to make, as the boundaries of parliamentary, District and county seats were often not contiguous, quite apart from the difficulty that the NF may not in local elections have fought all the wards of a parliamentary seat, or all of the District wards in a county seat. Hence comparisons may not be precisely equivalent, and the data must be regarded qualitatively rather than quantitatively.

In the four cases where a complete comparison can be made between a previous result, the NF's best result and a following one, the pattern is for the NF vote to have increased very sharply from a low level – on average 3.6 per cent – to a relatively high one in 1976, a mean of 16.7 per cent, and then decline in 1977 to an average of 8.2 per cent. In these cases the NF was unable to maintain stable growth. This pattern, it may be noted, was followed in Leicester, where comparisons are less swayed by boundary and candidate difficulties than elsewhere. This impression of instability is sustained when the four areas where data is available upon a 'best' performance and a successive one are considered. In the 'best' election, the average was 14.95 per cent, in the successive one 7.8 per cent. In fact, in only two cases of those where a comparison may be made between a 1976 and 1977 result did the NF actually increase its share of the vote, in Wolverhampton (from 9.2 to 10.6 per cent) and Loughborough (8.6 to 10.6 per cent). Neither of these increases are dramatic or to such levels as to suggest that representation is likely in the near future. The NF, at least outside London where it remains to be seen whether or not its vote will hold up, does not appear to have established a very solid base for representation even in areas where its vote is geographically concentrated.

Party support: some possible explanations

The questions may be asked as to what kind of people vote for the NF, and why they do so. There is relatively little data available on the sociology of NF support, but what there is suggests that, while the NF draws from all groups within the population, it does best among the very young, the least educated, and the working class (Harrop and Zimmerman, 1977; Whiteley, 1978). The precise reasons for such differential support between social groups have not been investigated

Table 4 Electoral areas where the National Front in the general elections of 1970 and February and October 1974, or in the local elections of 1976 or 1977, has gained more than 10 per cent of the total vote

1	2		3		4	
Constituency/District	% NF in previous election		Highest % NF		% NF in after-election	
Leicestershire, Oadby and Wigston	–	–	20.9	(76)	11.3	(77)
Lancashire, Hyndburn	2.9	(74)	20.7	(76)	6.9	(77)
London, Bethnal Green	7.6	(74)	19.2	(77)	–	–
West Midlands, Sandwell	4.9	(74)	17.6	(76)	9.6	(77)
Leicestershire, Leicester	5.2	(74)	16.6	(76)	12.6	(77)
London, Stepney	–	–	16.4	(77)	–	–
London, Hackney C	–	–	15.1	(77)	–	–
London, Newham S	–	–	15.0	(77)	–	–
London, Deptford	4.8	(74)	14.5	(77)	–	–
Leicestershire, Hinkley and Bosworth	–	–	13.6	(76)	6.5	(77)
London, Newham NE	7.0	(74)	12.7	(77)	–	–
Surrey, Spelthorne	2.3	(74)	12.6	(76)	NA	–
London, Peckham	–	–	12.1	(77)	–	–
Hertfordshire, Watford	1.5	(74)	12.0	(76)	3.6	(77)
London, Hackney S and Shoreditch	–	–	11.7	(74)	9.0	(77)
London, Walthamstow	5.5	(74)	11.2	(77)	–	–
West Yorkshire, Bradford	–	–	10.7	(76)	4.5	(77)
Staffordshire, Tamworth	–	–	10.6	(77)	–	–
Charnwood, Loughborough	8.6	(76)	10.6	(77)	–	–
West Midlands, Dudley	2.8	(74)	10.6	(77)	–	–
West Midlands, Wolverhampton	9.2	(76)	10.6	(77)	–	–
London, Leyton	5.4	(74)	10.4	(77)	–	–
London, Islington S	–	–	10.3	(77)	–	–
London, Bermondsey	4.8	(74)	10.2	(77)	–	–
London, Wood Green	8.0	(74)	10.2	(77)	–	–
London, Tottenham	8.3	(74)	10.1	(77)	–	–

empirically but various suggestions may be made. The same factors which may account for the relative youth of NF members may also explain the appeal of the movement to young voters. The attractiveness of the NF to the lesser-educated probably in part reflects the association between education and class, and in part the fact that the lesser-educated are more inclined to be intolerant of racial minorities than the more educated, intolerance which may be translated into NF support (Lipset, 1963, pp.109—10). The greater support among the working class may reflect the fact that manual workers and their families are more likely than non-manuals to live in or near to a socio-economic milieu where there has been significant decay and decline which is blamed on the blacks (as Phizacklea and Miles suggest in chapter 5), and this could lead to NF voting.

The following general explanations may be advanced as to why people vote for the NF, including 1, racism triggered by the presence of a large black minority in the community, 2 racism dependent upon the 'threat' of further black immigration into a locale, and 3 generalized disaffection with the major parties. Evidence for each of these will be considered in turn. There are, however, further possible sources of support for the NF, for example, its opposition to the Common Market, its extreme anti-communism, its illiberal policies on education, its support for capital punishment. But to assess these and to follow-up possible psychological motivations, survey data would be needed.

National Front electoral support as white 'backlash' against the presence of a large black minority in the community

Perhaps the most obvious interpretation of NF electoral support is that it is a manifestation of dislike of black people because of skin colour, or their culture, or the alleged social and economic problems 'caused' by blacks, created or triggered by the presence of a large black population in the local community. Obviously, if this were the case, it would be expected that the NF would gain a relatively higher share of the white vote in areas with substantial black populations than in areas where there were few or no blacks. To evaluate this it was necessary to find indicators of the proportion of the community who were black, and of the NF's share of the white vote. The former was found by utilizing the data of the 1971 Census on the proportions of the population who had New Commonwealth roots in each parliamentary constituency, which are reproduced in Butler and Kavanagh (1975, pp.285—306). The appropriate figure was found for each parliamentary seat contested by the NF in 1970 and the two elections of 1974, and for those Districts or county seats within Districts where the boundaries were approximately comparable with the parliamentary ones. The areas were then grouped according to whether more than 15 per cent, 10 to

15 per cent, 5 to 10 per cent or less than 5 per cent of the population had New Commonwealth roots. The NF share of the white vote was estimated by weighting the actual NF share by the proportion of whites in the electoral area. This measure is an approximation, and may suffer from various sources of error which, however, may be self-cancelling (Taylor, 1978, p.26).

The hypothesis may be re-stated in that, if it were generally valid, it would be expected that the NF's share of the vote would be highest in areas where more than perhaps 10 or 15 per cent of the population had New Commonwealth roots, and lowest where less than 5 per cent had such roots.

Table 5   Weighted mean National Front shares of the vote in electoral areas with varying racial compositions

Election	% of population with New Commonwealth roots							
	More than 15%	N	10–15%	N	5–10%	N	Less than 5%	N
1970	6.7	1	4.3	2	5.5	2	2.7	4
Feb. 1974	4.5	6	3.7	7	4.3	16	2.5	25
Oct. 1974	5.3	7	5.6	16	3.9	21	2.3	45
1976	–	–	18.9	1	12.0	1	–	–
1977 outside London	–	–	13.1	2	6.8	4	3.5	7
GLC	9.0	14	9.6	15	6.7	23	4.8	40

The data do lend some general support to this interpretation. In all cases the NF did least well in areas where the proportion of the population with New Commonwealth roots was under 5 per cent, compared to those over 5 per cent. The difference between the NF's share in the former as compared to levels in areas where 5 to 10 per cent had New Commonwealth roots was, however, comparatively small at an average of only 2.3 per cent. There was also some tendency for the NF to run better in seats where 10 to 15 per cent of the population had New Commonwealth roots compared to those where the proportion was 5 to 10 per cent, as evidenced by the October 1974, 1976 and 1977 elections, although not in the earlier ones. Given the difference in the numbers of contests, it may be right to stress that the pattern in the former should be accorded more weight than the latter. However, the relationship between the level of the NF's vote and the incidence of black populations does not clearly stretch further upward. In both the

October 1974 and in the 1977 GLC elections, the NF did slightly worse in areas where more than 15 per cent of the population had New Commonwealth roots than where 10 to 15 per cent could be so classified, although it did slightly better in the former in 1970 and February 1974. Again, on the principle that the data may be weighted according to the number of cases, the pattern in the later elections may be of greater significance than that in the earlier ones. It may, on this basis, be concluded that the level of presence of a black population influences the level of the NF vote, but only up to a certain point.

National Front electoral support as white 'backlash' against the prospect of an increase in the size of the black minority in the community

A second possible interpretation is that NF support may be a function not just of the level of black population within the community, but also of the electorate's perceptions of the changes of an increase in that level. Whites living outside areas with major black concentrations may fear that blacks will move into their community, or where there is an existing small black population, augment it, with consequent alleged effects upon property values, the availability of housing, the solidarity of the community, the character of the local environment and crime rates. The NF may be regarded by whites as the final hope to maintain, or at least prevent 'further' deterioration in, the standards of their community. This may be considered as an explanation of NF voting in two senses. First, at times when sudden immigration takes place, of the kind following the expulsions of Asians from African countries, whites in areas where the newcomers might be expected to settle may express their fears by voting for the NF. It is significant that the very high NF votes in 1976, just after the admission of the Malawi Asians, occurred in the areas where it was anticipated they would go to - the West Midlands (Sandwell and Wolverhampton), Leicestershire (Leicester, Oadby and Wigston, Loughborough) and Yorkshire (Bradford and Leeds). The threat of a very large - at least in terms of the estimates of the press - increase in their black populations seems to have motivated support for the NF, support which, as the threat was shown to be rather empty, diminished in 1977. The second sense in which the threat of further local immigration may be important is where movements of an existing black population from neighbouring areas might be expected. In areas where the black population is less than those in surrounding ones, voters may consider that there is a real prospect of 'overspill', which they may perceive as 'threatening' their own community. Thus 'fear-motivated' support for the NF may be found among white voters living in such milieu.

To try and test the latter hypothesis it was necessary to derive some measure of the extent to which the white electorate might feel 'threatened' by black immigration. It would have been best if degree of perceived threat could have been defined using survey data, but as none was available, it was only possible to use the Census. The degree of 'threat' was assessed for each electoral area by comparing the highest proportion of the population with New Commonwealth roots in all constituencies bordering upon it with the proportion within it. The suggestion is that where there was a significant positive difference, the population was more likely to feel 'threatened' by black immigration, or further black immigration, than where this was not the case. The level at which the discrepancy became significant was taken as where the difference was more than 10 per cent. Areas where the difference was under 10 per cent or negative were regarded as less likely to harbour voters who feared 'invasion'.

Several caveats are in order concerning this approach. First, there is a strong implicit assumption that there is some 'minimum rationale' for feelings of 'threat', that these are motivated by the presence nearby of a black population larger than that in the locale. This may not necessarily be the case, as some people living many miles away from multiracial areas may feel threatened, however improbable this seems. Second, it is posited that the significant reference point for voters is the black population in the immediately surrounding neighbourhood. It is of course possible that, particularly in the areas bordering upon larger cities, the reference point may be slightly further afield. Finally, it would have been desirable to have discriminated more finely between levels of discrepancies within areas, but this was not possible because of the small number of cases.

The proposition may now be re-cast in that it would be expected that the NF's mean share of the vote would be greater in seats bordering upon a much larger black population relative to their own than in those where this was not the case. In order to control for NF voting 'triggered' by the level of the black population within the area as distinct from 'threat' motivated voting, the cases were grouped by the percentage of the population with New Commonwealth roots and divided within these groups according to the 'objective' possibility of 'threat' operating. It was only possible, because of the need to maintain an adequate 'spread' of cases, to investigate the proposition for seats contested in the two 1974 elections considered collectively and the GLC 1977 election.

Table 6 Weighted mean National Front shares of the vote in the General Elections of 1974 and the GLC elections of 1977 in areas with varying racial compositions and degrees of potential threat from further immigration

	% of population with New Commonwealth roots							
	More than 15%		10–15%		5–10%		Less than 5%	
Difference between highest % with NC roots in neighbouring areas and that within area	>10%	<10%	>10%	<10%	>10%	<10%	>10%	<10%
1974	–	4.9	5.3	4.9	4.2	4.0	3.7	2.0
N	–	13	4	19	7	30	14	56
1977 London	11.2	8.4	7.8	10.0	6.7	6.6	5.2	4.6
N	3	11	3	12	9	14	6	34

The data offer some support to the hypothesis (see Table 6). In six out of the seven cases where comparison could be made between mean support in areas with similar internal levels of New Commonwealth population but different degrees of external 'threat', the NF's vote was higher in those where there was a more than 10 per cent discrepancy between the greatest proportion in surrounding seats and that inside the area than in those where the discrepancy was less or negative. The exception, where the reverse occurred, was those areas of London with proportions of the population with New Commonwealth roots of between 10 and 15 per cent. The reason is that in two seats where the 'threat' was small - Bethnal Green and Newham N E - the NF won quite disproportionately high shares of the weighted vote compared to others in the category, an average of 18 per cent compared to 7.2 per cent. These were two out of only four seats in London where the NF did not have to contend with Liberal competition and, as will be argued later, picked up a vote which might otherwise have gone to the Liberals. If these exceptional cases are excluded, and comparison made between seats in this category where both Liberal and NF candidates fought, the mean NF vote in seats where no threat could be established was lower by 0.6 per cent than in comparable areas where 'threat' voting could be considered realistic. Taking this into account, the data lend full support to the proposition.

National Front electoral support as reflecting protest against the major parties

It is common to assume that the NF's vote must, in some sense, represent racism. This need not be the case. One particular alternative which has attracted some attention is that of a NF vote as a protest vote against the major parties, one of essentially the same character as that for the Liberal party in 1974. Husbands (1975, pp.403–5) has suggested that the NF's vote in those elections was part of a vote which could have gone to almost any third party candidate. If the Liberals were available, it went to them, while if the NF stood, they gained. This was supported by an analysis of NF voting which showed that where the NF fought alone against the major parties it did considerably better than where there was also Liberal competition. Some limited evidence may be provided that this was still the case in 1977 in that the mean NF vote in London seats where they were not in competition with the Liberals was 11.3 per cent, that for those where they were 5.2 per cent. Elsewhere, I (Taylor, 1978, p.32) have investigated the extent to which the NF's GLC performance in May 1977 might have been explicable in terms of the party taking a larger share of a protest vote which had gone to the Liberals in 1974 but, consequent upon Liberal decline, went to the NF. No general support was found for this hypothesis.

Conclusion

The impact of the NF may usefully be assessed in terms of the distinction made by Lipset and Raab (1971, pp.498–503) between 'norm-oriented' and 'value-oriented' political movements. The aim of the former is to fundamentally re-allocate values in the political system: the latter are more concerned with taking political power themselves, with changing norms as a secondary objective. The NF has not, despite some growth in the 1970s, been successful in mounting a challenge for power or even representation, with a relatively low, and compared to

1976 declining, share of the vote. It may well be that future historians will regard the 1976 vote as a 'flash' vote similar to that for the Poujadists in France in 1956 (Williams, 1970, pp.60–3, 105), reflecting an immediate set of popular grievances which did not provide a basis for permanent growth. One is conscious in making this kind of assertion that much the same analysis could have been made of the Nazi party in 1928, when its share of the vote fell to 2.6 per cent, but which five years later won over one-third of the popular vote. If there was a complete economic collapse, a break-up of one of the major parties, or a sudden very large-scale influx of black immigrants, then the NF may gain quite dramatically in popular support. If, however, these can be avoided, as seems likely at the time of writing, it would be surprising if the NF made significant progress in the near future.

It may be argued that the main impact of the NF has been in assisting normative change, as suggested by Robert Miles and Annie Phizacklea in their introduction to this volume. There is, in Britain, a strain of hostility to black people among the white population which has been fairly constant in level and magnitude over the past two decades (Studlar, 1974, pp.371–81). If there was no vehicle for the expression of such opinions or possibility of them being translated into votes for a third party, then major party élites could probably have made a 'non-decision' to exclude them at least in some measure from the realms of political consideration (Bachrach and Baratz, 1970, pp.3–17, 104–9). The existence of the NF has meant that élites have had to respond to the climate of opinion more than they might otherwise have done. The effect of this, of course, has been to legitimize racism further, to the detriment of black British citizens, as well as to the once-true image of Britain as a tolerant, civilized society.

Bibliography

Abrams, P. and Little, A. (1965), 'The Young Voter in British Politics', *British Journal of Sociology*, vol. 16, pp.95–110.

Almond, G. (1954), *The Appeals of Communism*, Princeton University Press, New Jersey.

Bachrach, P. and Baratz, M. (1970), *Power and Poverty*, Oxford University Press, New York.

Benewick, R. (1969), *Political Violence and Public Order*, Allen Lane, London.

Butler, D. and Stokes, D. (1974), *Political Change in Britain*, Macmillan, London.

Butler, D. and Kavanagh, D. (1975), *The British General Election of February, 1974*, Macmillan, London.

Crewe, I., Sarlvik, B. and Alt, J. (1977), 'Partisan De-alignment in Britain 1964–74', *British Journal of Political Science*, vol. 7, pp.129–90.

Daniel, W. (1968), *Racial Discrimination in England*, Penguin, Harmondsworth.

Harrop, M. and Zimmerman, G. (1977), 'The Anatomy of the National Front', mimeograph, Department of Government, University of Essex.

Hughes, A. and Kolinsky, M. (1976), ' "Paradigmatic Fascism" and Modernization: A Critique', *Political Studies*, vol. xxiv, pp.371–96.

Husbands, C.T. (1975), 'The National Front: a Response to Crisis?', *New Society*, 15 May, pp.403–5.

Lawrence, D. (1974), *Black Migrants: White Natives*, Cambridge University Press.

Layton-Henry, Z. and Taylor, S. (1977), 'Race at the Polls', *New Society*, 25 August, p.392.

Lipset, S. (1963), *Political Man*, Mercury Books, London.

Lipset, S. and Raab, E. (1971), *The Politics of Unreason*, Heinemann, London.

Nugent, N. (1977), 'The Parties of the Extreme Right' in N. Nugent and R. King (eds), *The British Right*, Saxon House, London.

Rae, D. (1971), *The Political Consequences of Electoral Laws*, Yale University Press, New Haven.

Scott, D. (1975), 'The National Front in Local Politics: Some Interpretations' in I. Crewe (ed.), *British Political Sociology Yearbook*, vol. 2 *The Politics of Race*, Croom Helm, London.

Smith, D. (1977), *Racial Disadvantage in Britain*, Penguin, Harmondsworth.

Studlar, D. (1974), 'British Public Opinion, Colour Issues and Enoch Powell: a longitudinal analysis', *British Journal of Political Science*, vol. 4, pp.371–81.

Taylor, S. (1977), 'The National Front: backlash or bootboys?', *New Society*, 11 August, pp.283–4.

Taylor, S. (1978), 'The National Front: a contemporary evaluation', *University of Warwick Occasional Papers*, no. 16.

Walker, M. (1977), *The National Front*, Fontana, London.

Whiteley, P. (1978), 'The Decline of Partisan Allegiance in Britain and the National Front Vote', paper delivered to the Third Contemporary British Politics Workshop, Sheffield, 5 January.

Williams, P. (1970), *French Politicians and Elections 1951–69*, Cambridge University Press.

CHAPTER 7

The threat hypothesis and racist voting in England and the United States

Christopher T. Husbands

It is a truism that racist voting presupposes that the voters hold corresponding sentiments.[1] However, the beneficiary of racist voting can vary from one place or time to another. In the 1960s, for example, some Conservative voting in areas of New Commonwealth concentration such as Smethwick (in the West Midlands Borough of Warley) was interpreted as being inspired by racist sentiment. This conclusion was consistent with subsequently available evidence that not only did the great majority of the British electorate believe that too many immigrants had been allowed into the country, but also that many whites in areas of such concentration were more likely to believe that the Conservative Party would reduce immigration (Butler and Stokes, 1974, pp.303–7). Labour voting might be similarly motivated among at least some of those having a similar perception of the Labour Party.

Since the beginning of the 1970s, the rise in British politics of an explicitly racist party, the National Front (NF), further complicates such motivational attribution. Prima facie one would expect that much of the voting specifically attributable to racist motivation would gravitate to a party with the sort of strong anti-immigrant (and, by implication, anti-black) platform of the Front. However, racism is not necessarily the only motive for voting for even this party, despite its current image, and elsewhere the author (Husbands, 1975) has hypothesized the operation of a generalized protest sentiment or alienation to explain some voting for the Front in the 1974 general elections. However, to complicate the issue further, the two types of motivation, racism and generalized protest, are not mutually exclusive and both may jointly contribute to voting for the Front by the same individual.

Yet the political sociology of Front voting has almost certainly changed somewhat since the circumstances of the 1974 general elections. Whereas in 1974 the Front was probably not universally known as quite the sort of racist organization that more recent publicity has shown it to be or, whereas then some voters might have voted for it out of some sort of protest motive and despite its racist character, current Front support is more likely to be partly or wholly racially based. It is not that protest- or alienation-inspired voting for the Front does not now occur, but rather that it is much less likely to be the exclusive reason for such voting; racism will also be there as part of individual political motivation. This is suggested because the publicity given to the organization during 1976 and 1977 has insisted on its racial character to such a degree that one may expect that this particular feature has become very widely diffused into public awareness and that correspondingly Front voting has an increasingly conscious racial base. This argument is intended to justify the attribution of a particular type of materially based racism to that type of Front support which is to be found in certain urban areas of England.

The aim of this chapter is to show that, using a comparison between urban racist voting for George Wallace in the northern United States and for the NF in England, the latter is better explained by factors operating throughout the urban structure and is not simply a function of a localized fear of 'invasion' or of other micro-spatial processes, as tends to be the case with the Wallace vote. This will lead on to a consideration of housing and labour markets in the United States and England, from which it will be argued that racist voting in the former is better explained by the functioning of the urban housing market, whereas in most parts of England, the character of the urban labour market is at least equally decisive. An appendix considers the case of racist voting in London, which is different from such voting in other areas of England.

Theories of racist voting behaviour among whites

Contributors to theoretical and empirical work on the social and economic, as opposed to the psychological, dynamics of racist voting behaviour by white electors have adduced a range of predisposing causes which differ along at least two dimensions: firstly, in the degree to which they posit materially or economically based causal processes;

and secondly, in the degree to which they depend on the significance of the spatial or territorial relationship between the white population of voters and the non-white population against whom the former's racist voting is directed.[2]

One dynamic of racist voting, perhaps the most remote from an economic derivation, may be termed cultural antagonism; this expresses itself as an inability or a reluctance by a white population to accept the cultural practices of a proximate non-white group and may lead to a more general racial negativism. The possible participants of such cultural antagonism are various: types of music, ostentatious displays of some hitherto unknown religious practice, or perhaps culinary habits. Some of these possibilities are variously captured in a quotation from Roy Painter, a former NF activist who became part of the leadership of the breakaway National Party after the split of late 1975 (This Week, 5 September 1974; also quoted in Fielding, 1977, p.187):

> 'It's all very well for [the then Home Secretary] Mr Carr to come out with these platitudes while riding home in his XJ6 to Hadley Green, while old ladies in Tottenham have to suffer reggae music over 'em and the smell of curry beneath them'.

A second, and distinct predisposing dynamic of racist voting (which may or may not have an economic derivation) is fear that is induced by a perceived threat of 'invasion' (to use the loaded term of traditional Chicago-School urban sociology, e.g. Duncan and Duncan, 1957, p.16) from a proximate and distinct ethnic group. Such fear may be based either on the anticipation or the certain knowledge of the type of cultural antagonism introduced above as the first dynamic or it may have the economic character of the third type of dynamic to be introduced. Slightly facetiously, one may regard this second dynamic as the operation of a 'Seventh Cavalry' mentality in which voters are in continuous doubt about their circumstances and in perpetual dread of attack from 'Indians riding over the crest of the hill'.

The third dynamic of racist voting explicitly emphasizes the role of competition for scarce economic resources; however, the supply of these resources in turn differs in degree of spatial concentration. Housing, for example, is a strongly space-related economic resource since housing choice for most potential urban consumers is in fact severely constrained in terms of space. Jobs, on the other hand, are an urban economic resource upon whose supply there is usually a somewhat lesser spatial constraint for most consumers, less at least than in the case of housing; usually transportation limitations (although not to be underestimated in the context of a large American metropolis) or perhaps vigilantist activities (when one racial group deters members of the other from crossing over or moving into the territory of the former to take up labour opportunities) would be the major explicitly spatial restrictions on the take-up of jobs in an urban context. Finally, such scarce or allegedly scarce material resources as welfare benefits would normally be available according to criteria that, however arbitrary and bureaucratic their distribution might seem from other perspectives, were not directly space-related.

It should be noted that the relationship to urban space of the supply of these different types of commodity does not necessarily imply anything about the space-relationship of their respective demands; in fact, it is this latter factor, or more precisely the manner in which it interacts with the spatial distribution of supply, that is most crucial in predicting the distribution of racist voting with an economic dynamic.

Each of these three types of major dynamic has predictive implications for the locational distribution within a city of whites voting support for political candidates appealing to racial animosity. However, the empirical effect of each dynamic upon the spatial variation of such racist voting by whites depends on a further crucial factor, the degree of urban residential segregation between the white and non-white groups.[3]

Let us posit two opposite extremes of white/non-white urban residential segregation. The first is zero segregation of one from the other group; i.e. whatever areal sub-units are used (polling districts, wards, enumeration districts, blocks, census tracts, community areas, or whatever), the white/non-white ratio within each such sub-unit comprising the total city equals the ratio within the city as a whole. On the other hand, imagine also a situation of total or 100 per cent segregation between the two groups; in other words, all members of one group would have to be relocated in order to produce within each constituent areal sub-unit the inter-group ratio in the city as a whole.

Zero inter-group segregation

In such a segregation situation the implications of each dynamic for the spatial distribution of racist voting by whites would be as follows, assuming *ceteris paribus* throughout:

1 If the dynamic of cultural antagonism were significant, there would be no spatial variation in the level of whites' racist voting. Whites throughout the city would demonstrate in similar proportions their hostility against non-whites also located in their local residential areas.
2 The operation of the dynamic of a fear of anticipated invasion presupposes some minimum degree of residential segregation. This dynamic could not therefore operate in the zero-segregation situation, such fear being predicated upon the threat, not the actual experience, of inter-group integration of a white or formerly white area.
3 In an on-going zero-segregation situation dynamics based upon competition for scarce economic resources could have several differing implications for the spatial distribution of any white racist voting. The precise outcome would depend essentially on spatial variations in the net demand for a commodity within the white population. If both supply and demand of a resource were strongly space-related, as might be the case with housing, there would be a corresponding variation of racist voting levels, unless the interaction between this supply and demand were such as to produce some kind of levelling effect.[4] To the extent that demand for a resource is more evenly distributed throughout the whole city, as might be the case with some employment opportunities, there would be little spatial concentration of such racist voting.[5]

Total inter-group segregation

In this segregation,[6] 100 per cent white/non-white segregation could be realized by an almost infinite number of spatial permutations but a schematic ideal-typical representation in two dimensions, based on the concentricity of economic distributions that is assumed in the Chicago-School type of city, is reproduced in Figure 2.[7] Shown in this Figure by a dotted line is the spatial distribution that whites' racist voting might be expected to have in such a city if the 'Seventh Cavalry' mentality were its dynamic, or if such voting were due to competition for a resource such as housing with a particular space-related demand; also shown, by a dashed line, is the comparable spatial distribution when the dynamic is competition for a resource whose demand has constant level throughout the white community. (Shown too are the two respective values of the quartile coefficient of variation across the sixteen electoral areas included; this measure of variation is described in note 12.)

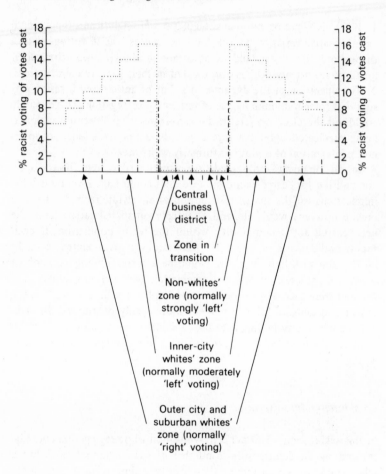

Figure 2 A schematic cross-sectional representation of an ideal-typical Chicago-school city with total white/non-white residential segregation showing economic and ethnic locations and examples of the hypothesized spatial distribution of racist voting in sixteen electoral areas under the operation of different causal processes

KEY

Quartile coefficients of variation
of distributions of racist voting
across sixteen electoral areas

Spatial distribution of
racially motivated voting
under the operation of
competition for a resource
without a space-related
demand   - - - - -   0.333

Spatial distribution of
racially motivated voting
under the operation of a
fear-of-invasion dynamic
or of competition for a
resource with a space-
related demand 0.625

Electoral area boundaries   — · —·

The following observations about this figure can be made:

1 In a residential situation such as that depicted in Figure 2, racist voting produced by cultural antagonism based on immediate experience would be an inapplicable dynamic, except perhaps at the point of contact between the two communities. Normally, however, such total inter-group segregation would imply the existence of a definite *ils ne passeront pas* racial dividing line between white and non-white communities and cultural antipathy between the two groups of the sort implied in the earlier definition would have little chance to take root.

2 On the other hand, in the total-segregation situation racist voting based on the fear of the supposed consequences of invasion would be particularly significant within those white areas adjacent to the non-white community. Throughout the city as a whole, such voting might be expected to have considerable variation in strength and to demonstrate a spatial distribution as represented in Figure 2, i.e. non-existent in electoral areas inhabited by non-whites, highest in white areas that are immediately adjacent to non-white ones, and then having a distance-decay curve as one moves along a radius to the periphery of the city.

3 The precise pattern of any white racist voting based on the third dynamic of competition for scarce resources would, as in the zero-segregation situation, depend both upon the spatial distribution of their demand within the white community and upon the spatial distribution of their supply. A commodity such as housing of a particular type and

standard would normally have a strongly space-related supply and one would also expect its demand to be equally space-related. If demand focused on a white area under threat of invasion, as would normally be the case, the situation would be identical to that already discussed above as part of the second dynamic, fear of invasion when such fear is based on a material issue; correspondingly, the spatial distribution of any racist voting would have the high variation pattern shown in Figure 2. On the other hand, to the extent that a net demand for a resource is distributed evenly throughout the white community, the spatial pattern of white racist voting would have maximum variation between black and white communities, but minimum variation within each community. Over both communities taken together it would therefore tend to have intermediate spatial variation when measured on an areal unit-by-unit basis. This pattern is also depicted in Figure 2.

Racist voting behaviour and the 'contact hypothesis'

This discussion on the spatial distributions of whites' racist voting is a particular extension of the varied and diverse literature on the relationship between the occurrence of prejudiced attitudes and/or behaviour and physical proximity to the ethnic group against whom such prejudice or behaviour is directed. However, the conclusions in this work are varied and contingent, while the precise dependent variable varies from study to study, a fact that results in confusion when it is ignored. After the initial qualified optimism of early studies of the 'contact hypothesis' (some, like Deutsch and Collins (1965)), based on integrated and segregated public housing projects in the United States and reviewed in Wilner, Walkley and Cook (1955) and Secord and Backman (1964, p.441)), some pessimism set in as subsequent work showed the alternative consequences in contact situations where contingent factors differed. The best that can be said for attempts to test the contact hypothesis is that their outcomes are 'mixed' (Molotch, 1972a, p.35n). This is not a satisfactory intellectual resolution of a theoretical difficulty.

In the late 1940s and early 1950s Shirley Star (1964) examined the degree of racial tension in areas of Chicago undergoing varying degrees of racial succession. The major purpose of her research was methodological, viz., to produce a measure of inter-racial tension, but her findings did show that, at least at that time, there was comparatively little variation between areas of the South Side of Chicago that were undergoing different degrees of succession. It is interesting to note that she found slightly less than average inter-racial tension among whites in areas where the process of succession was advanced than she did in areas where it merely threatened. However, the precise reasons for this were not explored, and they may be due to the character of those moving out of the first type of area. Hamilton also speculates, perhaps rather optimistically, that whites in transition neighbourhoods may be more sympathetic to blacks' rights than are those in all-white areas, since the latter will contain more of the types of bigoted whites who would be among the first to move from a transition community (Hamilton, 1972, p.416). Orbell and Sherrill, in a study of racial hostility by whites in Columbus, Ohio, found a somewhat complex pattern of relationships:

> Areas with a high proportion of Negroes are characterized by in-
> creasing white hostility as their status declines. . . . However,
> whites living in the areas that are virtually *without* Negroes are more
> hostile when the areas have higher SES. Antipathy toward Negroes
> is virtually equal in low-status areas close to Negroes and in high-
> status areas away from them (1969, p.50).

The British studies display a similar variety of implication and result, not least because the range of types and degrees of racist attitude and behaviour is often not acknowledged. At one extreme there is what one might refer to as 'low-level' racism, an attitude that is almost part of national ideology and is certainly not likely to respond to attempts to place it within any particular material or structural context. An example of such 'low-level' racism would be acquiescence in the state-ment that 'too many immigrants have been let into this country'.[8] Butler and Stokes report quite outstanding degrees of agreement with such a viewpoint (1974, p.303). There is little reason to think that this situation has changed in any marked degree (Marsh, 1976). Given the one-sidedness of public opinion on the immigration issue, it is not too surprising, even though it is statistically still possible, that Studlar (1977) concludes, with every apparent indication of bewilderment, that the racial context of the constituency in which a respondent lives has little effect upon the likelihood of his subscribing to the majority 'low-level' response on this item. While the variables being used by Butler and Stokes and by Studlar (who combines viewpoint and the strength with which it is held into a four-point ordinal scale) do contain variation, the consensus towards the exclusionist extreme and the fact that most British voters do have relatively little contact with immigrants together make it improbable that variations in such attitudes will be determined by immigrants' proximity.

The various studies carried out on the *Colour and Citizenship* survey data also tend to support the position that individual levels of prejudice are not related in marked degree to the proximity of New Commonwealth immigrants (e.g. Schaefer, 1975), but it should be noted than in the study's national sample prejudice was measured only by a two-item summed scale where both items were of the imagined-situation type in relation to employment. In a four-item scale, whose two extra items were an attempt to capture more abstract feelings towards immigrants, Schaefer (1975) found an average difference between the five boroughs on whose white populations the relevant survey was conducted; all five boroughs had proportions of those born in New Commonwealth that were above the national average.

In addition to 'low-level' or consensus racism, there is a type of racism bred of real experience. This is much more likely to be materially based and to be found where the work or housing situation puts whites in actual or potential competitive relationships with New Commonwealth immigrants. This is the type of racism to be found among inner-city whites (considered in chapter 5 by Annie Phizacklea and Robert Miles), and it therefore probably has some locational variation. This sort of 'experiential' racism is to be emphatically differentiated from that of the full-blown racial ideologue who argues that race is the major dynamic of human history and is the crucial and necessary basis of social division and organization.[9]

Merely 'experiential racism' obviously predisposes to National Front/National Party (NF/NP) voting, perhaps even to membership and activism, since not even all activists hold the full-blown ideological apparatus exhibited by, say, articles in the NF's *Spearhead* or *Britain First*, the publication of the now disbanded NP. Even so, many of those whom we may call 'experiential racists' do not for various reasons vote for the NF/NP, even if they are to be regarded as potentially mobilizable. Hanna (1974) argues that not only a New Commonwealth presence but also a good organizational effort are necessary for NF potential to be realized in actual voting; he is certainly correct about the latter factor, even if he is in fact over-simplifying in the case of the former. There is now ample evidence (e.g. Husbands, 1977a and 1977b) of right-wing NF support in strongly Conservative areas, far away from New Commonwealth immigrant settlement.

In fact, when one moves from analysing the spatial distribution of racist attitudes, of whatever type, to studies of the distribution of supposedly racist voting behaviour, the patterns become even more complex. Rasmussen (1973) has conducted an aggregate constituency-level analysis of Labour strength in the 1964 and 1966 general elections and has apparently assumed a racist orientation to be implicit in an anti-Labour vote (to be sure, there were Smethwick, Eton and Slough, and so on in 1964, but one imagines that some people did vote Conservative for other reasons). He reports negative correlations between constituency Labour strength and New Commonwealth concentration in North, Central, and Celtic Fringe regions of the country, and a corresponding positive one in the Southern region (1973, Table 6, p.139). From these findings he suggests an explanation based on the purported cosmopolitan character and tolerance of diversity to be found in London and the South; one wonders how he would accommodate current NF strength in London within this intriguing perspective. Of course, aggregate data may mask a variety of processes, and *ad hoc* explanations of this sort are always risky, despite any immediate intuitive appeal they may possess; Butler and Stokes's (1974) finding, already referred to, of variations by level of local New Commonwealth settlement in perceptions of the exclusionism towards immigrants of the major parties would be but one factor complicating and mediating any meaning behind these ecological correlations.

When it comes to actual NF voting, there are numerous observations of its relative strength in immigrant-settled areas (e.g. Michael Steed in Butler and Kavanagh (1974)), though many such statements apparently assume a direct mechanical relationship between the two variables, with little obvious awareness of any intervening role played by material or cultural factors. The study by Harrop and Zimmerman (1977) argues, on the basis of individual-level survey data on pro-NF sentiment, for a curvilinear relationship between aggregate NF voting strength and the constituency proportion of New Commonwealth settlement.[10] There are various interpretive difficulties with their data-presentation, including the obsolescence of the New Commonwealth settlement data and the lack of further controls. However, even if correct, this relationship might still imply any of several competing possibilities: the selective out-migration from the highest immigrant areas of more pro-NF-disposed whites, the existence of a threshold beyond which any mechanical effect of the local presence of immigrants is attenuated, or else differences in the material circumstances of the constituencies inside the various categories of immigrant concentration.

Thus, in summary, the whole corpus of research on white prejudice and non-white proximity contains a display of ambiguity and variety which is truly embarrassing for a collection of research efforts that have been continuing for thirty or more years. It is necessary to move beyond the tenuous inferences contained in most of the research on this subject, whether based on aggregate data only or combining individual and structural measurements, and it is hoped that the sorts of orientation to the subject to be advanced in the present paper may prove useful in this respect. The nature and location of the material bases of racism, at least as manifested by racist voting by whites in an urban context, are central to a successful specification and elaboration of existing findings on this subject.

The next sections of this paper introduce the two cases that are to be the central focus of analysis, George Wallace's Presidential candidacies in the United States and NF/NP voting support in England. The literature on the spatial distribution of voting for each of these two movements within an urban context is summarized and reviewed.

Intra-urban variations in voting for George Wallace and for the National Front/National Party

In the literature on voting for George Wallace there are several references to its urban spatial distribution in relation to proximate non-white areas. Rogin's (1969) study of Wallace voting in Gary, Indiana, in the 1964 Indiana Presidential Preference Primary found Wallace's support came from southern, white, working-class homeowners and from homeowners of southern European and eastern European stock; his interpretation was that these people were concerned about both the value of their property if black migration into their neighbourhoods occurred and cultural differences between themselves and this black population. Moreover, 'the closer suburban whites lived to the ghetto, the more likely they were to vote for Wallace' (1969, p.30). Several writers on the success of George Wallace's American Independent Party campaign in the 1968 Presidential Election have mentioned a similar phenomenon (e.g. Lubell, 1970, pp.90–1), and Lubell has interpreted this as a kind of territorial defence with both economic and non-economic components in its motivation.

Because most American cities have white/non-white indexes of residential segregation that are closer to the total-segregation situation than to the zero one (Taeuber and Taeuber, 1965; van Valley, Roof, and Wilcox, 1977), the implications of the various dynamics of racist voting already introduced, as these occur under total-segregation conditions, are most theoretically relevant in comprehending the facts on the spatial distribution of urban Wallace voting.

There are also a large number of references on NF/NP voting in contemporary Britain that implicitly or otherwise adopt an explanatory perspective implying a degree of spatial variation in such voting that is comparable to that found in the case of urban Wallace voting, despite the lesser levels of white/non-white residential segregation in English cities. Such explanations frequently infer the operation of the 'Seventh Cavalry' mentality, whether the fear is cultural, economic or both.

Several journalistic attempts to account for the NF's initially surprising appeal in the parliamentary by-elections at Rotherham and Thurrock in June and July 1976 relied on whites' supposed fears of some kind of immigrant takeover. (At Rotherham the Front won 6.0 per cent of votes cast and at Thurrock, 6.6 per cent; in 1971 only 1.2 per cent of the population of the Rotherham constituency and 1.0 per cent of Thurrock were of New Commonwealth birth.) Michael White, writing in the *Guardian* (14 July 1976), graphically expressed the 'Seventh Cavalry' dynamic: 'Its (the Front's) candidate, Mr John Roberts, is playing the Surbiton card, telling his audiences – many of whom came to Essex from the East End of London – that the immigrant hordes they fled from are poised to follow them.' A report in the *Sunday Times* (11 July 1976) made a similar diagnosis of Front appeal, remarking on the paradox of this support, 'even though there is yet no coloured immigration population of any marked size'. Martin Walker also explicitly invokes the fear-of-invasion hypothesis to account for part at least of the Front's success in Leicester (1977, pp.198, 218). And the Front's own accounts of its successes sometimes emphasize a comparable process. Martin Webster, the NF National Activities Organizer, gave his prognosis of Front support in the Rotherham by-election (*Sunday Times*, 20 June 1976): 'We shall do well in Rotherham. The presence of a strong immigrant population is not the vital factor. The Front does best when an immigrant problem is in sight nearby. We find this creates the better prospects.'

It is often difficult to assess the degree to which available aggregate election results bear out the truth or otherwise of this kind of diagnosis because ward and electoral division boundaries do not neatly run between mutually segregated white and immigrant communities and so the denominators of NF vote percentages therefore necessarily contain an uncertain proportion of non-Front-voting immigrant voters. However, as has been argued earlier, in a situation of high white-immigrant segregation, the operation of the fear-dynamic to increase Front voting would imply a tendency to high inter-areal unit dispersion in such support within a single city. While it is undoubtedly fair to concede that there have been particular instances of time and place when the 'fear-of-invasion' explanation has clearly been the most plausible way to explain Front support, it would be wrong – so this paper argues – to regard this as universally the most significant explanatory factory. Other things being equal, this implies a degree of spatial variation in Front support, measured areally unit by unit, that in some cases seems not to be present or is certainly not present to the same degree that one may find such variation in some of the urban support received by George Wallace. To the extent that such variation is lacking, Front support among whites must be interpreted by factors that operate with relatively equal effect over the whole of a particular city rather than by a dynamic with a specific micro-spatial basis. Moreover, the operation of the micro-spatial dynamic also implies the probability of a positive correlation between the unit-by-unit variation in racist voting in cities and their overall levels of residential segregation. Again, we shall present evidence disposing against such a positive correlation in the case of NF support.

National Front/National Party voting and George Wallace voting

Table 7 contains data that, while not permitting any definitive inferences, relate to the question of how far NF voting is determined at the micro-spatial level, particularly in comparison with the evidence of urban voting patterns for George Wallace in the American urban context. It also includes calculations of the areal dispersion of NF/NP support in the Greater London Council elections of 5 May 1977 and the significance of these higher coefficients is discussed in an appendix. Table 8 contains information that is as comparable as available data-sources permit on the distribution of Wallace's 1968 support within the Wisconsin counties of Milwaukee and Racine.

Before a detailed discussion of these two data-presentations an admission of their shortcomings and a defence of their usefulness notwithstanding are required. The initial figures on which calculations

Table 7 Variations in aggregate support for the National Front/ National Party/British National Party White Power Candidates in the County Council Elections of 5 May 1977; percentages of the total population born in the New Commonwealth, 1971; and indexes of residential segregation of those born in the New Commonwealth, 1971: selected English districts/boroughs and London

District/ Borough	Quartile coefficient of variation of NF/ NP/BNPWPC support by ward or electoral division (areal units in calculation)	% born in New Commonwealth, 1971[1]	Index of residential segregation of those born in New Commonwealth, 1971[2,a]
Bradford, Borough of	0.081 (7 electoral divisions)	7.1	41.7
Leeds, Borough of	0.246 (21 wards)	2.8	43.4
Leicester, Borough and District of	0.175 (16 wards)	8.2	16.8
Sandwell, District of	0.228 (12 electoral divisions)	4.7	15.4
Wolverhampton, Borough and District of	0.310 (10 electoral divisions)	7.5	17.4
Means:	0.210	6.1	26.9
Greater London	0.339 (92 constituencies/electoral divisions in 32 London boroughs)		
Inner London	0.383 (35 constituencies/electoral divisions in 12 London boroughs)		

Sources
[1] Office of Population Censuses and Surveys, 1972–3; 1975–6.
[2] Office of Population Censuses and Surveys, 1974.

Note
[a] The areal units on the basis of which these indexes have been calculated are parliamentary constituencies as at February 1974, of which there are three in Bradford, six in Leeds, three in Leicester, four in Sandwell, and three in Wolverhampton.

of dispersion have been carried out were the percentages of support among valid votes cast in the areal units concerned. In the case of multiple-seat contests with multiple NF/NP candidacies the mean number of votes per NF/NP candidate was used as the level of support and the denominator of the percentage was the number of ballot papers issued.[11]

The measure of areal unit-by-unit dispersion of voting strength used is the quartile coefficient of variation (Spiegel, 1961, p.84).[12] Because of vagaries from one to another District in the establishment of electoral divisions for county council elections, the areal units on which the coefficients have been calculated are not always similar in size, a deficiency that may unfortunately produce some slight spuriousness but is not possible to correct. Moreover, the degree to which the values of these figures are affected by the presence of immigrant voters in the denominators of the original percentages may vary in unknown degree from city to city. The figures in Table 7 giving the percentages of residents born in New Commonwealth of course suffer from some obsolescence, although the Ugandan Asian entry into Britain during the summer and autumn of 1972 is probably the only immigration wave of sufficient size that could have substantially affected the absolute value of these figures. The indexes of segregation in Table 7 suffer similar problems of obsolescence, and in addition have had to be calculated based on parliamentary constituencies as areal units; these indexes therefore have meaning only for comparisons between English cities and they cannot be used in comparisons with corresponding American figures shown in Table 8. The latter have been calculated on a census-tract basis; census tracts are usually much smaller areas than British parliamentary constituencies and the well-known and invariably negative relationship between the absolute value of a segregation index and the size of areal unit on the basis of which it had been calculated vitiates such inter-country comparison.

The English boroughs and Districts included in Table 7 are all those cities with significant New Commonwealth settlement in which the National Front, the National Party, or the British National Party,[13] individually or together, put forward a complete slate in all wards/ electoral divisions of the specified city or District in the County Council elections of 5 May 1977.[14] The two Wisconsin counties of Milwaukee and Racine included in Table 8 are the only two in the state with black populations of sufficient size to be able to expect any process of territorial defence to operate among 'threatened' white voters.

All but one of the five English quartile coefficients are lower absolutely than the values of the Wisconsin ones. All the obvious manifold

Table 8   Variations in aggregate support for the American Independent Party's presidential and vice-presidential candidacy of George C. Wallace and Marvin Griffin in the general election of 5 November 1968; percentages of the total population who were Negro, 1970; and indexes of residential segregation of Negroes, 1970: two Wisconsin counties

County	Quartile coefficient of variation of AIP support by areal unit[1][a]	% Negro 1970[2]	Index of residential segregation of Negroes, 1970[3][b]
Milwaukee County	0.296	10.1	87.0[c]
Racine County and Standard metropolitan Statistical Area	0.259	6.2	76.2
	0.278	8.2	81.6

Sources
[1]   Wisconsin Legislative Reference Bureau, 1969, pp.205–12, 218–19.
[2]   US Bureau of the Census, 1973.
[3]   Van Valey, Roof and Wilcox, 1977, Table 1, pp.833–4.

Notes
[a]   The areal units used in the calculation of these coefficients are rural townships (called towns in Wisconsin), villages, total cities in the cases of smaller cities, and individual wards within cities in the cases of larger ones; see Husbands (1972, pp.62–3) for a longer discussion of these categories.
[b]   The areal units used in the calculation of these indexes are census tracts.
[c]   This figure pertains to the city rather than to the county of Milwaukee. The Milwaukee SMSA in 1970 contained Milwaukee, Ozaukee, Waukesha, and Washington Counties.

problems with aggregate data of this sort would make one wary of imputing too much substantive significance to any individual comparison that supported the initial supposition of greater variation in the English case, but the fact that four of the five English cases have values consistent with this supposition is, if not totally conclusive, certainly suggestive. Thus, a comparison of the English and Wisconsin figures of area-by-area dispersion of whites' racist voting does suggest that the micro-level explanation based on supposed fears of in-migrating non-whites may be more relevant in the latter than in the former case. Even if it does retain some residual significance in the English urban situation, it is certainly not the only dynamic. It is equally necessary to consider the operation of city-wide factors disposing whites to racist voting.

Although what follows in the next two paragraphs may appear special pleading for a favourite hypothesis that is supported only with irritating reluctance by a set of uncertain and suspect data, it is fair to add that one may adduce particular factors which explain the status of Wolverhampton as an exception and which imply that the Wisconsin coefficients may be underestimates of what they are intended to measure. The embarrassment of the high Wolverhampton coefficient may in fact be partly an artifact of how administrative boundaries have been drawn. The old County Borough of Wolverhampton that existed at the time of the 1961 Census and then contained 150,825 inhabitants was affected by the extensive rationalization of local authorities that took place in the 1960s. According to The West Midlands Order of 1965 the new County Borough of Wolverhampton that came into being on 1 April 1966 contained substantial parts of the Bilston, Cosely, Tettenhall, Wednesfield and Willenhall authorities and so formed an administrative area that in 1961 would have had a population of 261,552. It is likely that some of the more peripheral electoral divisions of the present District (as the new county borough then became in the local government reorganization of 1974), while perhaps being away from local immigrant concentrations, are also less fully integrated into the economy of the rest of the town; if this were the case, their residents would be less affected by any competition with immigrants over the distribution of city-wide resources such as jobs. Certainly, if one omits two peripheral electoral divisions with lower Front support from the Wolverhampton calculation the quartile coefficient is reduced to 0.244.

The Wisconsin coefficients may in turn have been reduced by a particular feature of Wallace's support in these two counties of the state. In the 1968 election (unlike the 1964 and 1972 Democratic primary races), Wallace typically did not attract disproportionate, extreme right-wing support from usually strongly Republican areas; such potential Wallace supporters opted for the certainty and safety of Nixon and Agnew (Husbands, 1972, pp.248–61). However, somewhat atypically there were in 1972 in both Milwaukee and Racine Counties some usually heavily Republican peripheral precincts where Wallace collected levels of support as high as those he was attracting from inner-city whites. Whilst such suburban voters may well have been as racist in general attitude as inner-city whites (Campbell and Schuman,

1968, p.38), it is probable that the attraction of Wallace to them was based on his aggressively right-wing positions on such matters as foreign policy and law enforcement rather than on a specific racially motivated territorial defence. The existence of high Wallace support in some peripheral precincts of both counties therefore suggests at least a duality of motive within the Wallace constituency; more immediately from the present point of interest, it reduces the size of the areal unit-by-unit dispersion coefficients for each county.

Before finally leaving the discussion of the data of Table 7 one further observation can be made about the viability of a territorial-defence interpretation of NF voting. As will be recalled from the earlier discussion, the examples of greatest areal unit-by-unit dispersion in racist white voting would, under that interpretation, be expected in cities that are closer to the total-segregation situation than to the zero-segregation one. In fact, in this extreme case of zero-segregation such a dynamic is no longer theoretically feasible, but even in a less extreme, low-segregation situation there would be both theoretical and statistical reasons for expecting any white racist voting that was based on the territorial-defence dynamic to exhibit lower spatial dispersion through-out a city as a whole. Despite the admitted shortcomings of the data in Table 7 it is none the less permissible to point out that, taking the five cities as a group and on this occasion examining the covariation be-tween them on the two relevant variables, they contain no suggestion of a positive correlation between areal unit-by-unit dispersion in NF voting and the degree of white-immigrant segregation. Although one should interpret with some circumspection a relationship which is based on only five cases, it is noted with satisfaction that the product-moment correlation coefficient between these two variables is clearly negative, −0.43. If Leeds is omitted from this exercise on the perhaps reasonable ground that its rather lower percentage of New Commonwealth settle-ment makes it an exceptional case, the coefficient becomes even more robustly negative at −0.80. The low areal dispersion value of NF voting in Bradford, despite the borough's comparatively high level of segre-gation, is particularly noteworthy. The 1971 percentages of those born in New Commonwealth countries in Bradford's three borough con-stituencies were 5.4 per cent in Bradford North, only 0.6 per cent in Bradford South, and a substantial 15.2 per cent in Bradford West. Only the assertion that there has been a large increase in the immigrant proportion in Bradford South since the 1971 Census and/or that whites in all the six Bradford wards within this constituency saw themselves equally under threat of immigrant in-migration can in this context revive the relevance of the territorial-defence or 'Seventh Cavalry' hypothesis in explaining the 1977 NF performance in the city.[15]

Because of the ambiguities inherent in the data that are available for the type of hypothesis-testing being attempted in this paper, the inventive mind could doubtless offer alternative, perhaps equally consistent, causal scenarios. However, despite reservations, the cumulative impact of the various pieces of evidence presented so far has been to show that dynamics operating on a city-wide basis, while not perhaps being totally determining, are at least more appropriate in explaining white urban support for the NF than they are in understanding the superficially similar racially motivated voting for George Wallace in the American urban context. The following section attempts to extend this proposition by considering the different levels of relevance of labour-market and housing-market competition in the two situations. Specifically, it approaches this task using the two concepts of 'dual market' and 'split market' applied to the analysis of labour markets and then of housing markets.

Dual markets and split markets for labour and for housing

Despite the possible temptation to the uninitiated to use the terms 'dual market' and 'split market' as though they were synonymous, they in fact describe two very different phenomena. Dual labour market theory developed in the 1960s as part of an attempt to explain the continuing poverty of many black and Hispanic ghetto dwellers in the USA. The analysis of dual labour markets assumes a structured dichotomy between so-called 'primary' and 'secondary' markets, the features of which are summarized by Piore:

> the primary market offers jobs which possess several of the following traits: high wages, good working conditions, employment stability and job security, equity and due process in the administration of work rules, and chances for advancement. The . . . secondary market has jobs which, relative to those in the primary sector, are decidedly less attractive. They tend to involve low wages, poor working conditions, considerable variability in employment, harsh and often arbitrary discipline, and little opportunity to advance. The poor are

confined to the secondary labor market (Piore, 1971, p.91; quoted in Gordon, 1972, p.46).

The important distinguishing feature between primary and secondary markets is therefore differential emphasis on reliability and stability.

Primary markets are also distinct from secondary markets according to more general economic criteria: different characteristics of supply and demand; different consequent equilibria; but perhaps most significant from our present viewpoint, the fact that different job sectors vary in the degree to which they are to be classified as primary-market or secondary-market employment. Thus, a worker with a particular set of achieved and ascribed characteristics competes predominantly or totally in either the primary market or the secondary market. Only in atypical situations is former primary-market labour power to be found subsequently located in the secondary market. Likewise, secondary-market labour remains confined to this market.

This is a very different concept from that of a split labour market, where the significant division is held not to be between jobs in one sector and those in another, but between one and another group of workers potentially employable in the same job sector. Edna Bonacich has defined the split labour market as follows:

> To be split, a labor market must contain at least two groups of workers whose price of labor differs *for the same work* [emphasis added], or would differ if they did the same work. The concept 'price of labor' refers to labor's total cost to the employer, including not only wages, but the cost of recruitment, transportation, room and board, education, health care (if the employer must bear these), and the costs of labor unrest (1972, p.549).

Bonacich is careful to point out that not all multi-ethnic situations produce split labour markets. Where one ethnic group is predominantly entrepreneurs rather than employees or where there is parity of economic strength between two employee ethnic groups, a split labour market does not develop. However, Bonacich makes the important point that it is not merely the readiness of one ethnic group to work more cheaply than another, or rather perhaps its inability to refuse to do so, that creates a split labour market. A greater willingness by one ethnic group to work non-social hours or to work overtime whenever the employer requires it are also dynamics of a split labour market.

The concepts of dual-market and split-market can be applied to the housing market and there is a developing literature on dual housing markets, particularly in American cities, to account for the perpetuation of racial segregation and for the longer-term instability of the racial composition of apparently integrated neighbourhoods (Molotch, 1972a, pp.15—37; 1972b). The essence of the dual housing market is that two spatially separated markets exist, different in terms of their supply and demand functions and their respective equilibria. Blacks can generally operate only in the black spatial market and whites need to operate only in their own spatial market because, other things equal, the supply-demand ratio in the latter market for housing (whether for purchase or rent) of any particular given standard is greater than in the corresponding black market. In the past in the United States the spatial segregation upon which the dual market is based has been maintained by vigilantist tactics where whites have felt threatened (e.g. Spear, 1967, pp.211—13). However, more refined methods have subsequently evolved according to which estate agents and landlords perceive a dual market and collude in its maintenance, at least until a 'rogue' estate agent follows the dictate of economic advantage and lets or sells to a black consumer (Molotch, 1972a, p.24). Because of the overwhelming predominance of the dual housing market situation in American cities, racially mixed urban communities are rare and occur under only two sets of circumstances, the first involving some sort of integration but also containing strong tendencies to instability, while the second involves racial transition and has inherent dynamics of instability.

The first instance - and an extremely unusual one - exists when there is some very particular reason why whites both demand housing that is spatially and economically within the black market and are also prepared to pay 'black' prices for it. For example, whites live in the Hyde Park area around the University of Chicago, adjacent to one of the largest and most famous black ghettoes in the United States. However, such a community can be fragile and a variety of emerging new factors, ranging from race-related problems on the streets to gang problems in local schools, may make some potential white residents unwilling to move there.

The second type of racially mixed community usually exists only temporarily. As Molotch (1969) and others have argued (e.g. Wolf, 1963), the process of transition is usually ordered and sequential rather than the panic-induced flight suggested by some of the earlier writings on American racial succession processes. The integrated racial status of such a community, when a dual housing market operates in the larger city of which the community is a part, alters slowly over time until numerical predominance by the succeeding ethnic group is established and consolidated (Duncan and Duncan, 1957, p.11). It is only in such communities that the two otherwise spatially distinct housing markets have mutual contact and interact with each other. The result of this interaction is the establishment within the community concerned of what may be referred to as a 'split housing market', to continue the terminology of the earlier labour-market analysis. Just as the important characteristic distinguishing the split from the dual-labour market was the similarity of the jobs being competed for in the former, so the split housing market involves competition between two ethnic groups for the same houses within a particular changing or threatened neighbourhood of a larger city. The spatial segregation that both defined and maintained the dual market is, in this limited neighbourhood, suspended for the transition period, when a split housing market comes into being.

The central thesis of the present paper can now be stated as follows: the apparently greater spatial variation in the distribution of whites' racially motivated voting in the United States as compared with the comparable situation in England is a consequence of the greater salience in America of a space-specific competition for housing and of fears by whites located adjacent to black ghetto areas. A relatively greater role is played in an American urban economy than in many English ones by a secondary labour market within which black workers are disproportionately concentrated. Within this market blacks present little or no perceived labour competition to whites, who are more heavily based on the primary market. In the English case, however, the situation in many cities is somewhat different; true, space-specific housing-market conflicts and cultural antagonisms and fears are obviously frequently present, especially in London and other areas of high demand for available housing stock, but the character of the labour market is equally decisive in explaining National Front support in many cities, and this latter dynamic is less space-related than housing-market competition. Although immigrant labour arrived in this country as a replacement labour force for certain sectors of the economy (Foot, 1965, pp.11–15; Peach, 1968, pp.39–50), the contemporary situation of economic stringency has brought to the fore a split-market potential in Britain.

The United States and England compared

The dual labour market in the United States is a tool, usually deliberately used but sometimes accidental in its effects, that has come to protect white workers from undue competition from blacks.[16] Despite attempts in America to end discrimination in employment, many strongly exclusionist craft unions have successfully managed to maintain the relative racial homogeneity of some of the traditional preserves of white American skilled labour. Of course, this process has not been total and to the extent that inter-ethnic competition has occurred within the same labour market, a potential for white racist action such as Wallace voting is to be found. It may be no accident that the building industry, one of the formerly highly segregated trades into which American blacks most publicly and vocally sought entry in the 1960s, has a workforce that, though certainly atypical in many respects (Sexton and Sexton, 1971, pp.5–6, p.306), developed a reputation for non-economic illiberalism, both on subjects like civil rights for blacks and also on policy for the Vietnam War.

It is generally in the more space-related private housing market where the genesis of the inter-ethnic tension which predisposes to white racist voting in urban America is likely to be located. In white urban American neighbourhoods adjacent to expanding black ghettoes, the situation faced by anti-black resident whites wishing or needing to remain is inherently unstable because of the corrupting role of economic rationality upon those wishing and able to leave. Residents of some neighbourhoods facing imminent black in-migration have in certain American cities formed so-called 'block clubs' to orchestrate the sale or letting of local neighbourhood properties and so to prevent their being sold or rented to blacks. The activities in Chicago in the early 1970s of Father Lawlor, a Catholic priest whose parish was a white neighbourhood on city's South Side next to a black area, achieved considerable notoriety, if not long-term success.[17]

Despite attempts at solidarity, whites in racially threatened neighbourhoods are at a disadvantage because of the operation of the dual housing market, which may both facilitate the activities of so-called block-busters and also make it advantageous to whites who are able to move, whether or not for racially inspired motives, to sell to interested black purchasers. In the short term some whites, out of an idiosyncratic notion of loyalty to neighbours, may refuse to sell to a black purchaser, but eventually a seller will appear who is willing to sell to such a buyer.

The uncertainty that inner-city white Americans face in this situation, many of whom would find a move to comparable accommodation elsewhere in the city either difficult or impossible, predisposes them to territorially-based voting for candidates such as Wallace. The fear leading to such voting almost invariably has some material base in the housing situation, although there may additionally be a cultural hostility towards the other ethnic group.

By contrast, in analysing English racist voting, dynamics embedded in the labour-market situation are held to be more significant than in the comparable American case. New Commonwealth labour in fact fulfils an economic function that is different from that of many American blacks. While one may want to argue that parts of the British industrial structure have some aspects of the dual labour market to be found in the United States, the dichotomy between the two markets is undoubtedly less clear-cut and the overall national correlation of this distinction with English ethnic cleavages is less marked.

In fact, Doeringer and Bosanquet have concluded that: 'it would appear from the very limited evidence that coloured workers experience employment patterns resembling those in the United States', but if a dual labour market does exist, it is 'less sharply defined than in the United States' (1973, p.429). However, one proviso (which they themselves mention) even to this modest conclusion is that the typical pattern of a relatively high labour turnover of black workers in the American secondary market is, in Britain, reversed for those coloured workers in similar jobs as whites, a situation that was found to exist by the 1960s, if not in the 1950s (Wright, 1968, pp.153–8). This suggests that, at least in some industries (in this respect one thinks of Northern- and Midland-based declining industries such as textiles or foundry work), New Commonwealth labour may have become relatively entrenched against competing whites. Clearly, an argument based on entrenchment by coloured labour in certain industries would look suspicious in those places where, say, young West Indians have unemployment levels far higher than those of corresponding whites, but there is evidence from the wool industry, for example, that many employers have found immigrant labour equally acceptable and, most significant, in some cases actually preferable to available white labour (Cohen and Jenner, 1968).

The five English cities whose NF/NP support in May 1977 was analysed in Table 7 all have the status of areas whose traditional industries have been in decline almost since the end of the last war, a decline that has been accelerated by the present recession. In the post-war period, some of these cities also lost indigenous white labour to more expanding areas of the country or overseas, and this loss occurred at a rate greater than the decline of the traditional industries. Hence the need for the replacement labour force that was furnished by New Commonwealth immigration. In some instances, too, white workers will have eschewed employment in low-paying traditional industry in favour of more lucrative local opportunities. Some of the jobs into which New Commonwealth labour went could perhaps be regarded as having secondary market characteristics as the dual labour market economists would interpret it, even though this employment might also have some internal structure, such as in foundry work. Even so, and especially in the present economic recession, important sections of the white labour force, particularly the unskilled young, find themselves having to consider employment in a sector of the labour market that their white predecessors in the sellers' market of the relative affluence in the 1950s had no need to consider.

In the time since their arrival, some immigrant groups have become entrenched in these positions, making it particularly difficult for whites coming for the first time on to the local labour market to re-establish the previous dominance of their ethnic group. As McGrath (1976) shows in the case of Batley, white workers may well harbour or retain negative attitudes towards excessive overtime or shift working which could be held with economic impunity in an earlier period of affluence but which are an inappropriate luxury in present economic circum-stances. Thus, the often greater willingness of immigrant workers to work shifts or longer hours may introduce *de facto* a split market for labour. Furthermore, the former boom towns of the country that once attracted workers from regions with declining industries have been obliged to make economic retrenchments and are no longer capable of fulfilling this role. It may be significant for the type of material explanation of NF voting being advanced that unskilled and poorly educated youth were found to be most sympathetic to the NF by a recent survey (Harrop and Zimmerman, 1977).

The emphasis that has been placed upon the dynamics of labour-market processes in racially motivated voting in the British situation is not intended to preclude the role of housing-market competition. However, whereas in the case of the United States it is argued that the micro-spatial role of the housing market may be predominant, this is probably seldom going to be the position in this country where, as in

London, the labour market and the housing market are likely either to have material effects of comparable degree or where, as in various northern areas, the impact of the former may exceed that of the latter.

Karn (1969) has produced evidence from a Yorkshire town that Asian purchasers of housing do pay relatively more than white purchasers for the houses they buy, although they pay more when buying from each other rather than from white vendors. Moreover, they pay relatively more to go into areas densely occupied by their own countrymen. The first two of these factors support the presence of a split housing market model but, as Karn explicitly argues, the last piece of evidence implies the existence, at least inchoately, of a dual housing market in the area concerned. The findings of Fenton (1976) and Fenton and Collard (1977) also suggest the existence of a split housing market in Britain. However, it should be pointed out that if any English instances of dual housing markets are identified they will usually differ from the American ones in lacking the degree of inter-group residential segregation needed to support them: only if residential segregation increases in English cities to the level that one finds in typical American metropolises, would one expect territorially related racist voting to assume a greater prominence in Britain. In any case, Smith (1976, p.144) has shown that West Indian and Asian owner-occupiers are concentrated in the worst sort of housing for which there is little demand among the white population, certainly relatively less than might be expected in some American transition neighbourhoods.

However, the implications of this body of research for the spatial distribution of any racist voting are contingent. In a low-to-zero interethnic segregation situation any effects on such voting would be felt throughout the whole city if white demand were analogously distributed. This would in turn produce the same low level in the spatial distribution of whites' racist voting as would be implied by the process of city-wide competition in the labour market and it would not be possible to disentangle these two separate effects as contained within aggregate voting data. On the other hand, to the extent that high interethnic segregation is found and that whites' demand for housing also being sought by non-whites is spatially concentrated, one would obviously expect higher city-wide spatial segregation in the distribution of any voting so motivated. Few English cities have degrees of interethnic variation sufficient to permit such empirical effects to be observed. Because of this lesser segregation the localized 'transition community' of the American city covers, in the British case, a much higher proportion of a city's housing stock. Only in parts of London may there be exceptions to the implications of this statement since Peach (1975) has produced some ward-level calculations of West Indian segregation in London that approach those of some American cities.

Appendix: a note on London

In Table 7 there were presented two quartile coefficients of variation of NF/NP support in the Greater London Council (GLC) elections of 5 May 1977. One coefficient covered all ninety-two GLC constituencies/ electoral divisions, while the second covered the thirty-five in the inner London area. Both values were relatively substantial, higher in fact than the other comparable British coefficients and than those for the two Wisconsin counties presented in Table 8. These high values therefore imply both a higher degree of spatial variation in NF/NP support throughout inner London and in the metropolis as a whole and also a correspondingly micro-spatial explanation of this voting. In fact, the areal distributions of NF/NP support have a quite noticeable positive skewness and in their higher tail are located values for those areas of widely publicized NF/NP strength that are concentrated in parts of the East End. The NF won 19.2 per cent of votes cast in Bethnal Green and Bow (Borough of Tower Hamlets), its highest in the Greater London area, and Hackney South and Shoreditch with 19.0 per cent followed close behind, as did several other East End electoral divisions, albeit all usually on lower than average turnouts. It was in some of these same areas that NF strength in London was concentrated in the 1974 general elections, especially the second one (Husbands, 1975).

This pattern of support is suggestive if only because it was in precisely similar locations that Oswald Mosley's British Union of Fascists had popular strength in the 1930s, much more so than it ever had elsewhere in the country (Benewick, 1972, pp.217–34; Skidelsky, 1975, pp.327, 393–410; Volz-Lebzelter, 1977, p.94). Earlier, at the turn of this century, the strength of the anti-alien, anti-Semitic British Brothers League had also been concentrated in London's East End (Foot, 1965, p.89; Volz-Lebzelter, 1977, p.27).

This pattern and the continued ability of London's East End to produce this type of response invite speculation. One might very reasonably argue that during both the nineteenth and twentieth centuries this area has been forced to accommodate larger waves of successive different immigrant groups than elsewhere in the country and, stimulated by a similar situation, the political episodes are merely the same strongly hostile responses occurring at different historical junctures. The precise political vehicle may differ, the out-group may change from the Irish, through the Jews (Fishman, 1975, p.64) to New Commonwealth settlers, but the same response is independently occurring to similar objective conditions at different points in time. Alternatively, or in addition, one might want to argue the existence of some sort of ongoing tradition of intolerance with a long historical standing which those maturing in the locality imbibe as part of their political and general socialization. Parties like the NF would then merely be taking advantage of the presence of this culture of intolerance.

However, this latter dynamic, while plausible, does beg an obvious question about the reason for the initial establishment of such a tradition and one may additionally wonder whether it could be perpetuated merely as a local cultural value without some external agency of reinforcement. In analysing the origin of any such culture and the means of its perpetuation it is instructive to apply some of the insights in Stedman Jones's excellent *Outcast London* (1976). Jones's book discusses how the economic role of the metropolis fostered the growth of casualism in inner London and, by extension, militated against the development of a disciplined proletariat having a political consciousness expressed through working-class politics. London's East End was for a long time intractable to penetration by working-class-based political parties, and it preferred Conservative paternalism till well into the present century. Equally, its political orientations have a reputation for lability and volatility. If the economic circumstances of the metropolis failed to offer the base for a developed class consciousness in the time period covered in Jones's book, it may be reasonable to extrapolate at least some implications in his analysis to more recent times; the casualism in the history of the London docks and their final demise provide some intuitive support for the legitimacy of such an extrapolation. For reasons connected with its economic role, London may have had and may continue to have a working population that as an aggregate lacks the level of political, as opposed to economistic, consciousness which one can find elsewhere in the country in regions with a more established tradition of working-class political activity. Thus, without the protection such a consciousness affords, disproportionate parts of the East London population may be amenable to mobilization by any movement offering essentially scapegoating solutions to particular economic problems that are inherent in the nature of urban capitalist economic organization.[18]

In any case, it may also be, as has already been suggested, and as Phizacklea and Miles imply in chapter 5, that housing, and inter-ethnic competition for it, are more important in London's political economy than in northern and Midlands cities with comparable NF strength. If this is the case, housing market processes in the case of London may occupy unusual prominence in predisposing to NF voting. This possibility is consistent with the explanation of London NF support that has already been advanced for not only the East End proper but also a belt of electoral divisions emanating within a north and north-east sector away from the central area which indicate disproportionate NF support. Enfield, for example, is an area of relative NF strength. Even in the firmly middle-class areas of this belt, NF strength is higher than in areas elsewhere in London with similar social and economic profiles. During this century there has in fact been substantial migration out from the East End towards the periphery of the city. Even if still working in the old inner city, former East Enders were encouraged to move by a policy of the old Great Eastern Railway to promote rail commuting by working-class Londoners into Liverpool Street station (Pollins, 1964). In this present century many have moved out residentially along this radius taking with them their idiosyncratic political socialization that was originally nurtured by the distinctive economic circumstances of the old East End.

Notes

1 This paper is part of a research project comparing recent or contemporary right-wing political movements in four Western countries: England, the United States, the Federal Republic of Germany, and Italy. The movements being studied are respectively the National Front/National Party (NF/NP), the George Wallace movement in 1968 and 1972, the Nationaldemokratische Partei Deutschlands (NPD), and the Movimento Sociale Italiano-Destra Nazionale (MSI-DN). The present paper concentrates on the two of these four movements in whose appeal to the electorate race and/or immigration are incontrovertible issues and the distribution of whose voter support in urban contexts has a related variation.

The author would like to use this opportunity to thank the numerous reference librarians in municipal libraries and election returning officers who have kindly responded to his requests for various sorts of electoral data.

2 The introductory theoretical discussion to the analysis in this chapter assumes a voting population that is dichotomized into ethnic groupings, which are referred to merely as 'white' and 'non-white'. In the American situation to be introduced later these two groupings are respectively whites and blacks; in the British case they are indigenous whites and immigrant settlers of New Commonwealth origin.

3 The following discussion assumes the employment of the now traditional index of residential segregation, as used by Duncan and Duncan (1955) or Taeuber and Taeuber (1965). The theoretical interpretation of the index is independent of the relative proportions of the ethnic groupings within the agglomeration, although empirically in the American case higher proportions of black residents correlate positively with higher city-wide segregation indexes; see, for example, van Valey, Roof, and Wilcox (1977, Table 2, p.837).

4 Presumably both ethnic groupings would in any case have to have broadly similar aggregate demand for a change in their existing housing accommodation for any such competition to become intense.

5 An additional complication that deserves mention is the possibility of the white group's scapegoating the non-white one or falsely perceiving the latter to be a barrier to its own free access to the desired resource; however, according to the well-known dictum of W.I. Thomas one would still expect consequences similar to those of a genuine situation of white/non-white competition.

6 For the most satisfactory empirical exploration of the implications of total inter-group segregation one would require very small areal units for the calculation of figures of voting strength; also the electoral units and those from which a state of total segregation is inferred should be coterminous. As one departs in reality from 100 per cent inter-group segregation it also becomes increasingly desirable to know the proportion of non-white electors in each electoral unit whose aggregate voting propensity is calculated. As will become apparent, the available data do not meet these requirements.

7 In deference to reality it must be noted that, as Franklin Frazier's (1937) work of forty years ago showed systematically, the ecological distribution of black populations in American cities can seldom be represented as in the simple cross-section of Figure 2.

8 It might be thought that agreement with such a statement is not necessarily to be construed as any sort of racism, that both white and non-white respondents might genuinely believe this through other than racist motives. While conceding this possibility, it may none the less be said there is much supplementary evidence, albeit of a less structured kind such as reports from interviewers carrying out these interviewing assignments, that racism does underlie most cases of this type of response.

9 Such a total racially informed ideology would not normally be expected to have a material base; one might find it in at least a minority

of NF activists, although Scott (1975) argues that in many cases such activists only pick up the necessary ideological baggage after a period of appropriate socialization as members; their initial purpose in becoming activists was not ideological.

10 In fact, the relationship is not quite as obvious as these authors claim since the denominators of the respective percentages of NF sympathizers contain presumably non-NF-voting immigrants; however, when a necessary adjustment is made to omit these from the percentage calculations, the relationship does remain, though less markedly and probably within the region of sampling error.

11 Because some voters invariably cast less than N votes in an N-seat contest, even when each party has a full slate of N candidates, the number of ballot papers issued is always more, often quite appreciably so, than the number of votes cast divided by N.

12 This is the difference between the third and first quartiles of a distribution divided by the sum of those quartiles. It is a relative or dimensionless measure of dispersion whose value and consequent interpretation are independent both of the original units of measurement (even when, as here, these units are the same in all cases) and also of the central tendency of the distribution. As a quartile-derived measure it has characteristics, in terms of both advantages and disadvantages, that make it different from parametrically derived measures of dispersion; its principal virtue is that it has a definite meaning even when the parent distribution is strongly skewed or is otherwise non-normal.

13 The British National Party is a neo-Nazi organization active in parts of south and west Yorkshire. Four of its five candidates in Leeds called themselves 'British National Party White Power Candidate'.

14 This is clearly a necessary precondition for an attempt to compare areal unit-by-unit dispersion of support between the cases of the British cities and the American ones shown in Table 8; George Wallace, as a national candidate, by that fact alone ran in all locations of the country (except Washington DC). If one assumes that the NF would have done less well in those wards/electoral divisions where it did not run, the inclusion of districts or cities containing such wards would have introduced into the dispersion coefficients a degree of excessive homogeneity that might have been pleasing from the viewpoint of the hypothesis proposed in this paper but would none the less have been spurious.

15 The situation of Bradford is in fact a variable one. Between the District Council elections of 6 May 1976 and the county council ones of a year later the NF support per-candidate within the area of the old borough declined from 11.5 to 5.0 per cent. It should be said that there *was* a much more noticeable spatial variation in the results of the district elections of a year earlier, when the quartile coefficient of variation of NF and (in one ward) British National Party support percentaged on votes cast or ballot papers issued was 0.170 when calculated across the nineteen wards of the old borough.

Moreover, the 1976 value of this coefficient, when calculated upon the seven electoral divisions upon which the 1977 County Elections were fought, is a more substantial 0.327, a figure that suggests a quite significant territorial component affecting the 1976 elections that was absent or at least reduced in the circumstances of a year later. The effect of the hostile racial climate immediately preceding the 1976 District elections, sensitized by the provocative and sensational treatment in some of the national press of several immigration-related stories (see Walker, 1977, pp.196—7; Husbands, 1977b), may well have been temporarily to activate a territorial dynamic of the vote that could not be similarly roused by the Front in the slightly less overtly hostile racial climate of a year later.

16 In the case of the United States, Bonacich (1976) sees her split labour market model as a feature of an earlier era of American capitalism. Since the 1950s a split labour market has become increasingly less applicable, to be replaced by a dual market that produces continuously higher levels of black than white unemployment.

17 Nobody should doubt the depth of feeling on this matter in American cities. In 1971, after a long period of litigation, the Chicago Housing Authority was compelled by a judgment order to racially integrate its housing stock by locating future projects, built to particular specifications of size and building height, in white areas of the city (*United States District Court, Northern District of Illinois, Eastern Division, Gautreaux and Others* v *The Chicago Housing Authority, Civil Action* no. 66 c.1459). After considerable delay the authority published the location of the 275 sites in white areas where future public housing was to be built. By less than total coincidence this release occurred on 6 March 1971 during the city's mayoralty election campaign. There was a prodigious outcry from white voters in the areas concerned. Mayor Richard J. Daley, seeking his fifth term in the office, declared his opposition to the purported imposition of these sites on to these white communities and was triumphantly re-elected by a positive tidal wave of grateful white votes. Daley claimed to have his own plan for building public housing that would be carried out without the Federal funds that would have been available for the court-ordered scheme (*Chicago Sun-Times*, 10 March 1971).

18 The NF/NP strength in some of the London New Towns may be due partly to the East End origins of some of these towns' residents, who have brought with them a disposition toward a particular racist political response. However, as I have argued elsewhere (Husbands, 1977a) the expression of NF sympathy voting in New Towns is itself amenable to an economically based explanation.

Bibliography

Benewick, R. (1972), *The Fascist Movement in Britain*, Allen Lane, London.

Bonacich, E. (1972), 'A Theory of Ethnic Antagonism: The Split Labor Market', *American Sociological Review*, vol. xxxvii, pp.547–59.

Bonacich, E. (1976), 'Advanced Capitalism and Black/White Race Relations in the United States: A Split Labor Market Interpretation', *American Sociological Review*, vol. xli, pp.34–51.

Butler, D. and Kavanagh, D. (1974), *The British General Election of February, 1974*, Macmillan, London.

Butler, D. and Stokes, D. (1974), *Political Change in Britain*, Macmillan, London.

Campbell, A. and Schuman, H. (1968), 'Racial Attitudes in Fifteen American Cities' (Survey Research Centre, Institute for Social Research, University of Michigan) in *Supplemental Studies for the National Commission on Civil Disorders*, Praeger, New York.

Cohen, B.G. and Jenner, P.J. (1968), 'The Employment of Immigrants: A Case Study within the Wool Industry', *Race*, vol. x, pp.41–56.

Deutsch, M. and Collins, M.E. (1965), 'The Effect of Public Policy in Housing Projects upon Interracial Attitudes' in H. Proshansky and B. Seidenberg (eds), *Basic Studies in Social Psychology*, Holt, Rinehart & Winston, New York, pp.646–57.

Doeringer, P.B. and Bosanquet, N. (1973), 'Is There a Dual Labour Market in Great Britain?', *Economic Journal*, vol. lxxxiii, pp.421–35.

Duncan, O.D. and Duncan, B. (1955), 'Residential Distribution and Occupational Stratification', *American Journal of Sociology*, vol. lx, pp.493–503.

Duncan, O.D. and Duncan, B. (1957), *The Negro Population of Chicago: A Study of Residential Succession*, University of Chicago Press.

Fenton, M. (1976), 'Price discrimination under non-monopolistic conditions', *Applied Economics*, vol. viii, pp.135–44.

Fenton, M. and Collard, D. (1977), 'Do Coloured Tenants Pay More?: Some Evidence', *SSRC Research Unit on Ethnic Relations Working Paper*, no. 1.

Fielding, N.G. (1977), 'National Front: A Sociological Study of Organization and Ideology', Unpublished PhD thesis. University of London.

Fishman, J. (1975), *East End Jewish Radicals, 1875–1914*, Duckworth, London.

Foot, P. (1965), *Immigration and Race in British Politics*, Penguin, Harmondsworth.

Frazier, E.F. (1937), 'Negro Harlem: An Ecological Study', *American Journal of Sociology*, vol. xliii, pp.72–88.

Gordon, D.M. (1972), *Theories of Poverty and Underemployment: Orthodox, Radical and Dual Labor Market Perspectives*, Lexington Books, Lexington, Mass.

Hamilton, R.F. (1972), *Class and Politics in the United States*, Wiley, New York.

Hanna, M. (1974), 'The National Front and other right-wing organisations', *New Community*, vol. iii, pp.49—55.

Harrop, M. and Zimmerman, G. (1977), 'The Anatomy of the National Front', *Patterns of Prejudice*, vol. xi, pp.12—13. Summarized in M. Walker, 'Forecast of 25 Front MPs', *Guardian*, 5 July 1977.

Husbands, C.T. (1972), 'The Campaign Organizations and Patterns of Popular Support of George C. Wallace in Wisconsin and Indiana in 1964 and 1968'. Unpublished PhD thesis, University of Chicago.

Husbands, C.T. (1975), 'The National Front: a response to crisis?', *New Society*, 15 May, pp.403—5.

Husbands, C.T. (1977a), 'The Political Economy of Contemporary Cities and the Genesis of Right-Wing Movements: An Argument for New Approaches to the Study of Support for Right-Wing Movements, With Special Reference to the National Front/National Party'. Paper read at the Annual Conference of the British Sociological Association at the University of Sheffield, 30 March.

Husbands, C.T. (1977b), 'The National Front Becalmed?', *Wiener Library Bulletin*, vol. xxx, pp.74—9.

Jones, G.S. (1976), *Outcast London*, Penguin, Harmondsworth.

Karn, V. (1969), 'Property Values Amongst Indians and Pakistanis in a Yorkshire Town', *Race*, vol. x, pp.269—84.

Lubell, S. (1970), *The Hidden Crisis in American Politics*, Norton, New York.

McGrath, M. (1976), 'The Economic Position of Immigrants in Batley', *New Community*, vol. v, pp.239—49.

Marsh, A. (1976), 'Who Hates the Blacks?', *New Society*, 23 September, pp.649—52.

Molotch, H. (1969), 'Racial Change in a Stable Community', *American Journal of Sociology*, vol. lxxv, pp.226—38.

Molotch, H. (1972a), *Managed Integration: Dilemmas of Doing Good in the City*, University of California Press, Berkeley.

Molotch, H. (1972b), 'Why Neighborhoods Change: A Reply to Whom It May Concern', *American Journal of Sociology*, vol. lxxviii, pp.682—4.

Office of Population Censuses and Surveys (1972—3), *Census 1971, England and Wales, County Reports*, Part I, HMSO, London.

Office of Population Censuses and Surveys (1974), *Census 1971, Parliamentary Constituency Tables as at February 1974, England*, Parts I and II, Titchfield, Hants.

Office of Population Censuses and Surveys, (1975—6), *Census 1971, England and Wales, Reports of Counties as constituted on 1st April 1974*, HMSO, London.

Orbell, J.M. and Sherrill, K.S. (1969), 'Racial Attitudes and the Metropolitan Context: A Structural Analysis', *Public Opinion Quarterly*, vol. xxxiii, pp.46–54.

Peach, C. (1968), *West Indian Migration to Britain: A Social Geography*, Oxford University Press, London.

Peach, C. (1975), 'Spatial Distributions and the Assimilation of West Indian Immigrants in British Cities'. Paper read at the Thirty-fourth Congress of Applied Anthropology, Amsterdam.

Piore, M.J. (1971), 'The Dual Labor Market: Theory and Implication' in D.M. Gordon (ed.), *Problems in Political Economy: An Urban Perspective*, Heath, Lexington, Mass.

Pollins, H. (1964), 'Transport Lines and Social Divisions', in R. Glass *et al.*, *London: Aspects of Change*, MacGibbon & Kee, London, pp.29–61.

Rasmussen, J. (1973), 'The Impact of Constituency Structural Characteristics Upon Political Preferences in Britain', *Comparative Politics*, vol. vi, pp.123–45.

Rogin, M. (1969), 'Politics, Emotion, and the Wallace Vote', *British Journal of Sociology*, vol. xx, pp.27–49.

Schaefer, R.T. (1975), 'Regional Differences in Prejudice', *Regional Studies*, vol. ix, pp.1–14.

Scott, D. (1975), 'The National Front in Local Politics: Some Interpretations' in I. Crewe (ed.), *British Political Sociology Yearbook*, Vol. 2, *The Politics of Race*, Croom Helm, London, pp.214–38.

Secord, P.F. and Backman, C.W. (1964), *Social Psychology*, McGraw-Hill, New York.

Sexton, P.C. and Sexton, B. (1971), *Blue Collars and Hard-Hats: The Working Class and the Future of American Politics*, Random House, New York.

Skidelsky, R. (1975), *Oswald Mosley*, Macmillan, London.

Smith, D.J. (1976), *The Facts of Racial Disadvantage: A National Survey*, PEP, London.

Spear, A.H. (1967), *Black Chicago: The Making of a Negro Ghetto, 1890–1920*, University of Chicago Press.

Spiegel, M.R. (1961), *Theory and Problems of Statistics*, Schaum, New York.

Star, S.A. (1964), 'An Approach to the Measurement of Interracial Tension' in E.W. Burgess and D.J. Bogue (eds), *Urban Sociology*, University of Chicago Press, pp.181–207.

Studlar, D.T. (1977), 'Social context and attitudes toward coloured immigrants', *British Journal of Sociology*, vol. xxviii, pp.168–84.

Taeuber, K.E. and Taeuber, A.F. (1965), *Negroes in Cities: Residential Segregation and Neighborhood Change*, Aldine, Chicago.

US Bureau of the Census (1973), *County and City Data Book, 1972*, US Government Printing Office, Washington DC.

van Valey, T.L., Roof, W.C. and Wilcox, J.E. (1977), 'Trends in Residential Segregation: 1960–1970', *American Journal of Sociology*, vol. lxxxii, pp.826–44.

Volz-Lebzelter, G. (1977), 'Political Anti-Semitism in England, 1918–1939'. Unpublished DPhil thesis, University of Oxford.

Walker, M. (1977), *The National Front*, Fontana, London.
Wilner, D., Walkley, R. and Cook, S. (1955), *Human Relations in Interracial Housing: A Study of the Contact Hypothesis*, University of Minnesota Press, Mineapolis.
Wisconsin Legislative Reference Bureau (1969), *The Wisconsin Book, 1969*, State Office Building, Madison, Wisconsin.
Wolf, E.P. (1963), 'The Tipping-Point in Racially Changing Neighborhoods', *Journal of the American Institute of Planners*, vol. xxix, pp.217–22.
Wright, P.L. (1968), *The Coloured Worker in British Industry*, Oxford University Press, London.

CHAPTER 8

The effects of the presence of immigrants upon the local political system in Bradford, 1945-77

Michel Le Lohé

Introduction

In a chapter of this length one cannot hope to cover every aspect of the impact of immigrants upon a local political system and hence some matters are hardly discussed at all. Other points are considered in some detail in an attempt to produce a case study which is intended to illustrate a number of features which developed as a consequence of immigration. These are, first, that an additional set of issues arrived in the local political arena; second, that the major parties found themselves calculating the politics of net gain in bidding for an immigrant vote; and thirdly, that new minor parties developed in the system as a consequence of the presence of immigrants.

First the issues, often broadly and loosely described as 'race' and 'immigration'. For the purposes of this study these terms will be used in the same ways as the voters and party spokesmen use them; in other words, their definition is one of popular political parlance rather than of anthropology, sociology or law. What it all really amounts to is a debate about the attitudes to be adopted by whites to non-whites, ultimately irrespective of whether they were immigrants to the United Kingdom or were born here. The non-whites are commonly referred to as 'coloured' and that term is also adopted here.

Thus the issues for the white majority become the policies which are to be adopted towards 'them', them being the racial category identified on the basis of colour. Racial issues begin with the question of whether coloured people are to be allowed to immigrate and develop with the issues of how many and what types are to be allowed and whether they are to be encouraged to settle. There are then subsequent issues relating to discrimination, the provision of schools, houses and employment, matters relating to health and the tolerance of dress and ritual. All these issues have in common the notion of white and coloured, they are implicitly or explicitly racial and are therefore here described as racial issues. They are what is meant when the reference is to 'race' as an issue.

Second, the major parties found themselves not only developing new policies where race was an issue but also trying to do so within a matrix subjected to a host of conflicting considerations. They often began with some policy outlook developed from what could be termed their ideology, but soon found themselves adjusting this to new circumstances and at the same time balancing the advantages and disadvantages of pro-immigrant or anti-immigrant postures.

Third, minor parties of two broad kinds introduced themselves into the local system. On the one hand there was the Pakistan People's Party which appealed only to one group of immigrants and on the other hand there was the Campaign to Stop Immigration which appealed only to anti-immigrants. Subsequently party names were changed or just dropped but these two kinds of specialist appeals became a permanent feature of the local system.

These three features were, of course, all interdependent and although they are considered under separate headings, they also need to be brought together. There are other features, such as the intrusion into the local system of the politics of immigrant homelands, and the whole adds up to a system which is different. It would be wrong, however, to think of it as completely changed and things will be out of perspective if the system is not seen as continuing largely in the form of the traditional party contest.

The decision to go back to 1945 for the purpose of this paper was taken because it allows us initially to consider the impact of two different immigrant groups. There was a substantial group of immigrants from eastern and central Europe at the beginning of the period and a substantial group from southern Asia over the later years. The first group were aliens and white; the second were Commonwealth citizens but coloured. These two characteristics, and the numbers involved, are fundamental to any consideration of the impact of immigrants upon the system in Bradford.

In addition to the two groups already mentioned there were, of course, other groups, principally from Ireland, East Africa and the West Indies. Attention here is focused upon the groups locally described as the 'Polaks' and the 'Pakis'. Admittedly these are stereotypes and subsequent references to Asians are not necessarily accurate since they often refer to persons born in Europe or Africa. Place of birth may be legally important but, in this political context, it often does not matter where they were born but it does matter that they are coloured.

The 'Polaks' and 'Ukies'

There were some eastern and central European families already established in Bradford before 1945. They were relatively few in number, were mostly involved in the textile industry and were part of the élite group of employers. The groups which came to Bradford between 1946 and 1950 were much more numerous and also became involved in the textile industry but, in this instance, as employees.

Bradford textile employers willingly made the city a principal reception area for Poles and Ukrainians who immigrated under various schemes during this period. Bradford received considerably larger numbers of Polish immigrants than any other place in West Yorkshire and, with the large group of Ukrainians and Latvians who came in May 1948, the total number of east Europeans became substantial and was enumerated in the Census of 1951 as 5409. As a proportion of the population they amounted to only about 2 per cent and although there was some reaction to them amongst the indigenous citizens it was not a major issue. People complained that you could hardly hear anyone speaking English in the street any more and others complained that it was rather arrogant for millworkers to carry their sandwiches in brief cases. Some young men complained that they were taking 'our women' but, on the whole, reaction to them was minimal.

There are several reasons why their presence produced relatively little reaction and had no political impact but one might note, first, that the groups rarely spoke English and, second, they were distinguished by their 'Slav' appearance, haircuts and dress. Third, they were competing in the housing market and some of 'our lads', who had fought with 'Monty' still had no roof of their own. On the other hand it was generally believed that many of them had also fought with 'Monty' and 'you couldn't really send 'em back to Communist firing squads'. There were plenty of jobs anyway and 'You can say what you like but those Poles are hard workers'.

The group maintained their separate culture with a wide range of societies and organizations. There are today several Polish and Ukrainian clubs and there is both a Polish Catholic Church (St Czestochowa) and a 'Ukrainian Rite' Catholic Church which together claim a congregation of 4650. The children learn their parents' native languages, songs and dances and figure prominently in the Bradford Chess Club (which meets in the Latvian Club). The Ukrainian Boy Scouts are a separate organization and it was the Ukrainian Youth Folk dance team which represented Bradford in a television 'Top Town' competition.

The Poles and Ukrainians have had little impact on the local political system, first, because they were white and relatively few in number. Second, most of them remained aliens who can neither vote nor stand as candidates and their political activity therefore tended to be unrelated to Bradford politics, its focus being the politics of the Soviet Union. Hence, the Captive Nations Committee and other organizations have indulged in some anti-Soviet activity from time to time. On such occasions as the fiftieth anniversary of the Revolution or the visits of Soviet leaders there have been minor demonstrations and banners reading 'Freedom for Bielo-Russia' or 'Free the Ukraine'.

It was not until 1972 that a name associated with these immigrants appeared on a ballot paper when Z.H. Wysezcki contested University ward as a Conservative. The second occasion was in 1976 when Mrs Barszczak appeared as a candidate of the National Front. There has, however, been no distinctive involvement by this group of immigrants in the Bradford political system and their presence seemed an irrelevance to it. The same cannot be said of the Asians.

The major parties and the development of racial issues

It is important to outline the growth of the Asian community because the attitudes of the major parties and their tactical positions clearly develop in relation to this growth. Using census data and the electoral registers it becomes clear that growth really began between October 1957 and October 1958. The electoral register compiled on the latter date was the first one to show more than a thousand Asian names and this period coincides with the first occasion when race, or its euphemism immigration, appears as a political issue. It also coincides with the first occasion, 3 April 1958, when this issue appears to be discussed in the House of Commons.

Locally, at a public meeting on 11 April 1958, Mr A. Tiley, MP

(Conservative, Bradford West) told the Pakistan High Commission that, 'None of us object to coloured people coming to our land . . . . We should not be rude about them coming in such masses, we should be proud . . . the numbers must be controlled and we must stop any more coming in at the moment' (*Telegraph and Argus*, 12 April 1958). Later, in a newspaper article, Mr Tiley expressed concern that half the 4000 Pakistanis in Bradford were unemployed and he wrote to the Minister asking:

1 That no more should come to the country in general and Bradford in particular.
2 That some control should be exercised as to future numbers.
3 That some effort should be made to absorb the unemployed Pakistanis elsewhere – possibly on farms.

'Minister reassures Bradford MP on Pakistani Problem' was the heading given to a report of the Minister's reply. Mr Macleod stated that Bradford and Attercliffe were where they settled originally because the bulk of unskilled vacancies occurred in these places and that no action seemed necessary at that moment but 'Government Departments would continue to watch the situation created by the influx of Pakistanis into Bradford' (*Telegraph and Argus*, 1 May 1958).

The Labour Alderman, England, speaking as Deputy Lord Mayor, said that he hoped they would stay despite the slight recession. Alderman England (and that really was his name) praised the Polish workers and delighted the editor of the local paper who wrote a leading article on the subject. This article quoted and developed Alderman England's theme that 'Bradford's history shows that the city has always benefited from the influx of other races'. This view amounted to a belief not only that an 'influx of races' was beneficial, but also a belief that colour was irrelevant, and it was set in a context of claims that Bradford had both a tradition and the commonsense to absorb new waves of immigrants without real difficulty. For a time this became the standard liberal view and it was adopted in the pulpits and the press and by the party spokesmen. But that is almost twenty years ago and attitudes, particularly those of the parties, have undergone re-evaluation.

In the early years, there was actually competition between the Conservative and Labour parties to see which could claim the noblest posture. The Conservatives in 1960 accused their opponents of practising racial discrimination in the Transport Department. Their leader Alderman White (and that too is the real name) stated they were short of labour but the socialists say, 'So many coloured employees and no more' (*Telegraph and Argus*, 12 May 1960). The allegation was denounced by Labour spokesmen as 'a pack of lies' (*Telegraph and Argus*, 12 May 1960). Nevertheless, there was evidence which made it look as if the Transport and General Workers' Union had asked for, and been given, a statement that a quota of 23 per cent would be applied (*Telegraph and Argus*, 11 May 1960).

In 1961 Labour was again attacked, first, for publicizing a story that a coloured worker had deliberately self-inflicted an arm injury for which he received £4000 compensation which he used to establish himself as a landlord for his fellow countrymen (*Telegraph and Argus*, 2 May 1961). Second, they were attacked during the local election for attempting to 'terrorize the coloureds'. Labour distributed a pamphlet in Urdu which stated that the Conservatives wanted to send back the immigrants to the place from whence they came. Councillor Bishop for the Conservatives described this as absolute rot, and challenged his opponent 'to produce evidence of our wanting to send back home one man' (*Telegraph and Argus*, 9 May 1961).

At this stage the local Conservatives were clearly trying to win the hearts and minds of all honourable men and the immigrants. They also wanted their votes but it would be too simple and too cynical to explain the Conservative attitude solely in terms of electoral calculus. Many local Conservative leaders were devout and active churchmen who saw themselves as friends of 'our coloured brothers' and supported the policy stances of Councillor Bishop who was their spokesman on these matters and appeared to be guaranteeing the immigrants' votes.

Their votes, however, had been of little value because the Conservatives had lost that seat and there then followed a series of events which illustrated that the local parties were changing their positions. The most important of these events was the proceedings in parliament over the Commonwealth Immigrants Bill which began on 1 November 1961 and continued until the Lords' amendments were considered on 12 April 1962. Councillor Bishop found himself out of line with his party when he opposed the Commonwealth Immigrants Bill. Hugh Gaitskell also opposed it, yet many local Labour politicians did not share their leader's enthusiasm. Subsequently, in 1963, a leading Labour alderman published a letter asking his Labour MP, Mr McLeavy, to vote for the continuation of the Commonwealth Immigration Act (*Telegraph and Argus*, 18 November 1963). When the debate on its expiration took place in late November, neither

Mr McLeavy nor the other local Labour MP, Mr Craddock, voted with the Labour opposition, but abstained. Mr McLeavy, however, spoke in the debate and suggested that Labour in Bradford was developing a 'hard line' with the statement that, 'we cannot afford to be the welfare state for the whole of the Commonwealth' (*Telegraph and Argus*, 25 November 1963). The numbers of Asians in Bradford has continued to grow and local politicians were very aware that voters were talking about 'them'.

In the local elections of 1964, race was never mentioned. It scarcely received any consideration in the parliamentary election either. Electors were, however, known to be talking about immigration and associated problems, and it was clearly an issue which had salience. Yet before race could really become an issue, the different parties had to show different attitudes. At one point in Bradford the Conservatives had appeared as the pro-immigrant party but since the Commonwealth Immigrants Act there appeared to be no differences between the local parties. After October 1964, when Labour gained power nationally, but lost seats in Smethwick and Slough, the local Conservative Party began to adopt a harder line.

In the municipal elections of May 1965 race, in the guise of immigration became a major issue. The Conservatives followed their normal practice by publishing a large advertisement in the *Telegraph and Argus* which repeated the policy statement of most candidates' election addresses. Six points can be discerned, the first two being concerned with rates and capital expenditure, the third and fourth related to housing and the fifth to education. The sixth point was headed 'Immigration control is a must', and went on,

> Greater control of all immigrants is most desirable both in their own interests and the interests of the rest of the population. Failure to do this means the creation of even graver social and health problems for them, for ourselves and for our children (*Telegraph and Argus*, 11 May 1963).

Reports of speeches at Conservative meetings showed that race was developing as a significant issue. For example, the Conservative Whip voiced anxiety about developments by the Labour Council which would displace a coloured population (*Telegraph and Argus*, 11 May 1963). The Conservatives did very well in the municipal elections, gaining four seats from Labour and four from the Liberals. Many people believed that the Conservatives had learned the lesson of

Smethwick. In a municipal by-election in July, the Conservative candidate had a rehash of the policy points mentioned in May, but 'Immigration control is a must' was promoted from sixth place to first.

At this point it is appropriate to observe that there was and is no 'Local Government (Control of Immigrants) Act' and that success in the council election would not have empowered the electoral candidates to implement immigration control. Rather, it is suggested that this was, in effect, using code, in that it signalled that the Conservatives identified themselves with the concerns which electors were believed to have about the presence of Asian immigrants. This identification, if it were mutual, could have beneficial electoral effects.

Following the Conservative successes in these 1965 elections, both major local parties held discussions on party policy in relation to 'immigration'. A special private meeting of the three Labour MPs, the Labour councillors and other senior party members discussed the problem. It was decided to await the publication of the White Paper which, it was anticipated, would express firm views. When the White Paper (Cmnd. 2739) restricting vouchers was published in August 1965 it was felt, with something of a sense of relief, that the issue had been neutralized. As one senior councillor put it in private conversation, 'They've stopped talking about it in the clubs.'

Within the Conservative Party there was pressure to adopt an even harder line. Mr Tiley, the moderate Conservative MP for Bradford West, found himself disputing that he had agreed, in a party meeting, that there should be a ban on the dependants of immigrants. He was attacked in letters to the local press and was quoted as saying that there was a hard core of 'race-haters' in his party (*Telegraph and Argus*, 2 November 1965).

It seemed as though race might become a major local issue both at the general election and at the council elections in the early months of 1966. That this did not happen appears to be the result of the meeting, on 6 March 1966, with Mr Heath in London. Apparently, he told all the Conservative candidates that he did not wish the party to conduct campaigns on racialist lines, and any tendencies to put over a strong line in Bradford became restrained, with candidates adhering closely to immigration policy as expressed in the party manifesto 'Action not Words'.

In the aftermath of the general election, the local elections in May were rather quieter than normal. There were only five reports of meetings and none of these made reference to immigration. The last of

the four points in the Conservative election message, however, concerned 'race' and is worth reproducing in full:

> Without wishing to make Immigration an election issue, we say that
> this is a problem which affects the welfare of a community like
> Bradford because of the problems brought about by the large-scale
> immigration into our city. It would be wrong therefore if we did not
> make our policy known.
> 1 An immediate ban on all immigration except for special cases.
> 2 Stricter health checks under British supervision at points of
> embarkation.
> 3 Furnishing of proof as to availability of work and satisfactory
> housing.

It must be noted that the Conservatives had made all the running on
this issue. The Labour Party never introduced it and the issue was never
mentioned in any of their literature. The City Labour Party's conspiracy
of silence was deliberate. Members felt differently about immigration
and there could be rifts but, more important, members feared the
racialism which they heard in the clubs.

The silence of the Labour Party was accompanied by the silence of
the Liberal Party. Only the Communist Party, which had very few votes
to lose, risked making any firm election statement. In 1968, for
example, their election address stated, 'The Communist Party stands for
complete racial equality and fights racial discrimination in any form.'
Similarly, in 1969 the Communist address for the local election called
for action in eight spheres, the sixth being 'End all racial discrimination
in Britain' and the seventh 'End the Vietnam War'.

The Conservatives continued to refer to immigration in elections but
in 1968 'Immigration' was the seventh and last heading of their election
policy statement and it simply said, 'We will continue to press upon the
Government the need to bear a greater share of the growing cost of
coping with special problems such as educating immigrant children.'
The Conservatives were thus beginning to demote 'race' as an issue
although in 1968 they were in a rather ambivalent position. Mr Powell
was dismissed from the shadow cabinet by Mr Heath for his 'Tiber
flowing with blood' speech (*The Times*, 22 April 1968) but he had
spoken and he was still a prominent Conservative.

Labour broke their silence in Bradford in 1969 and their fourth and
final heading in the election address was 'Immigration'. Beneath the
heading it simply said, 'Moderation and tolerance towards all of

Bradford's people.' The Liberals still said nothing. The Conservatives complained that the Labour Government was not providing extra funds to pay for the additional services provided for immigrants.

By the 1970 elections the parties seemed to have forgotten that 'race' could be an issue, but it returned to prominence in 1971 when candidates of the newly formed Yorkshire Campaign to Stop Immigration contested the May elections. This group had, on average, a 14.9 per cent share of the poll but here the important matter is the influence which this had upon the major parties. The general opinion was that they, and their 'strong line', had stolen votes from the Conservatives. The Conservative group leader blamed the anti-immigrant group for the Tory losses and one newspaper made this a headline (*Yorkshire Post*, 14 May 1971). The other newspaper also stated that they just 'took votes that would have been Conservative' (*Telegraph and Argus*, 14 May 1971). Various local politicians were reported as agreeing. My own research does not suggest that this conclusion is absolutely proven, but it does substantiate the guarded assessments of Richardson and Lethbridge (*Race Today*, April 1972) and of Steed who stated that the Campaign 'probably took a few more erstwhile Tory than Labour voters' (*The Economist*, 29 May 1971).

One consequence of this was that the Conservatives changed their emphasis and made much more of the issue. At a by-election in September 1971 the Conservative candidate's election address had two headings stating the candidate's views. He first discussed employment and half of it reads as follows: 'Sweeping statements about more jobs being available if immigrants returned home serve only to divert attention from seeking realistic solutions to this problem.' The candidate's other (second) heading was 'Immigration' and it was actually longer than the first but it is worthy of reproduction as a primary source:

> The Conservative Government's legislation restricting further the entry of immigrants to this Country goes a long way in the right direction. The Conservative Party has tackled the problem with resolution and realism but I feel still stronger measures are needed and more attention needs to be paid to the problems that have already been created. Immigration is a national problem, and we must see that it is nationally understood.

Variants of this view have since been occasionally put forward by Conservative candidates but much more commonly they have been locally silent on the matter. Indeed their standard election addresses have ceased to mention the topic at all. Again they do not seem to need to talk about it in order to win and they are firmly in control of the District and unlikely ever to lose that position. Furthermore, they must be aware that what research is available indicates that the effect of the intervention by parties like the National Front appears to be advantageous to them, for they, nowadays, appear to attract more erstwhile Labour voters than Conservatives.

Race, then, has never been fully developed as an issue between the two main parties although, over the years, they both moved to less liberal positions. There were periods when it seemed as if local Conservatives might diverge from their national, almost bi-partisan, approach but moderate elements within their party prevailed. Currently, 'race' is an issue but the established parties are, more or less, on the same side and opposed to the National Front.

The major parties and Asian candidates

The presence of coloured immigrant electors suggest that coloured candidates could possibly acquire their votes, perhaps irrespective of their party labels. The parties, if they had any coloured members, would have to consider this and individuals might well see this as an opportunity for some kind of advancement. Indeed the advent of coloured candidates is likely to be associated with charges of opportunism and self-seeking careerism, whether they stand as Independents or under some party label. On the other hand charges of opportunism and self-seeking careerism are often appropriate in places where coloured men have yet to tread.

Dr Qureshi, a local general practitioner, became the first coloured candidate for a major party when he fought as Liberal candidate in Manningham. The Liberals had no previous record of activity in the area and there was no reason to expect that they would poll well but they made it a close three-cornered fight and some of their supporters, at the end of the day, were sure that they had a victorious breakthrough. At that election the Asians turned out to vote at about twice the rate of their white neighbours and the Asian vote has been a significant factor ever since that date.

The Liberals never tried again, yet if their aim had been a desire to show the way to other parties their purpose was fulfilled since, for the next election Labour put up a coloured candidate. This candidate, however, died suddenly and the Labour Party replaced him with a white man who became the last Labour candidate to win the ward until they fought again with a white man in 1976. The candidate adopted for the following year, 1971, was Manawar Hussain, a Bengali who had recently joined the party. He, however, did not get elected and his defeat was a remarkable reverse, for the swing in Manningham was 8.3 per cent to the Conservative Party whereas in the other eighteen wards it averaged 13.7 per cent to Labour. In a landslide victory, Labour held its own seats and gained 75 per cent of the Conservative seats but Manningham, which Labour had won comfortably the year before, became the second safest Conservative seat. It appeared as if Manawar Hussain had an incomparable talent for losing for this scale of disaster was far worse, for example, than that of David Pitt at the previous general election. Furthermore, he could be blamed for leaving the Conservatives in power for newspapers reported their overall majority as only two.

The Bangladesh connection was more significant than skin colour in explaining the Hussain disaster, but Labour selection committees could not be sure how much of a disadvantage colour had been. For the by-elections, caused by 'elevating' councillors to aldermen, Labour had to choose again from its panel and the selection committees appeared determined not to choose Mr Hussain or any of the other coloured candidates. This led to allegations of colour prejudice by Councillor Rhodes who wrote to Sir Harry Nicholas, General Secretary of the Labour Party, asking for an investigation (*Guardian*, 19 June 1971). The City Party Executive was able to defend itself against the charges, but it did appear that they lacked enthusiasm for coloured candidates who seemed to be certain losers.

The Labour Party was unable, however, to prevent Manningham ward from again choosing Mr Hussain as the Labour candidate for May 1972. Mr Hussain still had a solid group of supporters, mostly his own countrymen, in the Manningham Ward Party. They seemed determined and so he tried and lost again, with an even worse margin against him.

It could be suggested that, apart from spoiling contacts with Pakistanis, Mr Hussain was an embarrassment to the Labour Party on two counts. Firstly, he kept losing them their seats and, secondly, he kept making them look like racists. It was therefore a double advantage to take him out of the electoral arena and to move him on to the council by choosing him for an aldermanic vacancy. This was not a painless matter, for it would involve public criticism for breaking both a convention and an inter-party agreement, yet the Labour group chose, by ballot, Manawar Hussain for one of the vacancies in preference to a white candidate, a man who later became a leading councillor (*Telegraph and Argus*, 3 October 1972).

Aldermen, however, were to be phased out by re-organization in 1974, and thus Alderman Hussain and all the other aldermen would have to fight for new council seats in May 1973. Manawar Hussain now lived in University ward where Pakistanis were less numerous than in Manningham but there was a substantial Indian, mostly Gujerati and Sikh, community. Alderman Hussain recruited a number of his friends into the University Ward Labour Party and claimed that he was smeared by suggestions that this recruitment was designed to guarantee him a majority on the selection committee. The alleged inability of the newly recruited selectors to understand English raised questions about their ability to judge the merits of rival prospective candidates, and the adoption meeting was adjourned. There was, however, never any doubt that Mr Hussain's supporters were adequate in number and he was subsequently adopted for both the Metropolitan County Council and the Metropolitan District Council. In April 1973, he won his first election and he was also elected to the second tier a month later. Bradford County Borough Council continued to operate for the interim period and so it came about that the much rejected coloured man had achieved office with a vengeance, for he was now an alderman and a councillor twice over.

Manningham, the ward he left behind for District purposes, however, continued with a Bengali Labour Candidate, Choudhury M. Khan. Unfortunately, for Labour, he maintained the tradition of losing and it would seem that in Manningham any coloured candidate must have the support of the Pakistanis if he is to succeed. Indeed, one may conclude that coloured candidates anywhere can only succeed in circumstances where one or both of two factors are present. The first of these is that, to counteract loss of white support, a coloured candidate needs a safe seat, which normally means adoption by the Conservative or Labour parties. The second factor which may compensate for weaknesses in the first is that they can benefit from the support of a relatively undivided coloured electorate. These circumstances are not easily found, and consequently successful coloured candidates are rare and are not likely to become common until circumstances change.

The minor parties, Independents and the immigrant appeal

The first coloured candidates in Bradford were three who appeared as Independents in 1963. One of them was well organized and gained 446 votes (11.9 per cent) which demonstrated that a considerable coloured vote could be mobilized. The coloured candidate at Manningham in 1969 was the Liberal, Dr Qureshi, but in 1970 the Pakistan Peoples' Party (PPP) was formed and Mr Nawaz was nominated as their candidate. His purpose in standing, and what the policy of the PPP would be in Bradford's City Council Chamber, was something of a mystery. There was, however, an election address in English which explained its policy though it still remained difficult for people to understand. This was because it was plagiarized from the election address of the Social Credit Party which also fought in the ward, but which also had policies which few could comprehend.

Mr Nawaz gained 488 votes (11.2 per cent) and wrote to the town clerk asking him to arrange a fresh election. To the local newspaper he stated that the whole thing was a farce and insisted that he should have been counted as having 1500 votes. The only electoral irregularity proved in this election, however, was that two Pakistanis were guilty of impersonation. In 1971, Mr Nawaz had some trouble with the Pakistan Peoples' Party and did not get their endorsement at the next election. Instead he fought as an Independent but gained only 163 votes (4.1 per cent).

In 1973 a much better performance was made by Riaz Shahid who appeared to be appealing for Muslim votes. He was in dispute with the local authority which would not provide a girls-only school for his daughter who had reached puberty. There were probably other factors involved in promoting his candidacy but the most interesting feature was the result. He polled more votes than the Labour candidates and with 1033 votes came only sixty-one votes behind the third Conservative elected for the three-seat division. He actually claimed that he had won the election but that summary sheets carrying votes in his favour had been deliberately destroyed. Mr Shahid told a press conference that he was 'sure that the counting was rigged' and then said, 'I don't think the local authority wants to see a coloured Independent candidate in the council just in case he makes a nuisance' (*Telegraph and Argus*, 16 May 1973).

Riaz Shahid subsequently left the country and was not able to stand again. Other Independents have continued to appear, and two of them polled well against Manawar Hussain in the County Elections of 1977. The motives of these Independent Asian candidates are never satisfactorily explained, but it seems most probable that they relate to the acquisition of influence within the Pakistani communities. The point I wish to make here is simply that candidates of this type now appear to be a normal feature of the local political system.

The minor parties with an anti-immigrant appeal

The development of the first anti-immigrant organization in Bradford dates from June 1970 when Mr J. Merrick founded his Yorkshire Campaign to Stop Immigration (YCSI). He stated that 'Our aim is to raise some voice and we hope to have 30,000 members within two months. We would like to stop all immigration for we are not going to be accused of discrimination' (*Telegraph and Argus*, 18 June 1970). He went on to talk of repatriation and problems with immigrants in a manner which was consistent with the statements he had been making over a period of several months.

Mr Merrick had been elected to the city council as a Conservative in a landslide victory in 1968. This had been his first entry into Bradford politics and initially there appeared to be nothing that was unconventional about him. Like all other Conservatives he reproduced the standard party statement of policy including a reference to immigration. Another Conservative candidate in his personal statement reminded electors of his strong views about stricter controls on all immigrants but, in contrast, Mr Merrick simply said that he strongly believed in the sale of council houses to sitting tenants, a view which was not at all controversial for a Conservative.

When he came up for re-election he was described as 'a controversial figure on the council' (*Telegraph and Argus*, 6 May 1970) and although he was the official Conservative candidate he had resigned the Conservative Whip on the council. During the last part of his term of office he had asked questions in council about such things as expenditure on immigrant school children and the incidence of various diseases. The *Telegraph and Argus* leading article (5 May 1970) before the election stated, 'Councillor Jim Merrick's election leaflet is frankly disgraceful and the Conservative Party ought to be ashamed at allowing it to go out under their party label.'

Although Mr Merrick's electoral result was one of the better

Conservative performances he, along with several other Conservatives, lost his seat. Afterwards, as chairman of the local Conservative Party, he alleged that there had been irregularities by immigrant voters at the polling station. He did not ask that the poll should be invalidated but, 'one woman voted five times', and he wished to make sure that this sort of thing did not happen in future (*Telegraph and Argus*, 14 May 1970).

Since he had already made it clear that he considered the Conservative leadership was 'soft' on immigration and holding back the facts and, since he had already resigned the Whip, it was not entirely surprising that he should form a separate group only a matter of a month after being defeated. At the next council by-election he became a candidate, standing against an official Conservative. This action ultimately led to his breaking with that party, although he tried to retain his membership both of local Association and of two Conservative clubs, and they had to change their rules to expel him (*Telegraph and Argus*, 1 October 1970).

In this first contest Mr Merrick was described as an Independent candidate but it was quite clear what his policy was. The newspaper reported, 'He is fighting on the immigration issue as a representative of the Yorkshire Campaign to Stop Immigration and this is the first time feelings have been tested in this way' (*Telegraph and Argus*, 11 November 1970). In a letter to the newspaper he stated that he was not a member of the National Front and that the Yorkshire Campaign had no connection with the organization (*Telegraph and Argus*, 12 November 1970) but his election address made it clear that he held very similar views. That address included an attack upon the Race Relations Act of 1968 because it was 'an act intended to operate against the British people', and also regretted that, 'Leprosy, TB and other diseases alien to this country are now being accepted.'

The by-election result was a predictable Labour victory and Mr Merrick was bottom of the poll. Yet he gained 419 votes, 17 per cent of those cast, and that placed him close to the Conservative with 480 votes and the second place. Nearly coming second is a disappointment if you had hoped to come first but it was certainly not demoralizing, and the YCSI began to plan for greater things in the local elections of May 1971. It was reported (*Telegraph and Argus*, 18 March 1971) that a circular to the YCSI members expressed satisfaction with the by-election result and said that they would put, to their first full meeting, a proposal to contest every ward in the city. This meeting was reported as being attended by about 100 people and as resolving to fight all wards if necessary. This meant 'We shall give the other candidates seven days to tell us whether they are with us' and 'Any candidates who are not sympathetic with our aims should be opposed' (*Telegraph and Argus*, 1 April 1971).

This first full meeting established most of the claims and allegations which were to become standard for the YCSI. First, there was a conspiracy of silence about immigrant matters and the main parties and the press, particularly the *Telegraph and Argus*, were all involved in this suppression of the views of the majority of people. This kind of allegation about hushing things up was made in the year when Mr Merrick stated that the police were not releasing details of attacks on eight women because the attacker was an Asian. He believed that if the attacker had been white it would have been, 'blazed across the front pages of the local newspapers' (*Guardian*, 9 July 1971).

The YCSI claimed over a thousand members in Bradford but they did not fight all the seats in Bradford and were probably exaggerating their own strength. There is evidence to support this in the form of an electoral irregularity in Great Horton ward. The candidate there was the YCSI's treasurer who later explained (*Telegraph and Argus*, 3 May 1971) that, 'every candidate has to have ten signatures on his [nomination] paper and I managed to obtain six of these but the other four names were obtained by one of the helpers'. The helper involved forged three of the names because he got 'soaked through going to different houses' (*Telegraph and Argus*, 16 June 1971). He was subsequently fined £50, but one might note that the whole affair should have been quite unnecessary for, if the campaign's claims were correct, they should have had at least fifty members in the ward.

The literature and the public statements of the campaign became standardized with detailed changes as time progressed. One of these changes was that the size of the problems was escalated. In 1971 the election address mentioned infant mortality, TB and veneral disease but by 1972 leprosy and typhoid were added to that list. In 1971 the cost of special services to immigrants was over £$\frac{1}{2}$ million but by 1972 they were using the figure of over £1 million each year. In 1971 their heading 'Immigrant Births' stated that over 30 per cent of births in Bradford in 1969 were coloured and that it would approach 40 per cent in 1970, but in 1972 (when the heading was changed to 'Bradford Births') the figure had been raised to over half. The campaign's literature and their candidates' public statements varied the emphasis from time to time but they normally still covered their other principal themes.

These were, first, the numbers of immigrants and the danger of Bradford becoming an Asian colony along with the inadequacy of the three political parties to deal with this problem. There was said to be associated problems of illegal immigration, crime, drugs (Bradford was said to be the centre for Britain), depressed property values, overcrowded schools and so forth.

The YCSI did not raise any other issues but did emphasize two points, at least in the early days, about their own position. The first was that they were not racist or anti-immigrant. One might note here that Mr E. Powell was never prepared to allow himself to be described as such and nor was Mr Merrick in Bradford. Mr Merrick, in fact, gave public lectures on the Sikh religion and did so in a manner which suggested he had no bias whatsoever. Similarly another campaign candidate opened a public meeting with the statement, 'I would like to correct an impression. That is that I am anti-immigrant' (*Telegraph and Argus*, 11 May 1971).

The second of the themes was that their organization was independent. In his first letters to the newspaper Mr Merrick stated that he was not a member of the National Front and that the YCSI had no connection with it (*Telegraph and Argus*, 12 November 1970). In later letters he repeated that he was not a member and that there was no connection but added that 'no true British people need fear the National Front' (*Telegraph and Argus*, 7 May 1971). The election address for 1972 again stated that, 'in spite of allegations made by Communists and their extreme allies *we are not connected with any political movement or group*' (their emphasis). On the other hand the Campaign did distribute, about that time, a leaflet rubber-stamped by them which originated with the Racial Preservation Society. It was not until 1975 that Mr Merrick became a member of the NF and he fought elections as the candidate of the campaign until 1976.

The YCSI changed its title by substituting British for Yorkshire and then the BCSI, as an electoral organization, was succeeded by the National Front. There was, however, continuity and overlapping membership and the only difference seemed to be that the NF raised a wider spectrum of issues including economic policies and the EEC. Mr Merrick remained the dominant figure although his best electoral performance came not as an NF member, but fighting as a BCSI candidate in May 1975 in the Bradford Moor ward. He gained 1051 votes which represented 28.7 per cent of the votes cast and since the Labour and Conservative candidates were neck and neck, it looked as if he might get elected.

With immigrants occupying rooms in four-star hotels, enormous publicity over demonstrations in Bradford, the Hawley Report, growing unemployment and numerous other factors it did initially look as if J. Merrick, the National Front candidate, had his best chance in May 1976. Other National Front candidates improved their performances in Bradford but Mr Merrick actually dropped both votes and his percentage share. It therefore seems as if support for these kinds of candidates tends to fall away after an initial impact.

The National Front had a monopoly of the anti-immigrant candidates in 1976 except for one candidate from the British National Party and their performance in that year was indicative of growing strength. Consequently in 1977 they fought on a much more extensive scale. In Bradford this proved a major disaster for them and their average share of the poll fell to just over 5 per cent. Yet it should not be thought that this means the demise of the Front for it is likely to have rises and falls as did its predecessor in Bradford. The fact is that it, or some successor movement, is probably a permanent feature of the local political system.

Conclusion

This case study has outlined some of the effects of the presence of immigrants upon the political system and the situation is constantly changing. For example, it is becoming more relevant to talk of Bradfordians of Asian stock. The two principal points that I would choose to emphasize are, first, that the local political system is changed but not dramatically. The local political scene is still dominated by the Conservative and Labour parties. They are still disputing the levels of public expenditure and the opportunities for private enterprise. They are still arguing the need to maintain the stock of council houses as opposed to selling them off into private ownership. They are still attacking or defending the subsidy to Bradford Boys' Grammar School or the record of the comprehensives. Yet other issues are now added, not least racial issues. These racial issues, nowadays, tend not to be between the two main parties. They seem broadly agreed upon the policies to be adopted, a good example of which is the policy of dispersing coloured school children. If 'race' were to become the issue between the two major parties, then the system might change out of all recognition but this has not happened and they are united against those for whom it is 'the issue'.

Second, there is considerable fluidity, even volatility, in the importance of the issues, the positions of the main parties and performances of the minor parties. Mr Merrick who once, admittedly as a Conservative, was the elected councillor for Little Horton ward fought it again in 1974 and came fifth with only 122 votes, a 5.4 per cent share. Similarly the importance of some issue, which causes the major parties to appear as racists, may seem great at one point and is almost forgotten at the next. Events which have been mentioned, such as the Conservative victory at Smethwick in 1964 and Mr Powell's speech in 1968 or, other events such as the disturbances in Red Lion Square and the arrival of Ugandan Asians, appear to account, in part, for this volatility. The full explanation, however, has to take in many other factors principally, perhaps, the state of the economy, expectations about standards of living, the level of unemployment and the personal views of the party leaders. Yet it should always be remembered that, although the situation is volatile, ethnic voting and race can have overwhelmingly powerful effects upon a political system.

CHAPTER 9

Where race didn't divide:

Some reflections on slum clearance in Moss Side

Robin Ward

Racial divisions are sufficiently pervasive in British society to make political action which is racist in character a familiar phenomenon, even though the familiarity may be due to the publicity given by the media to a relatively small number of actions. Anti-racist political action is equally familiar, especially when it is designed as a response to racialist actions. Political action is also well known in situations where it is ethnic rather than racial distinctions that are at issue; in this case action is likely to be taken by members of an ethnic minority striving to legitimate practices which they value such as the wearing of the turban at work or on a motor cycle or the use of an ethnic language such as Welsh in situations where this is not the practice. In many cases, the effect of such political action is that race or ethnicity reinforces divisions between those who are so defined. But because racial and ethnic divisions are so pervasive we should not overlook the possibility that those who in more familiar contexts may be divided by action based on racial distinctions, whether political or not, may also jointly engage in political action which has no direct relation to race or ethnicity.

Because black people are relatively recent arrivals to Britain, because they maintain, and are keen to retain, their cultural distinctiveness and because they are concentrated in a narrow sector of the housing and employment market, situations in which they have, recognize and act upon political interests in common with white British are less evident. Collective action is common at work where white and black have similar economic interests and there is well-developed machinery for acting to maintain or improve a shared economic position. But action by black and white designed to secure common political interests which goes beyond the routine of the parliamentary and local government vote is not well documented. While I was engaged in fieldwork in Moss Side, Manchester, in the late 1960s, a decision by the council to slum clear the area gave rise to a series of housing movements, all characterized by a multi-racial membership and constituency and all seeking to secure interests which were not directly related to race or ethnicity, by persuading the local political authority to take particular forms of actions.[1]

It might be held that, whereas people frequently see their housing interests as placing them in competition with other individual householders to secure housing which they equally desire (see Lambert, Blackaby and Paris (1975) on how, for example, the institution of the 'queue' for entry to public housing serves this function), slum clearance would give those involved a set of common interests in which collective political activity is more likely. Silburn, writing on urban redevelopment in inner Nottingham, argues, for instance, that

> the fact that the whole area was scheduled for comprehensive redevelopment by the Corporation was in itself a 'communalising experience'; it meant that . . . everybody in the district had a common set of problems in his relations with the local council (1975, p.392).

However, his analysis goes on to stress that, despite this, the reactions of local residents were heavily influenced by divisions both between those with distinctive housing interests and also between those identified as distinctive sets of residents:

> In St Ann's, for example, there was a widespread hostility between those who had lived in the area a long time, and newcomers to the district. This hostility was particularly marked in the case of coloured people or newcomers from overseas. Again there was another level of antipathy felt by the 'respectable' working-class residents towards alleged 'problem-families', whose presence was blamed for an overall lowering of social and personal standards (1975, p.395).

Given that Moss Side, too, was equally multi-racial and had witnessed a similar slide into disrespectability as newcomers replaced old-timers who moved further out towards the suburbs, the development of multi-racial housing protest movements on a substantial scale calls for explanation. In this paper a brief summary of their career is followed by an attempt to analyse some of the implications of the events observed.

The development of housing action movements in Moss Side, Manchester

Despite its early reputation as a high status suburb for the middle class of Manchester, in the period leading up to the Second World War, when the suburban exodus of previous residents which had started before the turn of the century gathered speed, there was a conjunction of circumstances which made inevitable the development of Moss Side into a stigmatized zone of transition. There was a severe housing shortage, exacerbated by a large programme of slum clearance which began in the decaying area of workmen's cottages adjacent to Moss Side. Those who were out of work were ineligible for council tenancies, as were poor families newly arriving in Manchester. Absentee landlords and main tenants saw this as a chance to make large profits by 'farming' housing, i.e. sub-dividing them into rooms, without structural alterations, and letting off each room to a separate family. The unemployed were particularly desirable tenants because landlords were thereby guaranteed a maximum rental income from the Public Assistance Committee. The lowering of 'standards' that this form of living led to, in addition to the structure of economic interests, facilitated the growth of prostitution in the area. Those held responsible for this were the poor white subtenants and the landlords (also white) who, while exploiting their tenants, were obliging the ratepayers to subsidize their profiteering and were apparently unconcerned with the rapid decline of the area.

Thus, when West African and West Indian seamen came to Manchester in increasing numbers during the Second World War and settled in Moss Side, the process of social stigmatization was already at an advanced stage. Welsh, Irish and Polish communities in Moss Side were succeeded by West Indians (mostly from Jamaica, and forming by far the largest proportion of the black population), Africans, and a cluster of Sikhs. The exodus from Moss Side continued and as a result pressure on housing diminished throughout the period from 1945 to the late 1960s, despite the arrival of several thousand black people in the area; so by the mid-1960s single family occupation was again becoming the norm in many parts of Moss Side. However, the housing was mostly eighty to one hundred years old, and although it had been solidly built for the commercial and business élite and for the artisan class in Manchester, much of it had been occupied intensively for some decades, and in 1969 the council gave notice of their intention to clear a large part of Moss Side.

This gave rise to issues which could be construed at different levels. Individual households were clearly concerned with their personal circumstances, and meetings at which local authority staff and representatives were available tended to be used to press particularistic enquiries. However, for a long time after the original announcement of the decision to slum-clear the area, there were also basic questions which concerned large numbers of residents equally: for those who felt certain of the offer of a house, when would clearance take place, where would people be rehoused, in what kind of buildings (houses or flats) and how could they find out; and for those who were unsure whether they qualified for an offer of rehousing, how could they find out, and if they found they were ineligible, how could they press for favourable consideration?

Residents in Moss Side were not short of organizational forms to act as 'vehicles' for action designed to secure their interests during the period of slum clearance. Local clergy, and social and community workers had been active constructing an organization called the Moss Side People's Association (modelled on the Notting Hill Social Council), which was intended to provide a framework within which local residents could discuss how to arrest the decline of Moss Side and in particular how to deal with problems that arose as a result of the decision to clear the area (for a full account, see Wheale, 1974). In addition political activists took the decision to move into Moss Side as residents and become resource people enabling local residents to develop an organized response designed to secure their interests in the face of the forthcoming slum clearance. The 'Housing Action Group' (HAG) and 'Housing Unions' which were formed as a result had far-reaching consequences (see Wheale, 1974; Duncan, 1970; Hammerton, 1971). The activists imported a model of community action which suited well the situation confronting Moss Siders:

> The group sought to aid 'neighbourhood power', defined in terms of greater democratic control by the residents over the decision that most radically affected their lives. The present powerlessness suffered by people in an area like Moss Side could only be overcome by collective organization and action around major issues that

united the whole neighbourhood, and no issue was seen as more
deeply affecting the people's lives in a way common to them all
than that of clearance and redevelopment. As a result of this
approach, the common live-and-let-live of the community against
the odds was emphasised rather than the great conflicts within the
district or the dire cases of extreme poverty. In a parallel way to
'black power' the politics of 'community power' sought to build
up a common image of pride and dignity among residents through
an affirmation of the community tolerance of Moss Siders etc. and
through a united fight against the *real* enemy – those most directly
controlling the life of the neighbourhood symbolised in the Town
Hall (Duncan, 1970, p.2).

So, shortly after the news that the area was to be cleared, there were
organizations with varying political stances ready to assist Moss Siders'
fight for a fair deal, and looking for issues about which there was the
widest common concern. They were not set up as institutions of the
truce, although there appears to have been an attempt within the city
council to use the People's Association as a buffer between itself and
the Housing Action Group, which for much of the time was a subcommittee of the People's Association (see Wheale, 1974, chapter 3).
They were designed to protect interests in a situation that was clearly
recognized as one of conflict.

It is not possible here to give a full account of the development of
protest activity. It is important, however, to summarize the salient
features of this activity for our purposes, noting in particular those
aspects that bear on race relations in the area. As previously suggested,
there was a basic division between the interests of those assured of the
offer of a council tenancy, whose main concern was with how the
allocation process would work (would they be offered a house or a flat,
and what areas would they be offered), and those who were uncertain
of being made an offer (and therefore concerned with eligibility rather
than allocation policy). The Housing Action Group, the most significant of the bodies that emerged, set out in particular to represent the
interests of the first category. Above all it sought to press for local
housing to be made available to Moss Siders (from Moss Side they could
watch council homes being built across the road in Hulme, proudly
described as the largest redevelopment site in Europe) and for houses
rather than flats wherever possible. It is interesting to quote the comments of the chairman of the Housing Action Group, a steel erector

born and bred in Moss Side, on the significance of the opening meeting of the group:

'We called a meeting of the Housing Action Group – this was about rehousing problems – and there were well over five hundred people at this meeting, something like two-thirds white and a third black, which is roughly the proportion in the area and I made the point at this meeting that I felt that it was tremendously important that we made an effort to be rehoused together – that we'd got something special – we'd got a well-integrated community, and in the state of the world today it would be nice to sort of say "Look how good this is, we should preserve it"; that we should say "Rehouse us all together, white and black, not perpetuate a black ghetto, that's the last thing we want." What we want to do is to perpetuate an integrated area and I put this to the meeting of five hundred people, and nobody said that this wasn't what they wanted. I said, you know, "Is this what we are about, is this what we'd like to see?" and just about everybody said yes. And it was a nice moment, it was a very good moment.'

On occasions race became relevant to the working of the Housing Action Group. Duncan comments that 'those strongly prejudiced against the blacks' were the first to drop out and refers to a flirtation of black members of the group with a militant black power organization (1970, p.3, p.5). For most of the time, however, the Housing Action Group was non-racial in its policies while being multi-racial in its composition, and the same can be said of the People's Association and the Housing Unions too (see Wheale, 1974): they were multi-racial groups serving the non-racial interests of a multi-racial resident population.

These organizations suffered from growing pains, intermittent crises, splits and frustrations, but except in the instance cited above, these were not related to the skin colour of the members or any racial implications of the policies. The ferment of activity in Moss Side over the rehousing issue attracted several descriptive and analytical accounts of events during this period (Jackson, 1969; Duncan, 1970; Hammerton, 1971; Wheale, 1974). They are concerned, however, with interpreting events in terms of implications for housing or community action or political organization: none of them contain more than passing references to any race relations aspects of the course of events and a relatively low level of racial conflict within the area is either stated or appears to be assumed (see Duncan, 1970; Hammerton, 1971, p.7). That race was *not* seen as an issue in this period of protest activity is surely itself significant.

Second, the Housing Action Group and Housing Unions were felt by the activists to have failed, in that they gave rise to élitism, and the chance to attain a 'mature political community' was missed (Hammerton, 1971; see also Duncan, 1970); but they were far from unsuccessful in terms of their avowed aims of enabling ordinary residents in Moss Side to influence decisions about their rehousing. As well as a series of well-attended meetings being organized, 3000 signatures were obtained for a petition demanding talks with the council on the possibility of local rehousing through a form of phased redevelopment; there was a great deal of door-to-door visiting designed to get owner-occupiers to object at the public enquiry for their particular Compulsory Purchase Order (there were a hundred individual objections at the first public enquiry); a survey of the rehousing wishes of local residents was carried out; a newspaper was produced with a circulation of up to 1400 which gave a blow-by-blow account of the fight with the council, detailed alternative designs for redevelopment which would allow the residents to achieve their objectives and published a stream of current information relevant to progress over the rehousing issue; and a Housing Action Group candidate at the local elections polled 767 votes and raised the turnout by 1000 (in the second Moss Side ward the Labour candidate supported the HAG platform and doubled his majority) (see Duncan, 1970; Wheale, 1974).

The demand that the housing type that residents wanted should be made available (i.e. for the majority houses and not flats), at least influenced the planning of subsequent council developments, which in Moss Side were to consist entirely of the high-density, low-rise properties which the residents favoured. The demand that housing should be made available in the areas that residents wanted, and that they should not be arbitrarily dispersed over the city led to at least one block of new flats in the area being reserved for Moss Siders instead of being filled with anyone who happened to be available at the time and greatly enlarged the support in the Town Hall for the principles of phased development (Duncan, 1970; Wheale, 1974). After demanding two-way consultations with Town Hall departments, the group succeeded in obtaining a great deal more discussion with relevant officials. Finally, the most clear-cut success of all, the campaign of the Carter Street and Monton Street Housing Unions for equal rights to rehousing for *all* residents, including single lodgers who had previously been subject to more stringent conditions of eligibility, led to a change of council policy which resulted in over a hundred families and single people in an early clearance area getting offers of council housing instead of eviction letters and an estimate that 'over 1,000 more Moss Side families will now get rehoused as clearance continues' (*Moss Side People's Paper*, November 1970).

Whether these groups would have achieved a greater or lesser degree of success if they had adopted a less militant stance towards the Town Hall can only be a matter of speculation. The fact remains that issues of widespread relevance were identified and pursued, significant improvements were achieved in some aspects of the rehousing process, and large numbers of Moss Siders, black and white, were involved in protest activity in a variety of ways.

Before concluding this account of housing action movements and race relations in Moss Side, it is worth referring briefly to three other developments. First, in the highly cosmopolitan blocks of Hulme where many Moss Siders, especially the lodgers, were rehoused there has continued to be a tradition of organized resident activity which has brought together black and white through the recognition of common housing interests. An organizer of one such tenants' association described the situation as follows:

'Well, we formed this, you know, this tenants' association, it's black and white. If you join anything in Moss Side, you don't join it because it's a black organization – I'm not saying there isn't black organizations, and I believe in certain things that black organizations must be, you know, must exist. But there's also white organizations in Moss Side. But in lots of things we've got to join together. You know, when you're fighting the Town Hall on, you know, tenants' association, clearance, anything, you've got to fight it together. I mean it's no use saying, well, we'll keep separate; you've got to fight these things together.

I think it opens people's eyes. A lady came up to me the other day and she's from the other side of Moss Side that's not even cleared yet – and she said to me, "Can you get in touch with . . . for me?" I said, "Yes, what's it about?" "There's this couple" she said, "which definitely needs rehousing, living in shocking conditions, can you do anything about it? I know you're in this, you know Tenants' Association, and I know you did a lot of work with

the Union on Moss Side." So I said, "Yes, I'll see him about it."
Well I mean this is a great thing. That was a white woman that came
to me, not a black woman.

   You know when you're doing these things, you're working
together, you're not looking to say, well this black and white business, it's not there, it doesn't exist. When troubled times come to
Moss Side, it doesn't exist.'

The tradition of non-racial protest activity has continued since then,
fuelled by a succession of crises arising out of defects in the buildings
(e.g. Morris, 1974; *Sunday Times*, 15 December 1974; *New Society*,
5 June 1975). In May 1975 a resident's candidate came within a
few votes of being elected to the city council and it seems likely that
the common interests which residents have in fighting the Town Hall
over improvements to their housing situations will continue to provide
a spur to joint activity unrelated to race or ethnic origin.

   Second, on the fringe of the part of Moss Side that was cleared
and just outside the survey area is a large block of housing built about
the turn of the century where residents have for some years, with the
active support of a community worker, been pressing for the area to be
declared a General Improvement Area. The comments of the community worker on residential succession and race relations in this part
of Moss Side are of considerable interest.[2] The basic division among
residents in this district is between 'roughs' and 'respectables' and this
cuts across the division between white and black; there are lots of
rough whites and respectable blacks. West Indian families have been
living in the district for some time and are generally accepted. White
residents have somewhat different feelings towards the Asians, largely
in view of the cultural differences which are not nearly so significant
in the case of the West Indians. The only real worry in the sphere of
race relations, which is shared by West Indian parents as well as white
families, is the activity of young blacks. The thing that concerns most
residents, and again this is unrelated to skin colour, is the activities of
'kerb-crawlers'. Following the demolition of the lodging house area,
prostitutes moved out to the adjacent districts of housing that were left
standing and since this block was just across the road from the slum clearance, it has felt the impact of prostitution. It is not the girls that are
blamed so much as the anonymous (white) clients in cars, without
whom prostitution would not exist. The pressure to make the area an
improvement area reflects the fact that in this district houses have a

substantial life ahead of them and single-family occupation is the normal arrangement. So with very little sharing at all in the area, this is not something which is held against black residents.

Finally, one part of Moss Side, where the housing was more modern and of better quality, was excluded from the slum clearance programme. This was the area where there appeared to be the highest amount of criticism of 'coloured immigrants' in answer to subjective questions about housing in a sample survey. The University Settlement established a residents' association in two streets in this part of Moss Side shortly after the development of militant activity in the districts scheduled for clearance, and its progress is also relevant to our present concern.[3]

About 30 per cent of the housing in this block is owner-occupied, and it was some of the owners who wanted to take advantage of grants to improve their house. All the owner-occupied houses and almost all the rented properties, too, were said to be occupied by single families. A meeting was called by a community worker from the University Settlement and it was decided to form a committee, which had a secretary from St Kitts and one other West Indian member. Their strategy, in contrast to the abrasive encounters between the Housing Action group and Housing Unions and the Town Hall, was one of friendly co-operation: they were saying to the Town Hall, in effect, 'How can we help you to help us?' This evidently drew forth a most positive response from the authorities and led to steady progress in obtaining improvement grants, so that by mid-1975 only two owner-occupied houses had not been improved, and with the council deciding to create a Housing Action Area, there was a prospect of the rented houses being improved as well.

It became clear early on that white and black would benefit equally from this process. Whites saw that it was best for all the houses to be improved, and blacks could see that the whites were not getting anything special. In fact West Indian and Asian families were prominent among those who came forward early on to have their houses improved. There was some variation in the kind of improvements that were made (Asians, for example, went for showers rather than baths), but far from racial differences being a problem, 'the spirit of the people was wonderful'. There had been little movement in the area recently and more houses were being improved in adjacent blocks. It was assumed, however, that if any houses did go on the market, it would most likely be black families moving in because of the adverse publicity surrounding Moss Side in the media.

Analysis

In fact, as noted above, there is little indication in the available literature that local residents in working-class areas, whether multi-racial or
not, have been particularly successful in protest movements designed to
achieve a fair deal when faced by urban redevelopment (see Lambert
and Weir, 1975, ch. 8). Studies in Birmingham suggest that, partly
because of structural factors and partly because of strategy by the local
authority, local residents tend not to perceive that they have common
interests in such a situation (see Lambert, Blackaby and Paris, 1975;
Lambert, 1975). Thus, when common housing interests are not easily
identified, it is difficult to gauge how far racial differences are an
impediment to joint action in terms of interests that are recognized to
be common.

Again, some of the literature produced by the French Marxist school
of urban sociology associated with Castells analyses housing protest
movements in which immigrants are involved (see the literature cited in
Pickvance, 1975; see especially Olives, 1972). But here immigrants are
guest-workers, so that while this gives rise to protest movements, such
activity is not based on common housing interests of locals and immigrants, but consists of protests about immigrant housing problems by
radicals from the receiving society.

This literature does, however, provide a conceptual framework for
analysing the development of protest movements which has been
usefully summarized and developed by Pickvance (1975) and which
can structure the discussion of developments in Moss Side following
the announcement that most of the survey area was to be slum-cleared.

Pickvance summarizes this framework for analysing urban protest
movements as follows:

> It comprises the following elements, in terms of which any protest
> movement is categorised: the issues at stake (or 'stakes'), the 'social
> base' affected or concerned, the organisations present, the 'social
> force' constituted, the opponent, the demands made, the mode of
> action adopted and the effects on the urban system and political
> system resulting. These elements are then related in the form of
> hypotheses, e.g. the lower the socio-economic level of the social
> base the greater the chances of implantation of a revolutionary
> political organisation, providing it has a local base (1975, p.202).

In reviewing the comparative success of housing action movements in Moss Side it seems appropriate to pay particular attention to 1, the issues raised, 2 the organizational means, and 3 the social base in accounting for the social force that was constituted.

The issues

Despite the 'communalizing' effect of slum clearance, commentators seem agreed on the great diversity of interests among those in clearance areas. I have already quoted Silburn's (1975) stress on the diversity of interests in St Ann's, Nottingham, that were generated by the decision to redevelop the area. He describes the progress of one housing action group, the St Ann's Tenants' and Residents' Association (SATRA) which was preoccupied with the demand for improvement of houses, thereby giving itself a natural appeal to owner-occupiers. This led to more and more of its time being taken up with an increasingly narrow range of issues, while the majority of the local population, who were tenants and who were in many cases very much in favour of the proposals to clear the area, did not have their point of view clearly and forcefully expressed. In this case, then, the diversity of views did not prevent a vigorous protest movement developing, but the organizational means available were used to concentrate on a narrow range of the issues that were thrown up by the decision to clear the area.

However, in a redevelopment area in Birmingham described by Lambert (1975), as in Byker, Newcastle (see Batley, 1975), effective political action of this nature was notable for its absence, and Lambert puts great stress on the diversity of interests in the area. He summarizes the housing class situation as follows:

Although in 1971 the area *appeared* as if it was mid-way through a clearly planned redevelopment scheme and was a typical run-down working-class slum, in which there could be identified common interests and a common set of relationships to those who managed rehousing, in fact there was extraordinary diversity of owners, and tenants, some included in redevelopment, others not; some already acquired, others waiting; some with well-defined legal rights and a wide spectrum of housing opportunity, others utterly dependent upon the offer of Council accommodation. All, however, were unconsulted, unclear and uninformed, and so they were unaware of such common bases for interests and power as might exist. Hostility, suspicion among and between neighbours of different ethnic groups was most marked. Scepticism and resignation characterized attitudes to official policies, proposals and plans (1975, pp.421–2).

By way of contrast, Wallman (1975) has described a situation where the threat of slum clearance generated identical interests among residents in a single street in Waterloo, London, and led to a collective response.

In Moss Side there was certainly a wide variety of interests and associated issues to be raised as a result of the decision to clear the area. But the diversity of interests did not put residents in substantial conflict with each other. Most of them accepted that Moss Side was doomed. There were plenty of complaints about individual fit houses having to come down and about inadequate compensation being offered. Indeed this was one of the issues raised by the Housing Action Group. But it was still widely accepted that the houses had to go.

Those who knew they were entitled to a house and were concerned that the right offer should be made, and those who seemed unlikely to be made an offer at all had different interests but they were not seen as in conflict. There was potential conflict over access to a small number of highly desired local houses on a small parcel of land too small to take one of the large blocks of flats currently being built. But there was general agreement in pressing for houses, not flats, to be built for all who were affected by demolition, though it became increasingly clear that it would be those in subsequent clearance areas who would benefit.

Those affected by the drift of prostitution to the 'better end' of Moss Side following the clearance of the traditional patch also had different interests, as did those pressing for improvement grants in adjacent streets, but in neither case were their interests in conflict. Whether or not these issues were satisfactorily pursued depended on the range of organizational means available. Whereas in St Ann's SATRA concentrated on a single issue and other interests which threatened the effectiveness of their campaign were somewhat neglected, in Moss Side a range of organizational forms emerged which allowed a variety of issues to be presented and demands made.

Organizational means

Pickvance (1975) places great stress on the organizational means that are necessary for an urban protest movement to develop, basing his analysis at this point on Rex's conceptualization of the use of voluntary associations in conflict situations. However, although at least six housing movements, raising different issues and representing different sets of interests, developed in response to the declaration of Moss Side for slum clearance, they were all created largely or entirely for this purpose, rather than being existing organizations adapted for the purpose. In almost every case, although the movements were dominated by local people, they were set up and fashioned by outsiders, such as community workers and students (some of whom took up residence in the area), social workers, clergy and councillors.

Relations between organizations were not entirely free from conflict. The Housing Action Group, which had a particularly abrasive relationship with the Town Hall, started as a subcommittee of the Moss Side People's Association, an organization heavily influenced by a group of professionals who pressed for similar interests in a much more conventional way. Some of those leading the Housing Action Group saw that the problems of single lodgers, who were ineligible for rehousing, were more urgent than continuing the existing struggle for fair treatment for those already eligible for rehousing and broke away to form the Housing unions. This led to a brief period of conflict between the two groups of members and their respective organizers, a conflict which could be seen in terms of competition for organizational means to pursue their particular issues. But there was no real conflict of interests, only diversity in the issues that were being pursued and in the sets of residents involved.

Social base

Thus, given the availability of organizational means and issues of wide concern, following Pickvance, it seems reasonable to infer that whether or not a social force developed would depend on the nature of the social base. Homogeneity in the social base has been widely recognized as an important contributory factor in the development of effective community action (see Pickvance, 1975; Silburn, 1975; Dennis, 1972), but the most distinctive characteristic of Moss Side was its multi-racial composition. As Pickvance stresses, however, in assessing the social base it is necessary not only to consider the individual characteristics of those affected but the social structure:

We need to know not only, for example, the class and ethnic composition of the social base but to what extent class and ethnic divisions are reflected in the social structure – are they important criteria of differentiation in social practice or not? Are inter-class and inter-ethnic relationships, informal groupings, organisations etc. existent or not? Only when we know this can we determine to what extent a social base is likely to act in a united way, or is likely to act in a fragmented way along class or ethnic lines (1975, p.204).

Pickvance further stresses the need to analyse the value orientations of those who are affected by an issue, instancing Rex's delineation of the urban status system and ethnic identity as two forms of consciousness which may cut across and prevent the development of housing class consciousness (1975, p.204). That is, what is relevant is not the objective distribution of ethnic, socio-economic and demographic characteristics of the population in itself but the nature of the local social structure and the value orientations to which such factors give rise, which will alternatively impede or favour the development of a common protest movement, regardless of the distribution of individual characteristics.

Elsewhere, I have argued at length that the process of residential succession whereby Moss Side became the primary multi-racial district in Manchester took place in a way that resulted in racial distinctions receiving less emphasis than in some other situations that have been documented (see Ward, 1975). Certainly during the course of fieldwork local residents with a variety of political persuasions went out of their way to stress the extent to which within Moss Side a considerable degree of accommodation between different racial groups has been achieved. Consider the following comments. From an English trade unionist:

'Moss Side to me is a very integrated area – I don't think race plays an important part here. It may play an important part outside the area but you know here where we live most of us get on very well together. My daughter came in crying and said, "There's a little boy across the street's taken me bike and he won't give it me back" and my wife went to the door and said, "Which boy is it?" and she said "That one over there with the red jersey and the black hair"; and the thing was that he also had a black face but she'd never noticed this. And you know it was completely irrelevant to her that his skin was black – she just didn't notice. It would be nice if she could grow up like this, but of course outside pressures will spoil it before long.'

From a Polish woman who moved out of Moss Side to the suburbs with her family for health reasons:

'You've got Jamaicans, West Indians; they lived next door, a family of them. We were very friendly with them, we neighboured, but we didn't go in each other's houses a lot because they were busy out working at Dunlops. Their children played with my children, they came in my house. When they were sent home sick from school, the children of the West Indian family, they used to come into my house because they were at work. And we used to meet in the street, we were very friendly. Oh, very nice.'

From the daughter of an African seaman and an English mother:

'Well, we do have racial differences, it's natural to have racial differences in a normal community, but it doesn't, you know, go like Smethwick, and other places. You know, we seem to sort our own problems out in Moss Side. We argue about our kids and things like this but never get it to the extent that it's going to be big publicity.'

From a West Indian:

'Well, I never believed in integration but somehow I happened to change my mind from my experience in the past say seven or eight years, the way in clubs, the way I see young black girls and young white girls, they all drink together, they all enjoy themselves together. When I look on the road I see young white lads and young black lads, they walking together, they play together in the park.'

From an Irish woman rehoused locally:

'Well, of course, moving into the new houses, it's not like it was in the old Moss Side, though every second house is black and white now and they're very friendly with one another, going into other's houses, and if there's anything they can do for one another, shopping or anything, they'll be very friendly.'

Such views are not entirely representative. All but one of the residents quoted lived in the lodging house area of Moss Side. But they represent a substantial number of residents who lived in the area for many years and their accounts of race relations are reminiscent of earlier descriptions. As one woman put it:

'Moss Side is an economic condition, where people are pushed into sympathy. If a girl is an unmarried mother, the people in the local shop won't say "Oh, how terrible", they'll see the best and say "She's sticking to her kids" and help her. And it's the same with their racial attitude: white to black; black to yellow. Moss Side is staying together more than other types of communities because people are tolerant of each other. It's none of that Coronation Street myth – that went out with my grandmother – people leaving their doors unlocked. They mind their own business now. Yet they are thrown together.'

This multi-racial sub-culture, in which status differences as well as racial differences that are salient in more select areas were devalued, must be set aside the comments of the substantial minority, mainly in the better parts of Moss Side, who expressed criticisms of black Moss Siders. Such criticisms, however, rarely led to conflict. Hammerton, while recognizing that there was discrimination, speaks of white pride and black relief over the fact that racial conflict was 'relatively low-keyed' (1971, p.7). Duncan, an organizer of much of the local protest activity, refers to 'the community tolerance of Moss Siders' (1970, p.2; see also Wheale, 1974, p.149). Such descriptions of 'community tolerance' in Moss Side suggest that in the context of the prospect of slum clearance, there was a good deal of potential for joint political action by residents to secure their common housing interests, regardless of racial status.

Conclusion

I have described how residents in Moss Side engaged in a variety of forms of collective political action following the decision to clear the area. Such actions are the more distinctive in view of the multi-racial composition of each of the categories of residents involved. The explanation I set out was based on a model whereby the essential conditions for a social force to be constituted are compatible, clearly defined issues, organizational means and a relatively homogeneous social base.

In Moss Side, first, the prospect of slum clearance gave rise to a set of divergent interests and corresponding issues, but these were not in conflict (whereas if a large body of residents had been pressing for improvement in the areas scheduled for demolition, it is difficult to see how conflict could have been avoided or how political action could have been so effective). Second, a wide range of organizational means were made available, so that all the main issues could be effectively articulated and acted on. Third, the social base was relatively homogeneous, despite its multi-racial character. In so far as different life-styles existed in Moss Side, these tended to coincide with the different housing interests thrown up by the prospect of clearance: single persons in lodgings had particular interests, as did families who formed the established population in the areas scheduled for clearance and those in the respectable end of Moss Side on the fringe of the redevelopment area. Each of these categories of residents was multi-racial and residents regarded the housing interests they held in common as more significant than any racially defined distinctions.

Failure to develop such a social force might be due to heterogeneity in the social base, a conclusion that might easily be reached where racial or ethnic divisions were significant. However, it might equally reflect conflict over, or the lack of a clear understanding of, the issues involved, or the lack of suitable organizational means. Indeed a conjuncture of favourable circumstances in all three respects may be relatively rare. Given the degree of obsolescence of much of the housing stock in the inner city, circumstances similar to those discussed in this paper seem likely to recur, despite the current preference for improvement instead of slum clearance. Whether a longer established population of black people in inner areas scheduled for clearance will make the social base more or less homogeneous and the implications of this for the creation of an effective social force engaging in successful political action remains to be seen.

Notes

1 For a fuller analysis of residential succession and race relations in Moss Side, see Ward (1975).
2 I am indebted to Ian Robertson for the following description.
3 For the following account I am indebted to Mr H. Higgins, the organizer of the association.

Bibliography

Batley, R. (1975), 'An explanation of non-participation in planning' in C. Lambert and D. Weir (eds), *Cities in Modern Britain*, Fontana, London.

Dennis, N. (1972), *Public Participation and Planners' Blight*, Faber & Faber, London.

Duncan, C. (1970), 'Which Community, What Fight? A Critical History of Community Action in Moss Side' (duplicated), University of Manchester.

Hammerton, P. (1971), 'Towards the Political Community: a Study of Moss Side'. Unpublished BA (Econ) thesis, University of Manchester.

Jackson, B. (1969), 'One Point of View: an Account of the First Year of the Moss Side People's Association' (duplicated), University of Manchester.

Lambert, C. and Weir, D. (eds) (1975), *Cities in Modern Britain*, Fontana, London.

Lambert, J.R. (1975), 'Housing Class and Community Action in a Redevelopment Area' in C. Lambert and D. Weir (eds), *Cities in Modern Britain*, Fontana, London.

Lambert, J., Blackaby, B. and Paris, C. (1975), 'Neighbourhood Politics and Housing Opportunities' in M. Harloe (ed.), *Proceedings of the Conference on Urban Change and Conflict*, Centre for Environmental Studies, January 1975, pp.167–99.

Morris, B. (1974), 'Challenging Rubbish', *New Society*, 29 August.

Olives, J. (1972), 'La Lutte contre la Renovation Urbaine dans le Quartier de "la Cité d'Aliarte" (Paris)', *Espaces et Sociétés*, 6–7, 9–27 (English translation in C.G. Pickvance (ed.), *Urban Sociology: Critical Essays*, Methuen, 1976, pp.174–97).

Pickvance, C. (1975), 'From "Social Base" to "Social Force": some Analytic Issues in the Study of Urban Conflict', in M. Harloe (ed.), *Proceedings of the Conference on Urban Change and Conflict*, Centre for Environmental Studies, January, pp.200–18.

Silburn, R. (1975), 'The Potential and Limitations of Community Action', in C. Lambert and D. Weir (eds), *Cities in Modern Britain*, Fontana, London.

Wallman, S. (1975), 'A Street in Waterloo', *New Community*, vol. iv, no. 4.

Ward, R.H. (1975), 'Residential Succession and Race Relations in Moss Side, Manchester'. Unpublished PhD thesis, University of Manchester.

Wheale, G.A. (1974), 'Citizen Participation in the Redevelopment of Moss Side, Manchester', MEd thesis, University of Manchester.

CHAPTER 10

'It's our country'

Michael Banton

'We may fairly be sure that the English democracy will never allow coloured labourers to be imported in any large numbers into this country . . . the opposition of the working classes would be furious.' So, on the eve of the present century, wrote Gilbert Murray (1900, pp.141, 150). He was a brilliant scholar, appointed Professor of Greek at Glasgow at the age of twenty-three, whose humanitarian work led him to be regarded as one of the most eminent Liberals of his generation. Yet such labourers were allowed free entry for a significant period, and when controls were introduced and then tightened, it was scarcely because the opposition of the working classes was furious. Why was Murray wrong, and does his error point to any important features of what some writers call 'working-class racism'?

Full employment

Murray expected that opposition would be generated by a fear of competition for jobs, so it is the relative absence of such competition during the period of greatest immigration that should be noted first. If, because of economic growth, the demand for labour exceeds supply, and there is no immigration, then there must be pressure to reduce the demand by increased capital expenditure, particularly upon automating work that has been performed manually. With a high demand for labour, workers are likely to abandon dirty jobs in order to move up the scale into the kinds of employment they find preferable. In such circumstances there is pressure to change wage relativities and increase the wages paid to men willing to undertake the least attractive kinds of work. If, however, the labour shortage resulting from growth is seen as temporary, it may be thought easier to introduce immigrants during the boom period; they can take over the unattractive jobs until the boom is over, when the native workers will become interested in them once again, so it will not be necessary to attempt the politically difficult task of changing wage relativities. After the boom is over it may be possible to send the migrant workers away, but if a policy of repatriation is not implemented, the tendency is, after a while, for the immigrant workers to adopt the job preferences and consumption habits of the native workers. They move up into more attractive sectors of employment and when the next boom comes the jobs at the bottom of the scale are vacant once more, creating a demand for a new wave of immigrants. As W.R. Böhning concludes from his analysis of the process, it could continue almost indefinitely (1972, p.55).

An economic interpretation of events would therefore suggest as a broad general explanation that white workers did not furiously oppose immigration because, 1, they were content that immigrants should undertake the jobs they themselves did not want and, 2, they were unwilling to see relativities changed to counter-balance the unattractive features of these jobs (this 'unwillingness' is, of course, partly a reflection of the way in which wages are negotiated). It is also worth pausing over Gilbert Murray's use of the expression 'working classes' in the plural. Many writers refer to the 'working class' in the singular because of a belief – for which a stronger argument could be brought a hundred years ago – that ultimately the criterion of whether or not a section of the population owned the means by which it produced goods or services would create a homogeneous working class and decide its political strategy. The examination of New Commonwealth immigration shows that sections of the postulated working class have diverse interests and that in an economy like Britain's some of these divergencies are increasing.

The British economy has not attained sufficiently sustained growth since the mid-1950s to furnish a good example of the interrelations between full employment, relativities, and immigration. Moreover, there are many factors other than wage rates which influence job-seeking behaviour. Workers in areas of high unemployment are reluctant to move to the cities where jobs are more plentiful but housing is scarce and they have no friends. Consequently, immigrant workers have been drawn in as a replacement labour force in the more marginal industries where wage levels are insufficient to attract British workers (Peach, 1968), and they are spread across a range of employment. This strengthens the tendency for them to find housing in the declining inner-city zones.

Another consideration is that of ethnic specialization. Members of an immigrant group frequently find a niche in the employment structure which suits their social organization (e.g. Kosmin, 1978), and allows them to compete more effectively (perhaps because the labour force is not strongly unionized). The natives then conclude that there is a cultural explanation for the immigrant's occupational concentration when this is not the case. Few of the Jewish immigrants in Britain in the late nineteenth century had been tailors or knew much about the trade. Many of the ethnic restaurants in Britain are run by people coming from regions in their homeland which have no particular reputation for their cuisine. Specialization in industrial employment may also be encouraged by more general economic constraints. One response to full employment is automation, but the capital demands can be heavy. If an unskilled, low-wage labour force is available it may pay employers to redesign their production process so that they break down relatively skilled jobs into unskilled ones, employ more workers, and still break even. The textile industry in Bradford was apparently able to sustain itself, despite increasing international competition, by installing machinery that required shift-work since immigrants would undertake shift-work at wages unattractive to native workers (Cohen and Jenner, 1968). Whether a long-term strategy for industrial regeneration should favour the use of capital to support a textile industry in Britain is open to question.

The full employment of the 1950s and the inclination among Asians towards ethnic job specialization reduced the disposition of native workers to see immigrants as competitors, but in the longer term worries on this score were bound to find expression. The 'industrial reserve army' which Marx, observing nineteenth-century population growth had predicted as a feature of the British labour market, became more of a reality, but this reserve army was mustering in the New Commonwealth rather than in Britain itself. Workers and employers alike are tempted to respond to competition by raising barriers and trying to restrict the arena within which competition is permitted. As one Josiah Tucker remarked as long ago as the eighteenth century, 'all men would be monopolists if they could'. Trade unions are particularly anxious to become monopolistic organizations, for they believe that they can represent their members' interests effectively only if all, or nearly all, the people in a particular occupation join the union and act in concert. Indeed, unions can be effective only if they can exert psychological or material pressure upon people to join. Once there is a fair degree of unionization it is unlikely to be in the interest of the individual non-member to join. He can rely upon the union to negotiate wage increases from which he will benefit whether he is a member or not. The chances of the union getting a better increase if it has one extra member are small, and so the likely additional benefit to the man thinking of joining will be less than what he has to pay in dues if he joins (Olson, 1965). If a trade union, or an association of trade unions, is to serve the interests of its members, it should therefore seek to prevent competitors entering the market; if this fails, it should insist upon immigrant workers joining unions so that their competition is limited by trade union solidarity and organization.

Divisions in industrial societies

Many of the conflicts between groups in industrial societies are alleviated by the social and geographical distance between them. People tend to compare themselves primarily with their close associates and to have relatively little understanding of the lives and problems of fellow citizens who live in other social compartments. When conflicts do break out they are likely to be the more fierce because of the lack of common understanding, but in between such occasions people can ignore overall disparities and follow their weekly routines which bring them into contact with only a limited range of their fellows. Many white citizens spend most of their time in the company of other whites of similar social class and meet whites of another class, or immigrants, only in relatively formal relationships at work or in shops. Many Asians resident in Britain also live enclosed in their own communities. As a result it is not altogether facetious to say that the most striking thing about racial relations in a country like this is how few of them there are.

Political activity is the major mode by which life in the various social compartments is interrelated. In politics people are forced to recognize the demands of those socially distant and come to compromises about the division of resources. The great strength of the Conservative Party is in the south of England, yet if it is to obtain a majority in the House of Commons the party has to advance a programme that will enable it to win seats in the north, in Wales, and in Scotland. It must seek to obtain the maximum number of votes from an electorate which includes both whites who see black and Asian immigrants as competitors and those immigrants themselves. In this way the political system is apt to domesticate any passions associated with divisions such as that of race and to place minority relations on a level with all the other issues that appeal to voters. Yet such a view leaves some important questions unanswered. Why was it the Smithfield market porters and the London dockers who marched to Westminster in noisy support of Enoch Powell's views about the dangers of coloured immigration? These men experienced no direct competition from immigrants, indeed they had probably never met any. Why is it that 'racial preservation' societies and the like seem to flourish in areas where there are no immigrants? It may be that the dockers, the ladies in the stockbroker belt, and the whites who feel left behind in some inner-city neighbourhoods, express attitudes which show some superficial resemblance, and yet these very phenomena themselves may be different in important ways and call for separate explanations.

Gilbert Murray's statement could be read as implying that since the introduction of 'coloured labourers' (to continue with his terminology) would conflict with the interests of the working classes, it would suit the interests of the ruling classes and that therefore hostility towards coloured people would be associated with 'left-wing' political views and sympathy towards them with 'right-wing' views. Quite to the contrary, there is a well-known argument that since coloured immigrants are not merely workers but a particularly exploited section of the working class (both in colonial and post-colonial territories and in the metropolis) it is both morally right and politically expedient that the native workers hold out the hand of friendship, and that all workers unite against the bourgeoisie. When these expectations are checked against the evidence, however, neither argument is borne out. It becomes apparent not just that many other factors enter into the formation of political attitudes but that there are unsatisfactory aspects of the tendency to locate all social and political attitudes on a scale that stretches between 'left' and 'right'.

This tendency is stronger in Britain than in some other countries, such as the United States, perhaps because the nature of the British two-party system encourages it. Britain achieved formal national unity earlier than most countries, partly because of its island character, while the circumstances of its economic growth also stimulated sharper class antagonisms than in more heterogeneous societies. It is therefore not surprising that attitudes towards a great many political issues, like public ownership of industries, can be placed on a uni-dimensional scale of Radicalism-Conservatism. But attitudes towards some other kinds of issue, like capital punishment, censorship, and legislation about sexual relationships, do not fit on such a scale. These attitudes fall on a different dimension and reflect other aspects of the lives and personalities of the people expressing them. Attitudes about race and immigration have, in this respect, rather more in common with attitudes about punishment, censorship, and sexual relations, than with attitudes about the nationalization of industries.

Over twenty years ago H.J. Eysenck undertook research into what he called primary social attitudes, and concluded that there were two major dimensions which he called Radical-Conservative and Tough Minded-Tender Minded. In these terms (and there was some evidence from Eysenck's own study (1951, p.199) to support this) attitudes related to 'race' (such as a belief in white superiority) lie closer to the Tough Minded-Tender Minded dimension. Since then Eysenck's research on this topic has been subjected to devastating methodological criticism (cf. *Psychological Bulletin*, 1956, vol. 53) and subsequent research has revealed a more complex picture, but the criticisms do not invalidate the claim that there is more than one dimension to political attitudes. Opinions about immigration are weakly associated with the sort of items that Eysenck would have counted as Tough Minded (Butler and Stokes, 1974, p.320). As has often been observed, authoritarians of the extreme left and extreme right have some important characteristics in common. It would be justified to fit political activity to a Procrustean bed of 'left' and 'right' only if the central problem of politics were that of the ownership of the means of production. This would then leave no means of dealing with the upsurge in the politics of nationalism and the problem of explaining why some nationalisms seem more 'left' or more 'right' than others. It would leave no avenue for exploring new political tendencies like the women's movement or the reaction against bureaucratic control.

The majority's complaints

Opposition to competitors is likely to be stronger when members of the competing group can be clearly identified, but there are factors other than perceived competition which enter into the generation of hostility, as Michel Le Lohé's chapter on Bradford has illustrated. As he pointed out at the conference on 'Racism and Political Action in Britain', competition from the natives of Sunderland caused resentment in 1937, yet, as he shows in his essay, the 'Polacks' and 'Ukies' after the Second World War apparently attracted little hostility. No doubt the availability of employment had a lot to do with this. The distinctiveness of the east Europeans' language and appearance did not seem to matter, and this invites a comparison with the small Chinese minorities for they have rarely evoked antagonism. Why then should there have been resentment of the Pakistanis whose way of living is no more challenging than that of the Chinese? Was it, as appears to be the case, that only when they were perceived as a relatively large, distinct, and increasing minority, could their presence become an issue? There seem to have been about 6000 east Europeans in Bradford in 1951 compared with possibly 4000 Pakistanis in 1958. Reading Le Lohé's chapter 8, as when reading other accounts of white attitudes at this time, it is difficult to determine quite what members of the majority were complaining about. They were anxious, to start with, lest there were more immigrants than there were jobs for them, and only after the enactment of the 1962 immigration law was there mention of immigrants being a charge on the welfare services and of their introducing health problems. The first of these was without factual justification, while the general atmosphere of 'concern' seems to have derived from a vague unease rather than any direct experience or pattern of personal conflict. Controls were not introduced in response to organized working-class opposition to immigration, but in anticipation of such opposition, spurred by a half-conscious recognition that an escalating conflict identified with racial differences could upset traditional patterns of support for the two major parties.

It would surely be reasonable to expect a much sharper list of complaints from whites in Willesden since this is a locality of relatively dense West Indian settlement and by 1976 relations between members of the majority and the minorities must have become closer. Yet one of the striking features of chapter 5 by Annie Phizacklea and Robert Miles is that so much of the hostility they report is very diffuse. It is not easy to guess precisely what are the complaints of the people who believe that there are 'too many blacks' or what lies behind the responses of whites who considered that blacks were 'a local problem in themselves' as if their very presence was objectionable irrespective of their behaviour. The authors remark that those people who formed part of their residential sample were in conflict over scarce resources in the field of housing. The authors are inclined to emphasize the rational process by which inter-group competition contributes to hostility and denote little attention to the irrational processes.

The psychological features are given more attention in chapter 2 by Neill Nugent and Roger King who stress the process of scapegoating whereby aggression is directed not towards the person or institution which is responsible for a person's discontents, but instead is displaced onto a scapegoat. Ethnic minorities can thus be made to bear a burden of complaints about matters which have nothing to do with them. This constitutes an explanation for hostility towards coloured immigrants and their descendants voiced by people who live in neighbourhoods where no immigrants have settled and by people who have no contact with those about whom they complain. It also constitutes an explanation for the vague and generalized antagonism voiced by white residents of an area like Willesden. At the same time it must be acknowledged that it is easy to present such a theory so that it seems plausible, and very much more difficult to test it. It can surely be agreed that scapegoating is important to the social psychology of movements such as those discussed by Nugent and King, while believing that scapegoating does not itself furnish a sufficient explanation.

In the Freudian theory, aggression is either direct, being expressed towards the agent of a person's frustration, or it is displaced, in which case there need be no connection between the scapegoat and the agent responsible for the frustration. Since socialization is itself a cause of frustration, it builds up a fund of free-floating aggression and some of this is likely to be displaced and to accompany any release of direct aggression. This formulation, however, has nothing to say about an intermediate possibility which should be of primary concern to sociologists, namely that hostility can be systematically related to the pursuit of goals with which inter-group differences are only incidentally connected. John Rex (1968) provided an excellent example of this when he analysed English housing patterns as being influenced, *inter alia*, by general aspiration to the 'suburban ideal' of 'relatively detached family life'. Because whites pursue this ideal in a particular kind of housing market so, he says, a certain spatial distribution of majority and minority groups results without anyone's having intended such an outcome.

This approach can, with advantage, be generalized further. It would probably be agreed that the preference for, say, a semi-detached sub-urban house, is strongest among couples with children of school age. Unmarried young adults may prefer to be closer to the bright lights, while retired people may be attracted by the prospect of a little cottage in rural Devon. In similar fashion, preferences may vary with person-alities and social characteristics. There is a familiar sociological contrast between the person who has a cosmopolitan orientation and the one with a local orientation. Members of minorities may prefer a socially heterogeneous neighbourhood where they feel less different from the majority, and perhaps have a greater feeling of personal security. Members of majorities may, other things being equal, prefer a homo-geneous neighbourhood. If the proportion of minority members rises beyond a certain threshold figure then the attractiveness of a neigh-bourhood to majority members may decline; some of the whites already resident there may leave and the character of the neighbour-hood will then change more rapidly. In the parlance of the United States, once the 'tipping point' is passed, the result is 'white flight'. In the parlance of economic analysis, a homogeneous neighbourhood composition may in the eyes of majority members be a 'public good' and, like the availability of recreational facilities or ready access to transport services, it may be counted as an amenity.

Formulated in this way, it is possible to make better sense of much that has been written about the relevance of territory to inter-group relations (a topic which Christopher Husbands has discussed in chapter 7 from a more specialized standpoint). Because of the popularity of some recent works by students of animal behaviour, any reference to a sense of territory is apt to be interpreted as assuming some instinct, drive or inherited disposition. The possibility of such a disposition is not assumed here. The argument is that, in a society recognizing private property rights, just as a man may buy a field and then consider it his territory, so a person who is born in a locality may believe that he has rights there more extensive than those of people who were not so born, and much more extensive than of those who, as is obvious from their appearance, are quite unlikely to have been born within 500 miles of the locality. Ideas of rights to territory are culturally formed and trans-mitted. They can contribute to the feelings of being 'at home' or being an outsider in which is supposed to be one's 'own' country, and they surely contribute to the feelings reported from Willesden that the government 'ought to think about their own people first'. One reason why it is important to see such statements as reflecting individual conceptions of native rights is that English people differ among themselves in the extent to which they make such claims or identify themselves territorially. Where, for one reason or another, there is a high proportion of people with a local as opposed to a cosmopolitan orientation, these feelings are likely to be general. References to territorial claims do not have to posit some special kind of instinct.

This way of conceptualizing certain aspects of inter-group relations resembles the argument of H. Hoetink that the attitudes towards one another of group members in segmented societies are determined by a number of 'milieu factors' including family, school, social class, and one which he calls the 'somatic norm image' (1967, pp.120–6). This expresses the group's socially determined standards of physical beauty and aesthetic acceptability. Hoetink's theory is easily misunderstood since he writes (in translation) 'each "race" has, in theory, its own somatic norm image, and considers its members aesthetically superior to others' as if he were implying that races are distinct social units with particular attributes. This is not his intention and his argument can, I suggest, be better understood as stating that in racially divided societies people will identify with certain groups; this will influence their preferences for associating with some people rather than others, or for being socially identified with some rather than others. (In the language of neo-classical economics, this is a question of the 'tastes' of people buying goods and services.) Their social position will influence the value people place upon complexion and other attributes of appearance among those with whom they interact. As Hoetink says, he measures aesthetic appreciation with reference to a norm while recognizing that no individual ever completely embodies the group's ideal. He might have added that many individuals will also differ in their evaluation of others' appearance, so that the norm must ultimately be a statistical average.

If Hoetink's reasoning is accepted, it can be said that the white residents of Willesden will to some extent share an image of what they wish their neighbours to look like, and to the extent that the neighbours fall short, these residents suffer a loss in amenity. Their feelings in this respect may not win much sympathy from many commentators, for sociological research workers are often young people who prefer neighbourhood heterogeneity and are critical of the social patterns associated with many forms of residential homogeneity. Other sections of the population often see things differently. Proposals to establish prisons, homes for delinquent youths, or hostels for socially inadequate people, can evoke the fiercest opposition from local residents. The big hospitals for mentally subnormal people were built outside the cities because respectable citizens wanted to put at a distance those of their kith and kin who could be a social embarrassment. These sentiments may be regrettable, but little is achieved by simply condemning them. Many people identify themselves with their neighbourhoods and care intensely about changes, even trivial changes, if these run counter to their ideas of propriety. Since people feel like this about these aspects of their environment it is only to be expected that, given the association between a dark complexion and lower social status, an increase in the proportion of dark neighbours is likely to be seen as in itself a loss of amenity.

But it is also important to emphasize that evaluations of neighbourhood homogeneity with respect to skin colour, social status, and other factors, are not constant, and can alter quite quickly in either direction as a result of new experiences or new perceptions. If a neighbourhood changes, some may find that they like a greater degree of heterogeneity more than they expected. Others may dislike it the more intensely. People left behind in a neighbourhood of white flight may come increasingly to feel that their social status must be low; they may so hate heterogeneity that they make martyrs of themselves. This suggests that perceived loss of amenity is from one standpoint a self-inflicted wound. In some circumstances juvenile rowdiness is to be expected and if a lot of the juvenile residents are blacks, the rowdies will be black. If the whites perceive them as blacks rather than as rowdies, they may in this way increase their own feelings of deprivation. In the evaluation of neighbourhood heterogeneity there is therefore an indeterminate element: political opportunists can make the residents feel more sorry for themselves than they otherwise would be or, by a different kind of leadership, residents can be introduced to aspects of their new circumstances from which they might be able to find new sources of satisfaction. Robin Ward's description of relations in Moss Side in chapter 9, and his research into subsequent rehousing, show that some white Mancunians are not bothered about the complexions of their neighbours and others like a measure of variety.

Nationalism

If people with different social characteristics vary in the valuation they place upon neighbourhood homogeneity, then it is likely that those with a local orientation, accustomed to living in a community of people who are similar in terms of social class as well as ethnicity, will be the most inclined to feel that heterogeneity implies a loss of amenity. The Smithfield market porters and London dockers have the reputation of being such communities; they may well value their solidarity more than do most occupational groups, and their inclination to celebrate that solidarity may cause them to disparage stranger communities almost as an accidental consequence. This by itself, however, does not explain their willingness to align themselves with a politician whom they should presumably have identified as a class enemy. To explain this it is necessary to consider the possibility that nationalism may serve as an axis of alignment which in certain circumstances is more compelling than the dimension of Radicalism-Conservatism.

An important characteristic of nationalism is that people identify themselves both with others of the same nationality in the present time and with others in previous generations. These historical identifications can be too easily taken for granted. For example, in a recent newspaper article (*Observer*, 11 September 1977) about the National Front in East London, one right-wing activist is quoted on the subject of immigrants as saying 'Edward the Confessor slung 'em out didn't he?'. From most points of view the speaker must have much more in common with a contemporary Asian worker in the East End than with an eleventh-century Anglo-Saxon monarch of Norman upbringing. How is it that the speaker comes to see the matter otherwise? A proper answer to the question would require a historical analysis beyond my competence, but it could well begin with the claim that the English political struc-ture in the nineteenth century incorporated the working class and persuaded its members that what Englishmen held in common was, at least in certain circumstances, more important than class divisions (cf. Nairn 1977, pp.37—44). That century saw in England not only the creation of the world's first working class, but a great expansion of population and a portentous expansion of literacy. Some of the best selling novels were the historical romances like Scott's *Ivanhoe*, Lytton's *Harold*, and Kingsley's *Westward Ho!* which conjured their readers into identifying themselves with Robin Hood and Anglo-Saxons suffering under the Norman yoke, and with the Elizabethans repulsing the Spanish Armada. They supplied the basis for a historical identification which, coupled with the growth of the empire, led to the enthusiastic working-class participation in the exaggerated celebration of such an intrinsically unimportant event as the relief of Mafeking.

This points to an important difference between Britain and the United States, for in the latter it is not practicable for the established workers to try to justify the exclusion of immigrant competitors by saying 'It's our country.' If the United States belongs to any ethnic group it is to the Indians, and the established workers are simply immigrants who have been there a few generations longer than the most recent newcomers. It can be dangerous to use labels like 'racism' and 'nationalism' if readers may take them to identify forces that impel people to behave in particular ways. It is less misleading to say that it is easier for a group to monopolize a resource when it can mark off, categorize and exclude a class of competitors by appealing to the claim that 'It's our country' as a justification.

Annie Phizacklea and Robert Miles (chapter 5) also refer to 'the prevalence of the view that blacks are protected by the law and thereby occupy a privileged position in British society'. This also is an observation that many readers will have difficulty accepting; they will say that the law only tries to limit a tendency whereby blacks are treated less favourably than others. But a substantial section of the population, and not only in the working class, do not perceive things this way. In effect they claim that once basic human rights to personal security, fair treatment, and the opportunity to earn enough to avoid starvation, have been met, other principles of social living can be settled according to the customs of the group that happens to own the country. If strangers want to work in England they must observe English laws, speak the English language and respect, if not follow, English customs. The claims they make can be compared with those made by the Malays who wish to entrench their rights in the face of competition from Chinese immigrants in Malaysia, or by the Fijians who want to protect themselves against Indian competitors. Through its membership of the European Community the British government has accepted certain obligations to provide education in their mother tongue for the children of immigrant workers and this is likely to be seen as further evidence for the view that immigrants are given special privileges.

An appeal to inherent territorial right is a way of legitimating the claims of the native group in respect of the newcomers. It is also a way of invoking a past in which relative status was more secure. The last twenty years have seen a movement by powerful and articulate groups in British society (especially by those who produce for the mass media) to legitimate a series of social identities previously considered deviant. Homosexual behaviour is presented as normal. Criminals are presented as people to be understood rather than condemned. Expectations of sexual propriety and marital stability have been weakened. Not only are coloured people now a familiar sight, but the Englishman is told that they have a right to cultivate a separate ethnic identity on English soil. These changes are all closer to the Tough Minded-Tender Minded dimension; their emotional significance is an embarrassment to the major political parties, and it is not easy to find a vehicle for expressing them in a political system oriented to the Radicalism-Conservatism axis.

It is consistent with such a perspective that much of the resentment expressed by the men and women interviewed in Willesden is not directed against the immigrants themselves. To account for this it may be helpful to return to the image of industrial society as divided into a number of partially separate compartments, and of politics as one of the chief ways in which life in these compartments is interrelated. The opposition to New Commonwealth immigration was not furious because the newcomers were making a valued contribution in carrying out the work the natives disliked. The benefits of their contribution accrued to the whole economy and population, but the greatest loss of amenity resulting from their presence had to be borne by the small section of the population that was left behind in the inner city as the labour aristocracy moved out. The greatest political tensions associated with racial difference arise at points like these where the political system is least effective in arranging brokerage between sections of the population, between whites as well as between whites and blacks. As Phizacklea and Miles remark (chapter 5), in Willesden blacks can be *seen* to live in houses in which white workers once lived and could live again, and to occupy jobs which white workers once held and could hold again. They were told forcefully that any white person who lived in the neighbourhood was bound to see things differently from a visitor. It seems as if a significant number of the people they interviewed felt that they had been let down by their own government and by people of their own kind. The result is that Britain now has on its hands what the *Observer* (31 August 1977) has called 'a severe problem of two-way racial grievance'. The minority have a grievance about discrimination; the majority find their living conditions have substantially deteriorated.

The position in the overall structure of an inner-city zone like Willesden is different from that of Moss Side in Manchester as described by Robin Ward (chapter 9). The residents of Moss Side with energetic, responsibly led, multi-racial residents' associations, were able to bring pressure onto the municipal government more effectively than were the residents of Willesden, and it seems as if the Manchester City Council was more able to respond to the demands of the residents, so that the clearance of the area did not lead to a sharper drawing of racial boundaries. In Willesden, the reference groups of the white and black residents cannot be adjusted as part of a bargaining process in which each party recognizes shared goals as well as competing ones, and in which each side makes concessions in order to achieve a basis for harmony. It is when the conventional political system cannot negotiate such conflicts that the growth of extremist organizations is to be expected.

If extremist movements like the National Front are to seek power through the electoral process they must present themselves as respectable parties and shed characteristics which others see as incitements to racial hatred. From this standpoint then, as Ivor Crewe remarked at the conference on 'Racism and Political Action in Britain', the best defence against the rise of the National Front is a strong Conservative Party. But other observers would contend that the main danger of extremist organizations does not lie in the votes they obtain so much as in their power to influence the framework of debate inside the major parties. In chapter 3 Caroline Knowles attributes great importance to the influence of the Labour left, in tacit alliance with the Communist Party, in persuading the Labour Party that the 'problem' of anti-Semitism was part of the struggle to protect the working class against fascism.

Legitimating ethnic distinctiveness

This interpretation of English attitudes assumes that phrases like 'It's our country' reflect a fairly general and fundamental element in orientations towards immigration, and suggests that these phrases should be seen as implying some kind of territorial right. It is a highly speculative interpretation. But if it should be true, what consequences would it have for members of the minorities? And how might different strategies on the part of the minorities affect the further development of majority attitudes? In seeking answers to such questions, it is important to compare the experience of similar immigrants in different countries, such as Italians in Britain and the United States, and of dissimilar minorities in the same country. In Britain Jews, Asians and blacks constitute minorities defined by reference to religion, geographical origin, and colour. These definitions have different implications for their relations with the majority. In referring to these groups as following different strategies it is necessary to note that the word 'strategy' normally implies conscious planning within a structure of command whereas the behaviour of members of these minorities for the most part lacks these features. Seen from a distance, their separate solutions to personal problems add up to a patterned response to a changing social environment. This response is here called a strategy for lack of any better identification.

One possible strategy for minorities is that of promoting assimilation. It should be remembered, however, that if assimilation is taken to be simply a process of becoming similar, it is not necessarily a one-way movement. English patterns of cohabitation and marriage have in recent years moved considerably towards those characteristics of lower class people in the West Indies. But when an immigrant minority enters an established society it is usually the minority that has to change most and the speed at which it does so will reflect the extent to which the majority holds out rewards for conformity to its expectations.

In North America the white attitude towards immigrants has varied with economic conditions, but a major theme has been: 'There's room for a lot more, especially from certain favoured nations, but let them come in at the bottom and work their way up.' In certain spheres of conduct it is important that immigrants demonstrate their loyalty to their new country and often they make the greatest display of patriotism. In Canada (or so I am told) it is often the immigrants from the non-French-speaking countries, like the Italians, Greeks and Ukrainians, who are the least sympathetic towards the Quebeçois who wish to promote the use of French. In the United States immigrants were expected to change in many ways, but no one was expected to change his faith. State and church were to be kept independent of each other. So it was perfectly legitimate for immigrants to organize separate communal lives on a religious basis and assimilation among white ethnics has tended to be a two-stage process whereby all Protestants move towards a common pattern; Catholics and Jews do likewise; and each group tends to interpret its religion in a more American fashion.

The English have pictured England as a country which sends emigrants to Australia, New Zealand, Canada and South Africa, and as one that has little room for immigrants of any kind. With a more uniform climate, a denser population, and a much more comprehensive system of social-class ranking, they have expected greater social conformity and tended to take loyalty for granted (during the McCarthy period when Americans were concerned about loyalty the corresponding British problem was one of security). In England ethnic identities have been legitimate only in the restricted sense that individuals are accepted as being Scottish, Welsh, and Irish as well as British. These are not hyphenated Britons, like Irish-Americans or Polish-Canadians, but members of ancient nations with rights in territories occupied by their ancestors before the United Kingdom was formed. The suggestion that there could be Indian-Britons as there are Polish-Americans is something new, and would be questioned by white English people who might well argue that if people want to be Indian they should live in India. This means that those who seek to advance claims on behalf of Indians permanently resident in England need to find a basis for legitimating their ethnic distinctiveness while claiming the standard civil rights of all citizens. They may be able to do this to their own satisfaction without convincing less sympathetic members of the English population. Perhaps these people can never be persuaded. Perhaps, also, doubts about the legitimacy of ethnic distinctiveness underlie the attitudes of whites in Willesden who insist that anti-discrimination legislation is a bonus awarded to the coloured minorities.

The Jewish immigrants who came to England at the end of the nineteenth century were distinctive ethnically as well as religiously. They did not organize as a political minority or cultivate their ethnic characteristics, but presented themselves as a religious group, and they have steadily shed those cultural characteristics which did not have a religious foundation. This could well have been in part an unconscious adaptation to English attitudes favouring claims to distinctiveness based upon religious faith more than claims stemming from ethnic identity, and there are some signs that Asians in Britain are also preferring to identify themselves in religious terms. The separate Jewish ex-servicemen's parades each November in commemoration of the country's dead in two world wars, serve as reminders that Jewish citizens fought and died for the country and that therefore they too have territorial rights.

Such studies as have so far been conducted among Asian minorities provide little evidence of debate about what is the best strategy for responding to the pressures of English society. It seems as if Asians in areas of dense settlement take for granted the maintenance of their ethnic distinctiveness and that there are conflicts between the generations about the best way to defend themselves within a pluralistic framework, as was evident in Southall in 1976 when many Asians felt threatened by English hostility. Minority views about strategy are to some extent reflected in ethnic voting preferences, but in the longer term it will not be surprising if more Asians express anxiety over the questions posed by Shiva Naipaul (*Sunday Times*, 13 June 1976): if Asians in Britain construct separate communities comparable to those they constructed in East Africa, why should not the outcome be similar?

It is with respect to black West Indians that the experience of the United States is most relevant. The 'American dream' provided no place for blacks: they were expected to assimilate to white patterns at the same time as barriers were raised to prevent their doing so. If the Italian-American felt that the rewards for conformity to White Anglo-Saxon Protestant expectation were insufficiently attractive, he could insist that he would remain as Italian as he could, and perhaps even return to Italy. But what was the black man to do? What was the alternative to conforming behaviour? It is in this context that the apparently extreme nationalist organizations like the Black Muslims were so important. They offered a comprehensive alternative identity. The ordinary black man benefited from this even if he never joined such an organization. He knew that he could follow this course if he wished, and the majority had to offer him something more attractive if it deprecated the growth of black nationalism. The nationalist movements were more significant than the number of their members would suggest, and they made a critical contribution to the growth of black consciousness in the 1960s.

In England, West Indian immigrants and their children have been subjected to the contrary pressures of attraction by a mass-consumption society and repulsion by what some call a racist society. John Rex discusses these contrary impulses in chapter 4, testifying that since black workers believe that trade unions cannot adequately advance all their interests, they approve of the activities of militant black organizations. Professor Rex does not here attempt to identify all the reasons for which they approve of them. Perhaps it is partly because they raise group consciousness among the minority, thereby strengthening the capacity of the black communities to organize themselves in a posture of defensive confrontation. The risk which such a strategy entails is that it may reinforce the tendency of the majority to categorize them as alien. But another factor behind such a strategy, I suggest, is that it publicizes the message that there is an alternative open to the black man other than the stark choice between assimilation on the one hand and return to the Caribbean on the other. Blacks are in a more difficult situation than Jews or Asians, for while it is possible to build a group based upon a distinctive religion or a distinctive culture, it is not possible to build one based on a distinction of colour. A difference of colour may be used by the majority to exclude a minority, but it can only be used inclusively, to bind people together, if members of a group have something positive in common and regard their skin colour as a sign of this positive possession. Even in a technological world, religion is still the most effective carrier of cultural distinctiveness and it is for this reason that I would expect Rastafarianism to gain more adherents among young people of West Indian origin in Britain. It offers a distinct view of the world that, as it develops, could become for some young blacks an equivalent to Hinduism or Islam.

In considering how different strategies on the part of the minorities might affect the further development of majority attitudes, it is well to follow the example of Annie Phizacklea and Robert Miles (chapter 5) in paying close attention to the development of racial categories. What is sometimes called 'race relations' consists of relations between people ascribed to such categories so that the phenomenon cannot appear independently of the categories. It is also well to ask whether the categories they describe are more than conversational: what kinds of behaviour do they actually influence? Such is the nature of our compartmentalized industrial society that the perception of blacks as different may influence the way whites talk and behave to other whites, but only indirectly influence black people. It is important to enquire into the sources of these categorizations (such as the heritage of empire, current mass media reporting of the United States, personal experience) and whether these sources are equally important for all sections of the white population, for it has not yet been demonstrated that 'working class racism' is different from the racism of the middle and upper classes.

Among both the majority and the minorities some individuals will have an interest in stressing the distinctiveness of the minority, others in minimizing it. Both sides can contribute to the development and hardening of categories. Minority members will initially build relatively small and inclusive groups consisting of kinsfolk and others who come from the same district in their homeland, then the range of these groups will be extended to everyone of similar ethnic origin, that is of similar language, religion, culture and possibly nationality. (On the question of ethnicity among Pakistanis, see Khan (1976); on the way that Barbadians who would belong to different social categories in Barbadian society are allocated to the same category in Britain, see Sutton and Mackiesky (1976, p.124).) The nature of this wider group will depend, of course, upon the kind of place immigrants secure in the native economic structure; if they specialize in a particular occupation this may reinforce their cultural distinctiveness. On the other hand, majority categorizations will be exclusive. Not many English people are aware of the differences between Sikhs and Gujeratis, Pathans and Mirpuris, or even between Indians, Pakistanis and Bangladeshis. Usually they are all lumped together as Asians and perceived as racially distinct. Gradually, more English people will perceive the inclusive, ethnic categories within the exclusive, racial ones, and over the course of time the differences between the two are likely to diminish.

In the early 1960s questions of race relations were debated almost entirely in the context of immigration control. 'Immigrant' became a synonym for 'coloured person'. This tended to distract attention from the significance of the differences between the various minorities and to create a single racial category to which all people of darker complexion were indiscriminately allocated. Since both black West Indians and Asians suffered from discrimination by the English, some observers expected that they would fairly soon come together and form a common political movement. This expectation was increased by the reporting of developments in the United States where people with any Negro ancestry and often of very pale complexion are counted as 'black' and assigned to a single category. But seen in world perspective the United States pattern is a very special case and there is no more reason to expect Britain to take this course than for the society to develop a continuous scale of colour gradation like that in Brazil and parts of the Caribbean. In the early years the English seemed to display more hostility towards the West Indians because they sought a greater degree of acceptance than the English wished to accord; in more recent times there seems to have been more hostility towards Asians because they are insufficiently inclined to adopt English ways. Differences from one city or neighbourhood to another also make it difficult to delineate racial categories. In Willesden the biggest minority is that of working-class blacks (indeed, in parts of the area they are a numerical majority). In some other localities there are relatively few blacks but many Asians, some of whom have their own businesses and are established employers; their success may stimulate jealousy and support an image of Asians as 'brown' Jews. In Bradford, according to Michel Le Lohé (chapter 8), people from the New Commonwealth are most likely to be classed together as 'Pakistanis' or 'Pakis' and the man in the street can be expected to distinguish between Asians and black people. The categories commonly employed are likely to reflect whichever minority among the coloured immigrant population is most numerous or attracts most attention. The process by which racial categories are developing requires empirical investigation sensitive to local variations and is not a matter upon which it is safe to generalize from theoretical principles or American parallels.

Conclusion

One of the objectives of this book has been to outline some of the features of white racism; in their introduction the editors warn that there is no simple relationship between racist ideas and racist political action since these ideas are held in association with a whole range of other ideas that also influence conduct. This concluding chapter has pointed to a way of examining the relationship between ideas and action, taking up the suggestion of an economist who presented the level of discrimination as determined by both the taste for discrimination and the price of discrimination (Collard, 1970, p.84). The discussion of H. Hoetink's (1967) argument has indicated some of the ways in which what he calls milieu factors – which are of a customary and contingent character – may create tastes or preferences that result in discrimination. But a consumer can satisfy one taste only at the expense of other tastes. He may prefer to have a neighbour of the same complexion as himself, but would he still choose the same house if he could obtain an identical property next to a neighbour of another colour for a purchase price £500 less? Or £5000 less? There will be some price differential sufficient to counter-balance anyone's taste for discrimination. I believe that such an approach is capable of more general development (Banton, 1977). Its most obvious limitation is that a focus on market behaviour at a moment in time appears to freeze the flow of history, and to overlook the forces that have caused people to hold particular preferences and for them to be involved with others in structured relations. But this is not beyond remedy.

Another handicap is that the very vocabulary of 'race relations' is too static. It carries the implication that individuals all belong in particular races that can be recognized by characteristics of a permanent or nearly permanent kind. In reality the groups that are identified by race are continually changing, but the racial designation conceals this. There can be no better example of this contention than the way the category 'black' (and its predecessor 'Negro') in the United States has maintained a dichotomy between 'blacks' and 'whites' that in other social structures has given way to a continuous gradation. The process by which people are labelled and placed in social categories is fraught with abiding consequences and the special insidiousness of racial categorization is that it appears natural, masking the social character of the operation.

This chapter began with a prediction of Gilbert Murray's that has not been borne out by events. An explanation of his mistake has been offered which stresses the significance of opportunities presented by cyclical variations in labour demand. All workers want to advance their interests by excluding competitors, either at the national frontiers or by monopolizing preferred sectors of the job market; when the competitors can be physically identified, exclusion is that much easier. If, however, newcomers can establish themselves in jobs, residential neighbourhoods, trade unions and political constituencies, on a basis that permits competition, co-operation and coalition, the development of majority attitudes will depend upon the part they play and the contribution they are perceived to make.

How a group's contribution is perceived does not depend upon a dispassionate kind of social accounting. It is influenced by the prior notions which members of the indigenous group have about their special rights and by the shared preferences which they take for granted. It will also be affected by the prejudices of the majority which, coupled with their reliance on the shifting categories of 'us' and 'them', so easily distort the perceptions. The burden of history is manifested in the preconceptions which members of groups bring to their interactions, and in the advantages which one party so often has in his dealings with the other. Seen from this standpoint, it is possible both to analyse marginal changes in discrimination as the outcome of taste and price, and to explore why, in a particular society and for particular sections of the population, levels of taste for discrimination and of price tend to fall within a certain range.

The editors have underlined the relevance of some of the continuities in the majority's reactions to immigration, so it is appropriate to recall that previous governments have used their power to regulate the price of discrimination. In the fifteenth and sixteenth centuries when refugees from France and Holland with valued skills were allowed to settle in Britain legislation obliged them to take English youngsters as apprentices so that their skills were shared and they did not become a separate group attracting animosity like the Jews (Plant, 1970, p.xiv). The present government is implementing a similar policy in maintaining a Commission for Racial Equality to see that apprenticeships and other avenues to higher rewards are not limited to one section of the population. To the extent to which this policy succeeds, it will hold in check the tendency which would divide the population into racial categories and present category membership as determining the rights which people can claim in a whole range of situations. If it is not held in check then the sentiment of 'It's our country', interacting with economic interest, could prove an explosive mixture.

Bibliography

Banton, M. (1977), 'Rational Choice: a Theory of Racial and Ethnic Relations', *SSRC, Research Unit on Ethnic Relations Working Paper*, no. 8.

Butler, R.D. and Stokes, D. (1974), *Political Change in Britain*, Macmillan, London.

Böhning, W.R. (1972), *The Migration of Workers in the United Kingdom and the European Community*, Oxford University Press, London.

Cohen, B.G. and Jenner, P.J. (1968), 'The Employment of Immigrants: a Case Study within the Wool Industry', *Race*, vol. 10, pp.41–56.

Collard, D. (1970), 'Immigration and Discrimination: some Economic Aspects', in Charles Wilson *et al.*, *Economic Issues in Immigration*, Institute of Economic Affairs, London, pp.65–87.

Eysenck, H.J. (1951), 'Primary Social Attitudes as Related to Social Class and Political Party', *British Journal of Sociology*, vol. 2, pp.198–209.

Hoetink, H. (1967), *Caribbean Race Relations: A Study of Two Variants*, Oxford University Press, London.

Khan, Verity Saifullah (1976), 'Pakistanis in Britain: Perceptions of a Population', *New Community*, vol. 5, pp.222–9.

Kosmin, B. (1978), 'Culture, Exclusion and Opportunity: the Influence of Ethnicity on the Occupational Patterns and Work Attitudes of British Jews', forthcoming in Sandra Wallman (ed.), *'Race' at Work*, Macmillan, London.

Murray, G. (1900), 'The Exploitation of Inferior Races in Ancient and Modern Times' in W. Hirst, G. Murray and J.L. Hammond, *Liberalism and the Empire*, Johnson, London.

Nairn, T. (1977), *The Break-Up of Britain: Crisis and Neo-Nationalism*, New Left Books, London.

Olson M. (1965), *The Logic of Collective Action*, Harvard University Press, Cambridge, Mass.

Peach, C. (1968), *West Indian Migration to Britain: A Social Geography*, Oxford University Press, London.

Plant, Sir Arnold (1970), Introduction in Charles Wilson *et al.*, *Economic Issues in Immigration*, Institute of Economic Affairs, London.

Rex, J. (1968), 'The Sociology of a Zone of Transition' in R.E. Pahl (ed.), *Readings in Urban Sociology*, Pergamon, Oxford, pp.221–31.

Sutton, C.R. and Mackiesky, S. (1976), 'Migration and West Indian Racial and Ethnic Consciousness', in Helen Safa and Brian Dutoit (eds), *Migration and Development*, Mouton, The Hague, pp.113–44.